# BOSWELL'S CREATIVE GLOOM

# BOSWELL'S CREATIVE GLOOM

A Study of Imagery and Melancholy in the Writings of James Boswell

Allan Ingram

BARNES & NOBLE BOOKS
TOTOWA, NEW JERSEY

© Allan Ingram 1982

All rights reserved. No part of this publication may be reproduced or transmitted, in any form or by any means, without permission

*First published 1982 by*
THE MACMILLAN PRESS LTD
*London and Basingstoke*
*Companies and representatives*
*throughout the world*

*First published in the USA 1982 by*
BARNES & NOBLE BOOKS
*81, Adams Drive*
*Totowa, New Jersey, 07512*

MACMILLAN ISBN 0 333 29476 9
BARNES & NOBLE ISBN 0 389 20157 X

*Printed in Hong Kong*

*To Glynis*

# Contents

| | |
|---|---|
| *Preface* | viii |
| *List of Abbreviations* | x |
| 1 Introduction | 1 |
| 2 Melancholy and the Imagination | 11 |
| 3 Madness and the Role of the Image in Thought | 45 |
| 4 The Pressures of Society | 65 |
| 5 Freedom and the Pen | 92 |
| 6 'Scribo ergo sum': the World of Boswell's Journals | 118 |
| 7 Balancing the Accounts: the *Life of Johnson* | 153 |
| 8 Conclusion: the Final Reckoning | 184 |
| *Notes* | 194 |
| *Bibliography* | 202 |
| *Index* | 211 |

# Preface

This book sets out to explore an unusual territory. It is about a way of thinking; it seeks to understand another person's mind. It claims to be neither biography nor pure literary criticism, although it owes a great deal to the methods of both. In particular, I have employed the tools of close critical analysis on passages from Boswell's journals with a view to laying open the structure of his thought through examination of the internal structuring of his autobiographical narration. This is not undertaken from the point of view of the psychoanalyst, but I am not primarily concerned, either, with making artistic judgements on Boswell's published works – though of course such judgements cannot fail to be implied or endorsed when writing about works such as the *Life of Johnson*. What I have tried to do is to extract from the wealth of material available *some* consistent patterns (among, I am well aware, many alternative patterns) which suggest how Boswell thought. Whether he turned his mind to family and friends, to society, to literature or law, or whether he turned it inwards to examine himself, how did the way he thought influence the subject he was considering, and affect the conclusions, if any, that he reached? Everything that he wrote reveals his inquiring and intensely self-conscious mind. Sometimes the way he expressed his thoughts can be seen to have led to artistic excellence – I am thinking here of particularly striking passages in the journals as well as his organisation of thirty years of collected impressions of Johnson. Elsewhere, the excellence of the expression consists in the purpose it served Boswell at the time. If we are able to come close to the mind itself, then we shall hope to emerge with an enriched appreciation of the journals, *The Hypochondriack*, the *Journal of a Tour to the Hebrides* and the *Life of Johnson*, but more important we shall emerge with the beginnings of an understanding of what it meant to be Boswell.

The first part of my study is an investigation of Boswell's use of imagery in the journals. The image, I suggest, is for Boswell a basic unit of thought, and as such provides us with invaluable evidence of the way his mind worked. Alongside this I attempt to place his temperamental melancholy in terms both of eighteenth-century attitudes and of modern philosophical and psychiatric theories. This framework is then used as the basis for an account of Boswell's literary mind, his attitude towards and practice of self-expression in both private and published works. Chapters 6 and 7 are largely devoted to this aspect of the study.

In general, I have cited the most accessible editions of Boswell, including the excellent volume on the making of the *Life of Johnson* by Marshall Waingrow, to which I am particularly indebted for Chapter 7. Similarly, my treatment of melancholy is based wherever possible upon material available to the inquiring reader. In the Bibliography, while giving a fairly comprehensive list on Boswell himself, I have made no attempt to cover exhaustively the subject of melancholy, as I consider this beyond the scope of the present work.

Few books of this kind are written alone, and for myself I have a debt of gratitude to express to those people who have been kind enough to supply me with advice and assistance. My thanks are due to Professor John Lucas, who recommended sources which have had a formative influence on my work, to Professor Arthur Johnston for his searching and constructive comments as external examiner of the thesis on which this book is based, to Lionel Kelly, Trevor Hussey and Tom Woodman, and to my wife and the other friends who have helped by discussion, criticism and encouragement. I am most grateful, though, to Professor James Boulton, who, as my supervisor at the University of Nottingham, gave detailed and valuable advice during every stage of my research. Without his expert and scholarly guidance, this work would have been a great deal more disorderly than I have contrived to make it.

A. S. I

# List of Abbreviations

The following are the abbreviations of titles of works referred to in the text and in the Notes. Full publication details are given in the Bibliography.

| | |
|---|---|
| BC | *Boswell's Column*, ed. Margery Bailey (a one-volume version of her edition of *The Hypochondriack*). |
| Bosw. | *Boswelliana: the Commonplace Book of James Boswell*, ed. Rev. C. Rogers. |
| BP | *Private Papers of James Boswell from Malahide Castle*, ed. Geoffrey Scott and F. A. Pottle, 18 vols. |
| Corr. I | *Correspondence of James Boswell and John Johnston of Grange*, ed. Ralph S. Walker (Yale Research edn, vol. I). |
| Corr. II | *Correspondence and Other Papers of James Boswell Relating to the Making of the 'Life of Johnson'*, ed. Marshall Waingrow (Yale Research edn, vol. II). |
| Def. | *Boswell for the Defence, 1769–1774*, ed. W. K. Wimsatt and F. A. Pottle. |
| Ex. | *Boswell in Extremes, 1776–1778*, ed. Charles McC. Weis and F. A. Pottle. |
| GT (i) | *Boswell on the Grand Tour: Germany and Switzerland, 1764*, ed. F. A. Pottle. |
| GT (ii) | *Boswell on the Grand Tour: Italy, Corsica and France, 1765–1766*, ed. Frank Brady and F. A. Pottle. |
| Hebr. | *Boswell's Journal of a Tour to the Hebrides with Samuel Johnson, LL. D.*, ed. F. A. Pottle and Charles H. Bennett (Boswell's manuscript journal). |
| Holl. | *Boswell in Holland, 1763–1764*, ed. F. A. Pottle. |
| Laird | *Boswell: Laird of Auchinleck, 1778–1782*, ed. Joseph W. Reed and F. A. Pottle. |
| Letters | *Letters of James Boswell*, ed. C. B. Tinker, 2 vols. |

## LIST OF ABBREVIATIONS

| | |
|---|---|
| *Life* | *The Life of Samuel Johnson*, ed. G. B. Hill, rev. L. F. Powell, 6 vols, vol. V containing Boswell's *Journal of a Tour to the Hebrides*. |
| *LJ* | *Boswell's London Journal, 1762–1763*, ed. F. A. Pottle (1951 edn). |
| *OY* | *Boswell: the Ominous Years, 1774–1776*, ed. Charles Ryskamp and F. A. Pottle. |
| *Player* | 'On the Profession of a Player': Three Essays (repr. London, 1929). |
| *Wife* | *Boswell in Search of a Wife, 1766–1769*, ed. F. Brady and F. A. Pottle. |

The following abbreviations for periodicals are used in the Notes and Bibliography:

| | |
|---|---|
| *ELH* | *Journal of English Literary History* |
| *JEGP* | *Journal of English and Germanic Philology* |
| *MLN* | *Modern Language Notes* |
| *PMLA* | *Publications of the Modern Language Association of America* |
| *SEL* | *Studies in English Literature 1500–1900* |

# 1 Introduction

(i) *The Image*

This study is based on the assumption that close examination of the imagery to which a writer has recourse can provide a peculiarly revealing insight into the mind that has conceived those images. The way in which a mind chooses to express itself is indicative of its habitual internal processes, and, until we understand something of these processes, we shall find it difficult to account for the direction that that mind sometimes elects to take, or to judge of its underlying ease or unease. By dissecting some of the images with which Boswell attempts in his journals to shape his experience, I hope to be able to make some helpful suggestions about his life-long mental unease of melancholy, and about his attitude towards the written word both as private record and as published statement.

The purpose of this Introduction is to indicate the meanings of the word 'image' that I consider relevant to my approach to Boswell. I have reduced these to four fairly distinct and manageable categories, three of which may be seen as consistent with meanings attached to the word by, for example, Johnson. My fourth category is a more exclusively modern meaning of the word, and for this reason I shall devote a substantial proportion of this chapter to relating this concept of 'image' to assumptions common in the eighteenth century.

First is the Lockian concept of an idea retained in the mind as an image is retained in a mirror:

> These simple ideas, when offered to the mind, the understanding can no more refuse to have, nor alter when they are imprinted, nor blot them out and make new ones itself, than a mirror can refuse, alter, or obliterate the images or ideas which the objects set before it do therein produce.[1]

This is Johnson's fifth definition of 'image': 'An idea; a representation of any thing to the mind; a picture drawn in the fancy.' He also elaborates on the subject to Boswell:

> He was particularly indignant against the almost universal use of the word *idea* in the sense of *notion* or *opinion*, when it is clear that *idea* can only signify something of which an image can be formed in the mind. We may have an *idea* or *image* of a mountain, a tree, a building; but we cannot surely have an *idea* or *image* of an *argument* or *proposition*.
> (*Life*, III, p. 196)

My second meaning is the image as a means of expression and communication. As Paul Fussell writes in the Preface to *The Rhetorical World of Augustan Humanism*,

> The chief critical assumption on which this book is based is that, the mind being a thing that must work by means of metaphors and symbols, imagery is the live constituent in that transmission of shaped illumination from one intelligence to another which is literature.[2]

Johnson's fourth meaning of 'imagery' is 'Representations in writing; such descriptions as force the image of the thing described upon the mind.' I shall, however, extend this definition from the purely literary image to include spoken imagery as well, which seems to have been a particularly important feature of eighteenth-century conversation. Both the spoken and the literary images are refinements upon the first meaning.

Third is a meaning which will become prominent in the relation between imagery and madness. This is Johnson's third definition of 'imagery': 'Forms of the fancy; false ideas; imaginary phantasms.' And the example Johnson gives, from Atterbury, is particularly relevant: 'It might be a mere dream which he saw; the *imagery* of a melancholick fancy, such as musing men mistake for a reality.'

To these I must add a fourth and extremely important category, the image a man has of himself, the composite and changing picture of himself to which he refers more or less consciously when undertaking even the most trivial action.

This, of course, is particularly vital in relations with other people, where an observer can always be assumed. Even if the subject is alone, though, he instinctively caters for a sort of viewer over his shoulder, what John Berger refers to as 'the *surveyor* and the *surveyed*' within the individual, as 'two constituent yet always distinct elements' of one's identity.³ Boswell's journals, as we shall see, seem to be addressed to a 'reader', who has a similar function to that of the omnipresent spectator.

### (ii) The Social Function of Imagery

The image of the self is a particularly important factor with regard to the place of the spoken image in eighteenth-century society, for imagery seems to have formed an essential part of polite conversation. This, as far at least as Boswell was concerned, was not always as an aid to communication, but often as decoration purely for its own sake. One's aptitude in this respect was a factor in one's acceptability and social standing, and the purely decorative use of imagery was intended to communicate something far more important than ideas or information. It was a means of impressing an image of the self on one's company, and of enjoying the gratification of having that image confirmed by the evidence that it was both accepted and highly estimated by one's fellows.

Most conversations recorded in Boswell's journals and in the *Life of Johnson* provide ample evidence of the part played by imagery in social intercourse. And Johnson himself, says Boswell, was 'delighted', upon reading through some of Boswell's accounts, 'to find that his conversation teemed with point and imagery' (*Life*, III, p. 260). Boswell records, too, the satisfying reception one of his own images met from Edmund Burke: 'I said the Advocate's change was too sudden. It was a child born in the 5th month after marriage. It was clearly illegitimate. Burke was highly pleased with this allusion, and said he'd take care it should circulate' (*BP*, xv, p. 213).

Boswell's pride in his 'multitudinous imagination' (*BP*, XVIII, p. 137), then, is not least a social pride. He takes particular care to preserve in his journals the good things he is able to say in company:

> I observed how curious it was to see an African in the north of Scotland, with little or no difference of manners. A man is like a bottle, which you may fill with red wine or with white. (*Hebr.*, p. 57)

> Erskine and I went to Covent Garden and saw *Love in a Village*. We were well entertained. We got into a dispute, and said several very clever things. 'Sir' said I, 'when you and I get into a dispute, we give a smart rap against each other like two flints, and out fly sparks of fire. But Macfarlane and you come together like two thick-quilted chair-bottoms, and out comes a thick cloud of dust.'
> (*LJ*, p. 106)

In fact, the good things that Boswell says provide a measure of the enjoyment he has received from any particular occasion:

> I had one good image: that Burke's indignation when the Members were leaving the house while he was relating the reasons of his resignation was like that of a Man at the fatal tree whom the crowd should leave just as he is making his last Speech and dying words: 'What! Will you not stay and see my execution?' (*BP*, xv, p. 107)

The image is made to be relished both by Boswell himself and by other people. At his best, he can give the appearance of being clever, lively, and one who enjoys life to the full, and, what is equally important, he can also *feel* that this is so. The image of the self conveys not least among many qualities Boswell in his role as image-maker. And the literary image, at least as far as its appearance in the journals is concerned, represents a twofold activity on Boswell's part. It has the function of making permanent both the spoken images of conversations that have actually taken place, and the mental images which have been developed to a degree sufficient for them to serve as material for future publication, either in spoken or in written form. The journal in this sense is a storehouse from which Boswell can draw when the need arises:

I had a store of delicious ideas. I considered that mankind are sent into the world to gather ideas like flowers.... Let us lay up our flowers in some order. Let us pull flowers of size and figure, nor fill our repository with trifling ones which have neither colour nor scent. However, let us not despise a flower because it is small. The violet, though scarcely perceived among the grass, has many sweets.

*(GT* (i), p. 63)

Simply by being written down, the image is given the chance of a wider circulation, and hence of being relished by a larger audience.

Pride in imagery, then, becomes inseparable from pride in self, for relish of the image necessarily entails relish of Boswell, again by himself as well as by others. Here we are approaching the Laingian exposition of the psychological need for 'confirmation', which will appear more prominently in later chapters of this study. The image of himself that Boswell wishes to project, including that of image-maker, is given reality in being accepted by others, and hence he is able to consider it as part of the true Boswell rather than just as a privately gratifying image.

In *The Mirror and the Lamp*, M. H. Abrams refers to Bishop Lowth's publication in 1753 of his *Lectures on the Sacred Poetry of the Hebrews*, in which Lowth assigns to poetry the task of imitation of 'whatever the human mind is able to conceive'. The most effective imitation, however, is of the mind of the poet himself:

Since the human intellect is naturally delighted with every species of imitation, that species in particular, which exhibits its own image, which displays and depicts those impulses, inflexions, perturbations, and secret emotions, which it perceives and knows in itself, can scarcely fail to astonish and to delight above every other.[4]

Lowth, however, seems to assume that the imitation is of the poet's genuine self, and that the artist is able to make an objective assessment of himself in order to create a just image of his mind in the work of art. This ideal situation may serve as a standard against which to set the 'normal' man's projections of advertisements for himself. It is not quite that the image of the self is a contrived one, but rather that by a process of trial and error most individuals are able to define themselves through the reactions of others: an image of the self is offered, accepted or rejected, adapted accordingly, and so becomes part of the 'real' self. If one happens to be, as Boswell was, a lively and persuasive off-stage actor, then more daring (and perhaps less 'true') images will be accepted – though, at the same time, a wide variety of convincing images may be evidence of a truly Protean character.

This process can be seen especially clearly during Boswell's time in Holland, and particularly in his relations with Zélide. He presents throughout his stay the image of a lively and entertaining young man, but one who is at bottom sound, moderate, sensible and consistent. It is only in his letters to Zélide after he has left Utrecht that a vain and changeable side of Boswell's character is allowed to break through:

> Forgive me for talking to you with such an air of authority. I have assumed the person of Mentor. I must keep it up. . . . I charge you, once for all, be strictly honest with me. If you love me, own it. I can give you the best advice. If you change, tell me. If you love another, tell me. . . . Answer me this one question: If I had pretended a passion for you (which I might easily have done, for it is not difficult to make us believe what we are already pleased to imagine) – answer me: would you not have gone with me to the world's end? . . . Zélide, Zélide, excuse my vanity. But I tell you you do not know yourself if you say that you would not have done thus. You see how freely I write, and how proudly. Write you with all freedom, but with your enchanting humility! 'I am proud of being your friend.' That is the style. (*Holl.*, pp. 306–8)

This effectively shatters the image which had been confirmed in Zélide's earlier reaction to him: she replies, 'I was shocked and saddened to find, in a friend whom I had conceived of as a young and sensible man, the puerile vanity of a fatuous fool, coupled with the arrogant rigidity of an old Cato' (*Holl.*, p. 321).

Boswell is all the time offering dominant and sub-dominant

images of himself in order to assess whether a particular role suits him: 'I loved to be a perfect Scots laird of the last age' (*Wife*, p. 74); 'I said people thought of a dram when I appeared as when a goose appears' (*OY*, p. 107). To know that someone will think of you in a way that you can govern, be it as a laird or only as a dram, is a great boost to personal vanity, and Boswell, as he boasts himself, had more than a fair share of vanity: he has 'a good organ of vanity' (*Ex*., p. 273), and can 'magnify all events in my own favour, and with the wind of vanity blow them up to size immense' (*GT* (i), p. 69). Even in the depression and sense of isolation of his melancholy we can sometimes detect him posturing from motives of personal vanity. In a letter to his future wife, Boswell complains of his father's scheme of remarrying:

> ... what I hinted to you shocked me so much that I declare I was thrown into the wildest melancholy, and resolved to go and at once break off all connection for ever, that I might no longer struggle with uncertainty and a kind of unnaturality.... Believe me, such a step in a family is terrible, and I fairly own to you that unless I had an absolute security against what might be done, I would renounce all relation. The worst is that a wild, ruinous scheme in some measure pleases my gloomy temper, and there is not a man alive to whom poverty and obscurity would be easier.
> (*Wife*, p. 235)

Here it is confirmation of his state of mind and of the justice of his opinion, together with admiration for his stance, that Boswell is seeking through this idealised image of himself. Boswell was clearly the last person to be content living in obscurity! It is the presence of the spectator that makes the idea seem attractive to him. In fact, Boswell's enjoyment of most experiences is enhanced if he can feel that he has a witness. As he tells John Johnston, 'Go, my friend, by yourself to Arthur Seat; think of me in distant regions' (*Holl*., p. 273). Elsewhere, writing of his proposal of marriage, the image used is for Boswell's benefit alone, and adds glamour and stature to his situation:

> I thought that if M. gave me a prudent, cold, evasive answer, I would set sail for America and become a wild Indian. I had

great thoughts of acquiring strength and fortitude, and could not regret much leaving all I had known, as I should adore God and be happy hereafter. (*Wife*, p. 254)

This, then, is Boswell the noble savage, combining the wildness of a Byronic hero with the religious devotion of a Pilgrim Father!

From this point of view, we can examine Boswell's tendency to regard himself as a fictional character – Macheath, Dorando, or the hero of his own life: his love for a chambermaid 'was so strange a scene in the play of my life', and his relationship with Miss Blair is 'another chapter in my adventures' (*Wife*, pp. 6, 87). The point here is not only that such a trick in thinking gives Boswell a basis for the image he is trying to project, but that it makes him feel a more compact and consistent person. The mental process, somewhat simplified and schematised, seems to be: Boswell steps outside himself in order to attempt self-description, chooses from the range of descriptions which suits his own attributes as he knows them, and applies the selected label, for example 'Macheath', and this, paradoxically, then makes it easier and more attractive for him to identify with himself, as he would with the hero of an actual play or novel. The effect is to give a false sense of detachment, and to distort his character by placing it within artificially narrow limits. He seems to be attempting a useful description of himself, but is in fact identifying with a more glossy and unreal self. Boswell even does this in order to see himself as a hypochondriac: 'Afternoon read a good part of *Hamlet*, to interest me in a melancholy character' (*BP*, XVI, p. 57). Boswell is rarely cast in a role that has no stature to it. His organ of vanity functions normally even, for example, during the race to save John Reid from execution: 'Honest Charles Hay would not leave me in my distress, but accompanied me, as honest Kent did Lear' (*Def.*, p. 308).

These images of the self, then, can produce a more attractive character from both a social and a private point of view, and can distract the eye from actual faults and inadequacies. The imagination, in fact, can act quite generally in the field of wish-fulfilment, as M. H. Abrams observes:

> In one fashion, indeed, men of this age conceived the imagination to picture the fictional satisfactions for all kinds of

desires, whether general or personal, noble or ignominious – in the activity they sometimes called castle-building, and we call wishful thinking. Dr. Johnson, for one, was acutely aware of the immense disproportion between what a man wants and what he is likely to get, and of the strength of the impulse to make up the difference in phantasy.... 'He then expatiates in boundless futurity, and culls from all imaginable conditions that which for the present moment he should most desire, amuses his desires with impossible enjoyments, and confers upon his pride unattainable dominion....'[5]

Boswell can frequently be seen encouraging himself in delusive imaginings, and 'building my castle in the air' (*LJ*, p. 337): 'Temple and I ... amused ourselves by building many aerial castles of future felicity when he would be with me at Auchinleck' (*LJ*, p. 267). He is especially inclined to use his capacity for making images as compensation in the eyes of himself and others for his actual inabilities: 'Mem.: know who you are and what you are. You cannot hire a troop of horse like Jamaica Dawkins, but you can make people say, "What images he has!" This imagination can raise up a troop of horse in a minute' (*BP*, xv, p. 199). This is an unusually clear example of the 'Dangerous Prevalence of Imagination'.

(iii)

Boswell uses imagery, then, in order to project himself onto the world, but he also uses it to look inwards and to attempt to achieve a greater understanding of himself. Or, rather, he tries to define what he feels within by wrapping it up in a suitable image and presenting it in pictorial form:

> When my mind was weak, ideas were too powerful for me. I am now strong; I can discern all their qualities but am master of them. I was formerly, in many articles of thought, like a boy who fires a gun. He startles at the noise, and, being unable to wield it, he can direct it to no steady point. I am now master of my gun, and can manage it with ease.
> (*Wife*, p. 123)

In the words of Mme de Stael, 'as soon as a strong passion agitates the soul, the most vulgar men ... call to their aid external nature to express the inexpressible which takes place within them'.[6] This technique of self-analysis will be seen with particular reference to Boswell's melancholy. Even in his earliest letters to John Johnston, his use of a private term, 'Antiquity' (cf. *Corr.* I, p. 30), for the disease indicates his need to express his feelings in a more definite and approachable form.

His greatest problem concerning melancholy, however, apart from the actual distress experienced during the fits themselves, involves the status of that experience: should he admit the bleak vision as real, or dismiss it altogether as idle imagination? The 'monstrous shapes' generated by his 'creative gloom' (*BP*, XVI, p. 166) cast doubt upon the reality of Boswell's images of health, and the healthy mind finds it increasingly difficult to dispel the insistent black cloud. There are, it seems, two world-views, and each invalidates the other.

These subjects are important for an understanding of Boswell's mental life, and they will receive due consideration in subsequent sections of this study. But it is melancholy, and in particular the role of the imagination in melancholy, that is the subject of my next chapter.

# 2 Melancholy and the Imagination

(i) *The Background of Melancholy*

One of the most concise of recent discussions of the medical background to melancholy is that provided by Professor Bridget Gellert Lyons in the opening chapter of her book *Voices of Melancholy*.[1] Professor Lyons traces the word back to its Greek origins in the four humours of which the human body was believed to be constituted, namely blood, phlegm, and yellow and black bile. The unbalancing of the humours resulted in illness, and the melancholy man, excessively cold and dry in temperament owing to the presence of unnaturally large amounts of black bile, was regarded as the most unfortunate sufferer of them all. He is prone to cancers, to epilepsy, to ulcers and paralysis and, not surprisingly, to depression of spirits. Later, too, he is described as afflicted with bouts of madness. Aristotle sees the excess of black bile as being responsible for sluggishness and despondency, but also, when heated, for varying degrees of inspiration. Such inspiration may range from intellectual and philosophical insights up to ecstatic frenzy.[2] Thus the melancholy man can be God blessed as well as God cursed: he is both the most fortunate and the least. His condition causes him long and unremitting suffering, but he may also experience periods of pleasurable, almost divine contemplation.

Even as late as Johnson's *Dictionary* we are still able to trace a dual aspect of melancholy, though for Johnson there is quite clearly no pleasure in the condition. His first definition, the medical, continues to attribute the disease to excess: 'A disease, supposed to proceed from a redundance of black bile; but it is better known to arise from too heavy and too viscid blood: its cure is in evacuation, nervous medicines, and powerful stimuli.' And his third, 'A gloomy, pensive, discontented temper', preserves virtually intact the tradition of despondency that persists from the classical period. Johnson's second definition, however, is his characteristically severe version of the pleasurable contemplation of Aristotelian melancholy: 'A kind of madness, in which the mind is always fixed on one object.' For Johnson the exclusive contemplation of one object is evidence not of divine favour but of the frailty of human sanity, and the supposed insights not universal truths but fruitless and mind-wearying obsessions.

Probably the most comprehensive English commentator on melancholy, though, was Robert Burton. Certainly he is the best known. Burton occupies a useful place in the history of melancholy, for his compendious *Anatomy of Melancholy* sums up so much that had been written on the subject from Hippocrates onwards – much of it repetitive, some even contradictory – that he provides an invaluable guide to the past and passing fashions in the debate, while at the same time, as a confessed melancholiac himself, preserving for us always the actuality of the disease and of its most enduring characteristics. He is not merely an academic summarising other people's arguments, but a man who is temperamentally involved in his subject and who is writing his book partly in order to divert himself from the very melancholy he is discussing.[3]

Burton is nothing if not thorough. He sets out to anatomise melancholy by placing it in the context of other diseases, by explaining it in the context of the body's physiology, by discussing its causes, symptoms, varieties and their characteristics, and by presenting the wide-ranging suggestions that have been put forward over the centuries for its cure. There are, for example, three distinct species of melancholy: head-melancholy, hypochondriacal or windy melancholy, and melancholy of the whole body.[4] Causes of melancholy may vary from God himself, to evil spirits and devils, to stars, parents, education, idleness or the eating of cabbage, which 'causeth troublesome dreams, and sends up black vapours to the brain'.[5] Similarly there are a wide variety of symptoms both of body and mind. Head-melancholy brings headaches, heaviness, vertigo and singing in the ears as physical symptoms, and fear, sorrow, suspicion and perpetual cogitation in the mind. Hypochondriacal melancholy is distinguished by rumbling in the guts, heat in the bowels, sour and sharp belchings and pain in the left side, while the mind is tormented by lasciviousness and troublesome dreams. Cures range from strict attention to diet, almost every available food and drink being forbidden on the authority of one or more writer, to the alarming remedy of boring holes in the skull 'to let out the fuliginous vapours'.[6]

Burton, however, is not neglectful of the pleasurable side of melancholy. So he begins 'The Author's Abstract of Melancholy',

> When I go musing all alone,
> Thinking of divers things fore-known
> When I build castles in the air,
> Void of sorrow and void of fear,
> Pleasing myself with phantasms sweet,
> Methinks the time runs very fleet.
>    All my joys to this are folly,
>    Naught so sweet as melancholy.[7]

And in his discussion of the progress of melancholy he acknowledges that at first it may be 'a most delightsome humour' during which one may 'dwell alone, walk alone, meditate, lie in bed whole days, dreaming awake as it were, and frame a thousand phantastical imaginations'.[8] Later in the disease, though, the melancholiac will discover that 'his phantasy is crazed' and, 'habituated to such toys', he finds 'fear and sorrow supplant those pleasing thoughts, suspicion, discontent, and perpetual anxiety succeed in their places'. So he becomes 'a cankered soul macerated with cares' and is precipitated into 'unspeakable miseries'.[9]

These are the products of the diseased imagination: 'Ghosts, goblins, fiends ... a thousand ugly shapes,/ Headless bears, black men, and apes.'[10] Reason becomes corrupt and cannot 'detect the fallacy'.[11] The imagination, presented by the memory with 'some object to be known', misconceives or amplifies it, misinforms, therefore, the heart, 'the seat of all affections', and by this means 'causeth all these distemperatures, alteration and confusion of spirits and humours'.[12]

Those who are melancholy 'see and hear so many phantasms, chimeras, noises, visions, etc.' because 'their corrupt phantasy makes them see and hear that which indeed is neither heard nor seen'.[13] Particularly when unemployed the 'phantasy is so restless, operative and quick, that . . . it will work upon itself, melancholize, and be carried away instantly, with some fear, jealousy, discontent, suspicion, some vain conceit or other'.[14] Not least among such 'vain conceits' are distressingly blasphemous imaginings on the subject of religion, for the devil himself finally seizes the opportunity to mingle with the troubled spirits and to suggest 'devilish thoughts into our hearts', 'insults and domineers in melancholy distempered phantasies and persons' and 'violently compels such crazed souls to think such damned thoughts against their wills'.[15]

Burton, then, was a mixture of scholar and melancholiac, a man whose encyclopaedic knowledge of this species of madness was supported by personal experience of at least some of its characteristics. During the late seventeenth and eighteenth centuries, however, there was much increased interest in clinical observation of the actual manifestations of madness and in examination of case histories. One consequence of this move was the realisation by commentators of the frequent proximity between unnatural depression and an equally unnatural elevation, or frenzy, of spirits – the melancholy – mania alternation, discovered by Thomas Willis. 'After melancholia,' declared Willis, 'we must consider mania, with which it has so many affinities that these complaints often change into one another.'[16] And the same observation was still commonplace a century and a half later. In his *Treatise on Insanity*, published in 1835, James Cowles Prichard notes,

> A state of gloom and melancholy depression occasionally gives way after an uncertain period to an opposite condition of preternatural excitement.... In this form of moral derangement the disordered condition of the mind displays itself in a want of self-government, in continual excitement, an unusual expression of strong feelings, in thoughtless and extravagant conduct.... Not unfrequently persons affected with this sort of disease become drunkards.[17]

What is most striking, though, is not merely that the commentators should agree on the observed phenomena, but that the terms in which they so frequently express themselves should also be remarkably similar. From the earliest writers onwards, melancholy is rarely discussed without attendant images of blackness and obscurity. Timothy Bright, writing in about 1586, speaks of 'gastly fumes of melancholy' and 'the dungions of melancholy darkenes'.[18] Sir Richard Blackmore, in his *Treatise of the Spleen and Vapours* of 1725, goes further and gives the mechanical reason for the association: 'antient Physicians', he says, 'imagined that it consisted in the Elevation of dark Fumes and Exhalations from the Matrice; which rising up in fruitful, but unwholsome Clouds, produce Sufferings in various Parts of the Body where they use to spread their unhappy Influence'.[19] And there are corresponding images in descriptions of manic frenzy: 'if', says Willis, 'in Melancholy the Brain and Animal Spirits are said to be darkened with fume, and a thick obscurity; In Madness, they seem to be all as it were of an open burning or flame'.[20]

Melancholy–mania, then, is not merely an observed alternation, but, as Michel Foucault argues in his book *Madness and Civilization*, is linked much more powerfully 'in the landscapes of the imagination', in the uniting in the same fire both the smoke that obscures and deadens, and the flame that ignites 'a kind of conflagration' in the spirits. The combination of mania and melancholy 'is a secret fire in which smoke and flame are in conflict; it is the vehicle of that light and that shadow'.[21]

So mania is fire, 'preternatural excitement' and intense physical activity, while melancholy is smoke, depression and inactivity. But the inactivity of melancholy is of the body, not of the mind. Blackmore's 'unwholsome Clouds' are 'fruitful' in that they produce 'a surprizing and copious Diversity of odd and ridiculous Phantasms' and fill the imagination 'with a thousand uncouth Figures, monstrous Appearances, and troublesome Illusions'.[22] These are the images of melancholy, not the images that describe melancholy, but the images that melancholy produces, the 'Phantasms and Passions' of which Richard Baxter warns we should take heed lest we ascribe them to God's spirit.[23] In Johnson's third definition they are associated with 'false ideas', and in Boswell's own descriptions of his mental condition, as we shall see, they are at the very heart of his complaint, proving more distressing and more dangerous than the depression with which melancholy is so often – and today so exclusively – associated.

Hobbes argued that it was madness caused by dejection that 'subjecteth a man to causeless fears'.[24] The range of such fears and fancies, however, could be enormous. At one extreme was the case, handed on from commentator to commentator, of the man who fancied himself made of glass, who must always take care lest he should be broken. But, more subtly, melancholiacs would be 'apprehending themselves forsaken of God',[25] or troubled by 'naughty, and sometimes Blasphemous Thoughts' which 'start in their Minds, while they are exercised in the Worship of God',[26] or they might even fear that their troublesome thoughts were themselves some sort of divine retribution, as in the case cited by Jeremy Taylor of the man who began 'to beleeve that this scrupulousness of conscience is a temptation, and a punishment of his sins'.[27] Timothy Bright had observed how difficult it was to distinguish 'what the difference is betwixt natural melancholie, and that heavy hande of God upon the afflicted conscience, tormented with remorse of sinne, and feare of his judgement'.[28] And it was always possible that one's melancholy 'Phantasms and Passions', far from being God-sent, might actually be the work of Satan himself. Johnson, in fact, illustrates 'phantasm', which he defines as a 'vain and airy appearance; something appearing only to imagination', by the passage from *Paradise Lost* where Satan is engaged in seducing the mind of Eve, 'Assaying, by his devilish art, to reach / The organs of her fancy, and with them forge / Illusions, as he list, phantasms and dreams.'

So, for a sufferer from melancholy in the eighteenth century, there were many more troubling aspects of the condition than just the dejection itself, particularly bearing in mind that these accompanying symptoms were such as would deepen the dejection. This effect was even more likely in a case such as Boswell's, where behaviour during the manic side of the alternation gave ample occasion for intense guilt during the melancholy side. The passions and excitements he feels and indulges at his 'inflammable' (*Wife*, p. 144) times are regretted at more sober and reflective moments:

So fiery is my imagination that if an object furnishes only a spark, I am very soon all in flame. As we went home I said, 'If I had been born only to adore that woman, it would have been enough.' Oh, can I not tame this turbulence of mind. (*GT* (i), p. 75)

And it can be seen how closely Boswell adheres to the patterns of descriptive imagery already established for discussions of melancholy–mania. He complains that 'I was still under the cloud which has hung on my mind, though with intermissions, for some time past' (*BP*, XIV, p. 58), or observes, 'I have straw or chips in my mind which a little matter will kindle into a blaze' (*OY*, p. 165). But, typically, Boswell usually contrives to make his use of the basic images distinctive by adding to them, making them more detailed, and often linking them with familiar, everyday objects. He has 'straw or chips' in his mind, but also 'I have more solid materials, hard coal and old wood, which require stronger heat to inflame them. I should, however, take care. A chimney has been set on fire and a house burnt by an inconsiderable kindling.' Or elsewhere the 'secret fire' remarked by Foucault becomes, in Boswell, a mental furnace: 'I was in good spirits, nay in high and fine flow of thought. My mind is a furnace. It melts and refines objects when there is a strong clear heat; but sometimes my furnace is smoky, and then the objects are blackened' (*OY*, p. 252).

But Boswell is also intensely aware of the active, image-producing side of melancholy, the ideas and fancies which arise during his periods of 'creative gloom' (*BP*, XVI, p. 166). In a *Hypochondriack* essay 'On Hypochondria', he actually describes in detail how it feels to be one suffering under a fit of melancholy. He begins with the descriptive image, 'There is a cloud as far as he can perceive', and says that 'he supposes it will be charged with thicker vapour, the longer it continues'. But Boswell soon turns to explaining how melancholy affects one's vision of the world, how it distorts and obscures:

> The world is one undistinguished wild. His distempered fancy darts sudden livid glaring views athwart time and space. He cannot fix his attention upon any one thing, but has transient ideas of a thousand things; as one sees objects in the short intervals when the wind blows aside flame and smoke.

Then comes the real perversion and hopelessness of deep melancholy, for, while the sufferer 'knows that his mind is sick, his gloomy imagination is so powerful that he cannot disentangle himself from its influence, and he is in effect persuaded that its hideous representations of life are true'. For the melancholiac, there seems to be no way out, no escape from the gloomy images, for 'In all other distresses there is the relief of hope. But it is the peculiar woe of melancholy that hope hides itself in the dark cloud' (*BC*, pp. 208–9).

Once under the influence of melancholy, there is no external standard on which the sufferer can rely for a sane perspective on his present bleak ideas. He is incapable of judging between his fancies, which appear to him real, and reality, which in his mind is distorted and unreal. Everything seems unstable and worthless, until finally, in Boswell's words, the melancholy man is convinced not only of his own personal worthlessness, of his being forsaken by God, but of 'the nothingness of all things in human life' (*BP*, XVI, p. 25).

### (ii) *Boswell's Melancholy*

*Hypochondriack* 39, 'On Hypochondria', presents powerfully the actuality of Boswell's melancholy. As the editors of *Boswell: Laird of Auchinleck* comment, it is 'one of the best essays in the series, and perhaps comes closest to being a personal testament' (*Laird*, p. 276). But the observations Boswell makes in the essay are in fact condensed from the experience of half a lifetime of suffering. In writing *Hypochondriack* 39, Boswell was drawing not merely on the experience of one attack of hypochondria, but upon the lived and recorded experience of over twenty years.

Almost any journal from almost any part of Boswell's life will present us with vivid and convincing accounts of his bouts of melancholy. One of the most uniformly bleak patches, however, is the time Boswell spent in Holland, the period of the lost Dutch journal. The surviving memoranda and letters give, though, more than adequate testimony of his depth of melancholy. In a letter to his friend Temple from Rotterdam, shortly after his arrival in Holland, Boswell describes the painful experiences of melancholy, the behaviour into which he is led, and offers, too, insights into several possible causes of his state of mind, not least among which is his dread of the impression his inadequacy will make upon his father.

> My dearest Temple, –
> Expect not in this letter to hear of anything but the misery of your poor friend. I have been melancholy to the most shocking and most tormenting degree. You know the weakness and gloominess of my mind, and you dreaded that this would be the case. I have been at Leyden; from thence I went to Utrecht, which I found to be a most dismal place. I was there entirely by myself and had nobody to speak to. I lived in an inn. I sunk altogether. My mind was filled with the blackest ideas, and all my powers of reason forsook me. Would you believe it? I ran frantic up and down the streets, crying out, bursting into tears, and groaning from my innermost heart. O good GOD! What have I endured! O my friend, how much was I to be pitied! What could I do? I had no inclination for anything. All things appeared good for nothing, all dreary. I thought I should never recover, and that now the time was come when I should really go mad. . . . I am distracted with a thousand ideas. The pain which this affair will give my worthy father shocks me in the most severe degree. And yet, alas! what can I do? . . . I cannot read. My mind is destroyed by dissipation. But is not dissipation better than melancholy? Oh, surely, anything is better than this. My dear friend, I am sensible that my wretchedness cannot be conceived by one whose mind is sound. I am terrified that my father will impute all this to mere idleness and love of pleasure. I am not yet determined what to do. (*Holl.*, pp. 7–8)

He is brought so low during his stay in Holland that even suicide presents itself to his mind: 'You was direfully melancholy and had the last and most dreadful thoughts. You came home and prayed' (*Holl.*, p. 184).

Nor is Boswell's melancholy confined to periods of his life during which he is undergoing some enforced abstinence. In Holland he is binding himself to the study of law, he finds the Dutch temperamentally uncongenial and the country itself uniquely dull. But even amid the excitement of London

Boswell is rarely free from the threat of melancholy depression. In the London journal of 1762–3, one of the brightest and most lively of his diaries, Boswell frequently records that he has been 'uneasy' (*LJ*, p. 137), 'very gloomy' (p. 254), or filled with unpleasing reflections:

> This afternoon I became very low-spirited. I sat in close. I hated all things. I almost hated London. O miserable absurdity! I could see nothing in a good light. I just submitted and hoped to get the better of this. (p. 145)

Even the anticipated pleasures of a jaunt from London to Oxford in the spring of 1763 which Boswell promises himself at the invitation of Sir James Macdonald prove a severe disappointment. His initial impression of Oxford is good: 'The ideas which I had conceived of that noble university were realized when I saw it' (*LJ*, p. 268). However, within a matter of hours his spirits have been 'flattened'; he finds that 'from my old notions of a college taken from those at Edinburgh and Glasgow' he has 'a kind of horror upon me from thinking of confinement and other gloomy circumstances'; and by evening, after supping with Sir James and several of his friends, he is thoroughly disillusioned.

> They were all students and talked of learning too much; and in short were just young old men without vivacity. I grew very melancholy and wearied. At night I had a bed at the Blue Boar Inn. I was unhappy to a very great degree. (Ibid.)

Next morning he gets up 'in miserable spirits. All my old high ideas of Oxford were gone, and nothing but cloud hung upon me.' After a second day in learned company he is further depressed.

> I now thought that human happiness was quite visionary, and I was very weary of life. After dinner we walked about the place. I tried to work myself up to a little enthusiasm, and took a draught of the water of Isis so much celebrated in poetry, but all in vain. We supped with Pepys, and I continued very bad. (p. 269)

## MELANCHOLY AND THE IMAGINATION

A visit to Mr Shepherd, author of *Odes Descriptive and Allegorical* and of *The Nuptials*, leaves him 'really pleased with this night's adventure' (p. 271), but upon returning to London he retains 'the most gloomy ideas of the University. My mind was really hurt by it. I thought every man I met had a black gown and cap on, and was obliged to be home at a certain hour' (pp. 271-2). Boswell remains 'unhinged' and 'low-spirited' for ten days after, though his suffering is not lightened by his insistence on seeing 'the melancholy spectacle' of two executions at Tyburn (p. 275).

Clearly, though, Boswell's melancholy, while unquestionably influenced by his immediate circumstances, is to a large extent temperamental. In the midst of lively company, in comfortable surroundings, Boswell can still find himself inexplicably floundering in the deepest melancholy.

> I was in miserable spirits. All was dark. I dined with Webster, who treated me as his guest at a military mess at the Tilt Yard. Really it must be observed that officers live rather better than any other society. They have less to do, so it is a more important object. I had this day the satisfaction of a very good dinner, genteely served up in an elegant room, and a good company round me. Yet was I melancholy. I considered them all as unhappy, tired, slavish beings singled out from the rest of mankind for toil and pain. I disliked the idea of being a soldier. I thought of refusing a commission. (p. 252)

Almost twenty years later we find Boswell's thoughts following the same kind of pattern. He is now a married man, father of a family, someone well-known in society in Edinburgh and London, and a published writer and journalist. And yet melancholy still intrudes into every activity.

> Went to the race with Maclaurin in his coach. Was sadly dispirited; thought myself insignificant and subjected to a wretched destiny. Had no clear thoughts of anything, no consoling pious feelings. Had been with Lord Eglinton once since Tuesday. Went to him today near three and had a consultation on the election with his Lordship and Mr. Wauchope, an express having brought letters from Major

Montgomerie and Mr. Hamilton of Sundrum. Had some pleasure in observing the Earl's sense and spirit, but was saddened by speculative clouds composed of the uncertainty of life, the forgetfulness of things years after their happening, and such dreary truths. Wondered how I had ever been active and keen in anyting.... I was grievously hypochondriac in the evening. Went early to bed and fell soon asleep. (*Laird*, pp. 386–7)

Less than four weeks later Boswell is once more finding his thoughts straying to suicide.

> I was very low-spirited today; and during this late fit, there has come into my mind the horrible thought of suicide. It was most effectually checked by thinking what a triumph it would afford to my enemies, or rather enviers, and how it would hurt my children. I had *some* rationality therefore in store. (p. 392)

Suddenly, however, he recovers. The entry continues,

> Dr. Dunbar's dining with me had appeared a heavy task. Sir John Pringle said very well, 'Have somebody with him with whom you are easier. Dilute him.' I had Grange; and, most unexpectedly, I was very well. (pp. 392–3)

It is during these middle years, 1777–83, that Boswell writes *The Hypochondriack*. I shall have more to say about these essays elsewhere, but for the moment it is worth noting just how many of the papers were composed while Boswell suffered from low spirits. No. 2, 'On Fear', is completed despite Boswell's being 'vexed and fretful' (*Ex.*, p. 189); he gets no. 24, 'On Censure', finished though 'in sad low spirits' (*Laird*, p. 136); no. 29, 'On Pity', is delayed while Boswell, 'low-spirited and languid and fretful', sits 'moping by my fire' (*Laird*, p. 180); and nos 47, 'On the New Freezing Discovery', and 49, 'On Identification by Numbers', are old essays made to serve, Boswell finding himself 'languid and sauntering' and 'very insignificant' (*Laird*, pp. 391, 401) when called upon to write. Altogether, so far as it is possible to tell, Boswell was either melancholy or unwell during the composing of at least twenty-two of the seventy *Hypochondriack* essays. His record of the days spent writing *Hypochondriack* 39 is unfortunately missing from the journal for the period, eighteen pages having at some time been removed. Boswell gets up on Friday, 15 December 1780 'in sad hypochondria. Had several law papers and a *Hypochondriack* to be written without delay. Was quite in despair. Could not see any good purpose in human life. Thought...' (*Laird*, p. 276) – and there the record ends. All that remains is the essay he then produced.

> The Hypochondriack is himself at this moment in a state of very dismal depression, so that he cannot be supposed capable of instructing or entertaining his readers. But after keeping them company as a periodical essayist for three years, he considers them as his friends, and trusts that they will treat him with a kindly indulgence.... Instead of giving this month an essay published formerly... I have a mind to try what I can write in so wretched a frame of mind; as there may perhaps be some of my unhappy brethren just as ill as myself, to whom it may be soothing to know that I now write at all. (*BC*, p. 207)

After this introduction, Boswell proceeds by selecting 'some of those thoughts, the multitude of which confounds and overwhelms the mind of a Hypochondriack' (p. 208).

> His opinion of himself is low and desponding. His temporary dejection makes his faculties seem quite feeble. He imagines that every body thinks meanly of him.... He envies the condition of numbers, whom, when in a sound state of mind, he sees to be far inferior to him. He regrets his having ever attempted distinction and excellence in any way, because the effect of his former exertions now serves only to make his insignificance more vexing to him.... He is distracted between indolence and shame. Every kind of labour is irksome to him. Yet he has not resolution to cease from his accustomed tasks. Though he reasons within himself that contempt is nothing, the habitual current of his feelings obliges him to shun being despised. He acts therefore like a slave, not animated by inclination but goaded by fear.... He begins actually to believe the strange

theory, that nothing exists without the mind, because he is sensible, as he imagines, of a total change in all the objects of his contemplation.... An extreme degree of irritability makes him liable to be hurt by every thing that approaches him in any respect.... He is either so weakly timid as to be afraid of every thing in which there is a possibility of danger, or he starts into the extremes of rashness and desperation.... Finding that his reason is not able to cope with his gloomy imagination, he doubts that he may have been under a delusion when it was cheerful; so that he does not even wish to be happy as formerly, since he cannot wish for what he apprehends as fallacious. (pp. 208–10)

This is Boswell's most concise statement of the symptoms of his melancholy, made not, as one might expect, in his private journal, but in an essay intended for publication. His most private experience is given to the world with honesty and with an uncharacteristic lack of pretension. This fact alone, quite apart from the content of the essay, makes *Hypochondriack* 39 an essential document for the understanding of Boswell's complex personality.

### (iii) *Imagination and Religion*

J. G. Zimmerman, in his major work on *Solitude*, first published in Germany in 1773, sums up much that the eighteenth century thought on the subject of melancholy, and observes many characteristics of the disease that may also be found expressed in Boswell's writings. Unlike earlier commentators, Burton, Bright or Blackmore, however, Zimmerman concentrates largely on the physical side of melancholy rather than on the theoretical. On the possibility of cure, for example, he declares, 'The influence of this dreadful malady is so powerful, that it destroys all hope of remedy, and prevents those exertions by which alone, we are told, it can be cured.'[29] Melancholy persons, he goes on, are most likely to seek out solitude, but of all men are the least able to benefit from it, for in retirement the 'desires and sensibilities of the heart having no real objects on which their vibrations can pendulate, are stimulated and increased by the powers of imagination', which is 'continually heaping fuel on the latent fire' of the passions until 'at length the labouring desire bursts forth, and glows with volcanic heat and fury'.[30] At the same time the 'unsubstantial images' raised by the imagination portray 'the form of things unknown in Nature, and foreign to truth,'[31] while within the mind, which is 'labouring under religious despondency', convinced of 'having irretrievably lost the Divine favour, and of being an object unworthy of the intercession of our Saviour', the imagination, says Zimmerman, 'being left, in Solitude, entirely to its own workings, increases the horrors which such thoughts must unavoidably inspire'.[32] To the religious melancholiac, solitude 'operates like a rack, by which the imagination inflicts the severest tortures on the soul'.[33]

The imagination, then, maintains a permanent and inescapable relationship with the tendency to melancholy. Clearly, in its function as the creative, image-making faculty it organises the experience of melancholy using those elements of external reality which most correspond to the sensations of the condition. This is what constitutes the rhetoric of melancholy upon which Boswell is able to draw in *The Hypochondriack* in order to touch the common imaginations of fellow sufferers and so inspire a sort of community of consciousness among his readers. But, secondly, the imagination itself produces, or seems to produce, the phantasms and fancies that inhabit the melancholy vision, or else casts the melancholiac's distempered ideas in so powerful a way that his weakened judgement is induced to take them for valid representations of reality.

But the imagination does have another recognisable function which may be related to the tendency to melancholy, and that is the combined creative and re-creative operation of reliving past experiences and rehearsing future ones. Johnson in his first *Dictionary* definition of 'imagination' quotes from Bacon: 'Imagination is of three kinds: joined with belief of that which is to come; joined with memory of that which is past; and of things present, or as if they were present.' This is one reason for Johnson's constant reiteration of the importance of activity and amusement, and of the misery of 'those that have slept in the shades of indolence, and whose retrospect of time can entertain them with day rising upon day, and year gliding after year'.[34] A flat and unvaried past will produce boredom and depression, while a future which promises equally unbroken monotony may lead the thoughts to a morbid obsession with death. For Johnson, one of the causes of melancholy is just this, 'an awful dread of death, or rather, "of something after death" ' (*Life*, II, p. 298), be it the horror of annihilation, or of being 'Sent to Hell, Sir, and punished everlastingly' (IV, p. 299). So he consistently points to idleness as the chief factor in leading the mind into melancholy. A vigorous and active mind will not need to turn in upon itself and dwell upon its own dissolution, and a full and varied life is the safest way to ensure a contented existence. To be wise or useful, moreover, man must fix his attention upon externals, 'adopt the joys and the pains of others, and excite in his mind the want of social pleasures and amicable communication',[35] while 'to be idle is to be vicious', for 'any wild wish or vain imagination never takes such firm possession of the mind, as when it is found empty and unoccupied'.[36]

The power of the imagination, then, should, for Johnson, be directed towards human relationships and towards religious devotion. The one will render a man useful during his present life, and the other will reassure him of his hope for salvation in the life to come. But even here man finds himself in a dilemma. One part of him makes him wish to enter into relationships of mutual love with individuals, and to feel benevolence towards mankind as a whole.[37] (It is, for example, upon this feeling that Swift is able to rely for the satiric effect of his account of the Houyhnhnms in Book IV of *Gulliver's Travels*.) Yet everywhere there obtrude disillusioning instances of man's inhumanity to man, such as Goldsmith's Man in Black finds in an account of the thief-takers:

> I read over the many hideous cruelties of these haters of mankind, of their pretended friendship to the wretches they meant to betray, of their sending men out to rob and then hanging them. I could not avoid sometimes interrupting the narrative and crying out, 'Yet these are men!' As I went on, I was informed that they had lived by this practice several years, and had been enriched by the price of blood; 'and yet,' cried I, 'I have been sent into the world, and am desired to call these men my brothers!' I read that the very man who led the condemned wretch to the gallows, was he

who falsely swore his life away; 'and yet,' continued I, 'that perjurer had just such a nose, such lips, such hands, and such eyes as Newton.' ... I threw down the book in an agony of rage, and began to think with malice of all the human kind.[38]

Similarly, the imagination that desires religious belief and the existence of a divinity worthy of adoration can also be the imagination that is led into gloomy superstition and religious fanaticism. (It is not, for example, by chance that Johnson was active in the detection of fraudulent ghost stories.)

These dilemmas, involving human relationships and religious belief, are fully appreciated by Boswell. He writes in highly emotional terms to his friend Temple in 1765,

> True disinterested, celestial friendship is rarely found. But that it really exists you and I afford a certain proof. Believe me, my dearest Temple – I wish you saw the generous tear which now fills my eye – believe me, my friend, that I have an entire confidence in *you*, and that the sacred flame is never extinguished in *my* breast.... My heart speaks.
> (*Holl.*, p. 217)

The 'celestial friendship' of such a man as Temple will prevent the 'sacred flame' in Boswell's breast from sinking into the smoke and blackness of despair at mankind, just as the influence of Rousseau, he says, will 'kindle' his soul so that 'the sacred fire shall never be extinguished' (*GT* (i), p. 230). And 'the principles of our holy religion', Boswell remarks in *The Hypochondriack*, should be 'firmly established' in the mind, and strengthened 'by the habitual exercise of piety' so that 'the flame may live even in the damp and foul vapour of melancholy' (*BC*, p. 210).

Fire, then, which has previously been seen as an image of mania, is also an image of faith in mankind and in the soul's salvation. But to court religious enthusiasm would, presumably, be to risk a blaze. The fire of imagination must be maintained at a constant and controllable level if the extremes of gloom and of conflagration are to be avoided.

In this context, it can be no accident that Boswell adopts, in discussing Christ's Atonement with Johnson during their tour to the Hebrides, the traditional image of Christ as a light to show men the true way. Christ himself says, 'I am the light of the world: he that followeth me shall not walk in darkness, but shall have the light of life.'[39] Boswell says,

> I would illustrate this by saying that Christ's satisfaction is like there being a sun placed to show light to men, so that it depends upon themselves whether they will walk the right way or not, which they could not have done without that sun, 'the sun of righteousness'. There is, however, more to it than merely giving light – 'a light to lighten the Gentiles'.
> (*Hebr.*, p. 64)

Christ, for the orthodox Christian, can be the surest and most consistent light, the best guarantee for relying upon those principles of religion whose flame will 'live even in the damp and foul vapour of melancholy'. But Boswell, of course, was brought up in the Presbyterian faith, and must surely have been aware that his view of the Atonement goes directly against Presbyterian teaching. According to the Calvinistic creed, 'natural man' has lost the free will by which he might have chosen to 'walk the right way':

> Man, by his fall into a state of sin, hath wholly lost all ability of will to any spiritual good accompanying salvation; so as a natural man, being altogether averse from that good, and dead in sin, is not able, by his own strength, to convert himself, or to prepare himself thereunto.[40]

Only the grace of God can restore the individual to something resembling his unfallen freedom:

> When God converteth a sinner and translateth him into the state of grace, he freeth him from his natural bondage under sin, and, by his grace alone, enableth him freely to will and to do that which is spiritually good; yet so as that, by reason of his remaining corruption, he doth not perfectly, nor only, but doth also will that which is evil.[41]

The influence of his religious upbringing remained strong throughout Boswell's life. In fact, as an incident in Rome makes clear, part of his imagination always laboured beneath the gloomy phantoms of Scottish Presbyterianism: 'Then St. Peter's in grand frame. Prayed fervent to the unchangeable Father of all to drive away melancholy and keep clouds of Presbyterian Sundays from rendering mind gloomy' (*GT* (ii), p. 70). In the light of the few details we have of Boswell's early religious education, it is hardly surprising that memories of Presbyterian Sundays are conducive to melancholy: 'I shall never forget the dismal hours of apprehension that I have endured in my youth', he says, 'from narrow notions of religion while my tender mind was lacerated with infernal horror' (*LJ*, p. 128); and 'The relief *now* was as when I used to say to myself when a child, "*The Devil's Dead*" ' (*Ex.*, p. 282).[42] For Boswell, it is the external splendour of Catholicism and St Peter's which leads the imagination into its 'grand frame'. As he writes in the *London Journal*, he is given 'to the most brilliant and showy method of public worship' (p. 80). And it is reason and Johnson which argue for a brighter and more flexible religion, for, while Johnson is often accused of religious gloom, by comparison with the doctrines of Calvinism his beliefs are remarkably hopeful and free from rigidity.

Yet the fire of Boswell's religious devotion can easily become 'the fire that never shall be quenched',[43] and imaginative elevation may quickly turn to melancholy under the influence of a more sin-conscious religion. For example, Boswell's sense of sexual guilt is aroused by a sermon in the New Church, Edinburgh:

> In the afternoon Mr. Walker endeavoured to prove that the eternity of punishment was nowise inconsistent with GOD's goodness.... 'God who cannot lie, hath threatened; and we cannot complain, as we have it in our choice to avoid the penalties.' 'But alas!' thought I, 'What shall be said as to men of wavering faith and strong passions?' The afternoon's discourse darkened the fine tints of Blair in the forenoon. But I found that my mind had internal force enough to dissipate the mist. I steadily thought that eternity of punishment *could not be*, according to my notions of the divinity. (*OY*, pp. 199–200)

Boswell's editors add, concerning the last sentence, 'With a return of orthodoxy, Boswell inked out this and the preceding sentence.' The arguments of reason never permanently 'dissipate the mist', for the Walker type of religion does not itself cause these guilt feelings, but merely brings nearer the surface something far more fundamental and intangible, something not accessible to argument and to reason. To find punishment promised for feelings of guilt may be a temporary satisfaction, and may even be taken as evidence of an ordered universe, but it cannot ultimately help the sensitive man come to terms with the disorder at the heart of his being.

The immediacy of religious rhetoric, however, is often irresistible, and Boswell is again affected three months later by another sermon, this time in Lichfield Cathedral:

> I was much pleased with the Cathedral service here, having never heard the music so solemn and so accordant with the words. I was quite elevated, but sensual connexions with women, particularly with the lady with whom I had been twice lately in London, came across me. I thought thus: 'These are Asiatic satisfactions, quite consistent with devotion and with a fervent attachment to my valuable spouse.' Mr. —— preached on these words, 'be steadfast and immovable', etc., and admirably represented the bad effects of relapsing into vice after a course of holy living. This struck me, 'for', thought I, 'what vice am I ever inclined to but sensual indulgence?' However, my former soothing sophistry returned. (*OY*, pp. 293–4)

Between religious guilt and soothing sophistry, the errant Boswell vacilates helplessly, and his behaviour is justified or condemned according to the mood of the moment. Sometimes the image of manic fire itself becomes part of the soothing sophistry: 'Thus my life slipped away in a delicious dream, while my principles of systematic morality were melted down by the fire of a heated imagination' (*GT* (ii), p. 20). Sometimes, Boswell attempts to externalise this sense, and encouraged by his image of heat, shows a particular tendency in Italy to blame his behaviour upon the climate. A Scots baron, he advises himself, should 'not remain in the Italian sun till his Caledonian iron is melted' (*GT* (i), p. 110). And to Johnston he writes that 'the climate of Italy affects me much. It inflamed my hot desires, and now it keeps my blood so warm that I have all day long such spirits as a man has after having taken a cheerful glass' (*GT* (ii), p. 110). In later years, though, he is able to face the problem more seriously, even though he may come to no conclusion:

> My mind was unquiet with the thoughts of having acted immorally. Yet I was not quite clear. A man is not steady in his conviction of the truth of a principle which his warm passions are ever melting and the transgression of which gives him pain. I said to Sir John I did not see any positive precept as to connexion between the sexes. He insisted that the rule was explicit enough, but rather avoided an argument upon it. (*OY*, p. 316)

Here is a problem which obviously troubles Boswell greatly, and which he earnestly needs to discuss with his friends, but friendship, celestial or otherwise, seems not to have stretched so far, and they appear to have rather 'avoided an argument upon it' than provided him with an opportunity for the frank seeking of advice. Boswell has to conceal his approaches beneath a mask of generality. Nor with Johnson is he able to talk openly of these things.[44] This in itself would lead to an enhanced sense of guilt, and of daring. Indeed, when in a light frame of mind, Boswell is quite capable of being jocular upon this very dilemma, as when Johnson advises him to take a course in something, so as 'to have as many retreats for your mind as you can', and Boswell remarks, 'I *thought* of a course in concubinage, but was afraid to mention it' (*OY*, p. 286). Generally, though, his sexual behaviour leads him to very real confusion and depression, which the power of reason is frequently unable to dissipate. The following journal entry is for 31 March 1776, only nine days after the last quoted example. Boswell has devoted the night to 'the whoring rage' and now, 'satiated by repeated indulgence', he returns to his London lodgings,

> cold and disturbed and dreary and vexed, with remorse rising like a black cloud without any distinct form; for in truth my moral principle as to chastity was absolutely eclipsed for a time. I was in the miserable state of those

whom the Apostle represents as working all uncleanness with greediness. I thought of my valuable spouse with the highest regard and warmest affection, but had a confused notion that my corporeal connexion with whores did not interfere with my love for her.... This is an exact state of my mind at the time. It shocks me to review it.  (*OY*, p. 306)

It is clearly his changeability that causes Boswell his greatest distress. He feels, at times, that he has no control over his own behaviour, and, moreover, no completely acceptable moral principles to serve as a consistent code of conduct. Boswell himself is his own example of the wretchedness and depravity to which man can sink, his own best reason for thinking with malice of all human kind. And yet at times the frame of mind which leads him into reproachable actions is seen as proof of his independence of spirit and his freedom to 'walk the right way or not'. Boswell, in fact, epitomises the plight of the individual living in an age of diminishing religious influence. When the requirements of religion are relaxing their active involvement in the conduct of everyday life, and Church service gradually reducing to a point where a weekly celebration is all that is required, then, quite simply, a man such as Boswell is allowed to think and act for himself. Yet, if, as Foucault argues, 'religion loosens its hold but retains the ideal forms of remorse of conscience, of spiritual mortification', then the individual is left to inhabit 'an empty milieu – that of idleness and remorse, in which the heart of man is abandoned to its own anxiety'.[45] In these circumstances, acting and thinking for oneself will present very real and confusing problems, problems which the individual will largely be left to his own resources to solve.

### (iv)  *Self-imposed Imagery*

In this light, then, we may go on to consider how Boswell attempts to impose, through the use of imagery, firm patterns upon his mind with the purpose of reassuring himself of his own orderliness and sanity. It will be useful, as a first example, to examine his use of images of machines – for what better antidote to unpredictability and changeableness than the consistency and permanence of a machine? And, in an increasingly technological age, more and more fascinated by machines, it is scarcely surprising that a man so conscious of new developments and so sensitive to changing trends should seek to express himself through imagery of this type.[46] 'My affairs', he writes in the *London Journal*, 'are conducted with the greatest regularity and exactness. I move like very clockwork' (p. 207). The benefit of moving 'like very clockwork' is the same as that of having plenty to occupy the mind: it brings with it, in Johnson's words to Boswell, 'what is no small advantage, security from those troublesome and wearisome discontents, which are always obtruding themselves upon a mind vacant, unemployed, and undetermined' (*Life*, II, p. 21). A settled and full routine will determine life away from idleness and the tendency to melancholy, and a mechanical mind need have no fear of being seduced by idle speculation or self-indulgent fancies. So, at the court of Baden-Durlach, Boswell observes, 'Here amidst music and dancing I am as cheerful as if nothing had ever vexed me. My mind is like an air-pump which receives and ejects ideas with wonderful facility' (*GT* (i), p. 178).

The idea of his mind as a watch, presumably derived from the stock seventeenth- and eighteenth-century analogy of God as the divine watchmaker, is a favourite image, which Boswell uses to take account of all the activities of his mental life. In *The Hypochondriack* he observes,

> As the main-spring actuates the wheels and other component parts of a watch, so the soul actuates the faculties of the mind; and as the main-spring of a watch may either be broken all-together, or hurt in different degrees, we may justly talk from analogy in the same terms of the soul.
>
> (*BC*, p. 48)

The idea occurs, too, in conversation with Sir John Pringle:

> He would insist that I was not yet in earnest to marry. I told him that I could not show him the inside of my mind as one does a watch, but that I was certainly conscious that my wheels now went calmly and constantly. He said, 'Vous avez encore un peu de vertige.' I was slightly angry and a good

deal diverted, as I was sure of my being quite a different man from what he had formerly known me.  (*Wife*, p. 287)

Here Boswell begins by using the image negatively – his mind is unlike a watch in one respect – but he then proceeds to adopt its terms in order to express his 'new' assessment of himself. He has at last, he thinks, in 1769, attained to calmness and constancy, and need no longer fear lapses into excessive behaviour, or the disorder of his mind-machine that he had described to Temple from Holland in 1764: 'I have thought, if my mind is a collection of springs, these springs are all unhinged, and the machine is all destroyed' (*Holl.*, p. 274). If the mind is a machine, its breakdown is an obvious extension to account for that melancholy the image was originally conceived to combat. Other aspects of the watch idea can also be useful. In *The Hypochondriack* Boswell writes,

> Perhaps it may not be for the advantage of everyone to keep a diary. Should a man of great force of mind, impetuous in understanding, and ardent in activity, examine himself frequently with nice attention, it might weaken and relax his powers, as taking it often to pieces will hurt the machinery of a watch.  (*BC*, p. 332)

But Boswell is arguing here against his own adopted maxim, 'know thyself' (cf. *BC*, p. 330), as well as against a lifetime's practice. He fears the melancholy that acute self-examination could bring by exposing inadequacies and delusions or by leading into areas of the mind where he could perceive no order.

For this reason, too, the mind must be kept fully occupied: 'A man's mind is like a —— glass. He must endeavour to find a variety of prints to look at; otherwise, let the glass be ever so good, he will tire of the sameness' (*Def.*, p. 277). The possibility of the mind as a distorting instrument is just hinted at in the name Boswell could not remember (his editors suggest 'optical glass'), and he points out, too, one of the causes of the melancholy which may affect even the finest minds – boredom. This is what threatens him at Sir John Pringle's, and which he expresses in a very effective simile of another type of machine:

> Dr. Hunter fell to telling a long story of the bad behaviour of Dr. Harwood, to which Priestley listened with avidity. Sir John Pringle nodded. I was patient for I suppose eight or ten minutes, but the story was so uninteresting, and Hunter spoke so tediously and so insipidly, that my mind was in such uneasiness as the lungs are when in want of air, when they are just teased with as much as keeps them in a wretched feeble motion. I could endure it no longer, and made my escape. (*OY*, p. 270)

Boswell's image conveys particularly well the mental suffocation of boredom, and is also very appropriate to an anecdote featuring the man who discovered oxygen. And, unlike several of his other attempts throughout his journals, it expresses a perfectly understood state of mind.

What seems to happen in this use of imagery is that Boswell is able literally to fix his thoughts to something that is external to himself, that has its own independent rules of operation and its own momentum. If his mind is a machine, then he is partially relieved of the responsibility for its well-being, his mind is in other hands than his – either regulated by the requirements of its internal mechanism, or else under the care of the celestial mechanic. Just as the demands of a rigidly enforced religious and moral code shift responsibility away from the individual onto the impersonal machine of the institution and its non-individual representatives, so the choice of a reliable way of looking at himself can to some extent alleviate the problems caused by the freedom to adopt a bewildering variety of mental perspectives. The more convincingly Boswell is able to regard his mind as a machine, the less will he be troubled by finding other adequate vehicles of expression for his own changeability – and, even if he remains unpredictable, he can still resort to placing the responsibility upon the structure of the machine rather than having to confront the effectiveness of his own self-accounting.

But, ironically, yet hardly surprisingly in a man of Boswell's pride of spirit and religious warmth, one of the ideas which most distresses him is that of a mechanical universe and the absence of free will:

> I felt myself in a sort of wild state of mind, metaphysical and fanciful, looking on the various operations of human life as

machinery, or I could not well describe what; and not in the plain steady view which I have had in the midst of a busy session. (*OY*, p. 27)

My state of mind today was still affected by Hartley and Priestley's metaphysics, and was continually trying to perceive my faculties operating as machinery. (*OY*, p. 212)

Clearly, if followed through, the mind as a machine denies the possibility of free will and individual choice, and implies a completely mechanistic universe, and these are implications that Boswell is not prepared to accept. It is one aspect only of the machine image that he finds useful – the capacity of a machine to act reliably and consistently – and any further application of the idea to the scheme of things poses too great a challenge both to his religious principles and to his fundamental pride in his individuality, in being Boswell. For this reason, these particular attempts at imposing order upon himself can only be partially successful, and, while they appear scattered throughout his journals, there is nowhere any really sustained effort by Boswell to think consistently of his mind in terms of a machine. This method of self-accountability leads straight to the chasm of Priestleian determinism.

One thing which Boswell does seem able to maintain with certainly, though, is that the power of reason alone, without the free play of the imagination, will constitute a denial of all that raises life above the level of the mundane. This, whatever the justice of his view, is the basis for his objection to David Hume. Hume has closed off part of his mind, and, even while he is dying, he remains earth-bound. Boswell writes to Mrs Thrale,

My notion is that he had, by long study in one view, brought a *stupor* on his mind as to futurity. He had pored upon the earth till he could not look up to heaven. He was like one of the brahmins, who, we are told, by a rigid perseverance in maintaining a certain posture become unable to change it. Or may we not with propriety compare him to the woman in the gospel, who 'was bowed down and could in no wise lift herself up' till healed by our SAVIOUR, who described her as one 'whom Satan hath bound, lo, these eighteen years'? (*Ex.*, pp. 27-8)

Hume, for Boswell, may be said to represent the logical conclusion of rationalism, and he is refutable only by widening the terms of the debate to include the evidence of the imagination. 'Reasonable beings', he declares in his journal, 'are not solely reasonable. They have fancies which must be amused, tastes which must be pleased, passions which must be roused' (*Def.*, p. 177). And this argument is also convenient in that it deals satisfactorily with the problem of Hume's renowned virtue. Hume's virtue is a problem because he has no apparent external principles upon which to found it, but Boswell's view allows him no imagination and hence no passions. Hume is virtuous because he has no inclination to be otherwise, and he seems to exhibit, in Boswell's mind, the mundane stance of complete equanimity. The atheist suffers death of the spirit, and is in danger of losing half of life's experience:

> As I would not wish to have my body of stone, so I would not wish to have my mind insensible. (*OY*, p. 54)

> I felt my own mind much firmer than formerly, so that I was not depressed tonight; and even the gloom of uncertainty in solemn religious speculation, being mingled with hope, was much more consolatory than the emptiness of infidelity. A man can live in thick air, but perishes in an exhausted receiver. (*Ex.*, p. 155)

It is better to live with the constant danger of melancholy, provided one is living to the full extent of one's imaginative powers, than to take up the position of a Hume. And, again, Boswell has effectively introduced an image from science which, as in the Priestley example, concerns respiration. A state of mind is powerfully conveyed in terms of a physical situation and the point is reinforced by the implied recollection of Johnson's many remarks upon emptiness and upon the mind as a receiver yearning to be filled. Hume's behaviour would deprive life of its enjoyment, and atheism would, as Boswell wrote to Voltaire in 1765, remove one means of combating the depression of melancholy: 'I am a melancholy man, I know not how. In this world my prospect is clouded. I cheer my hours of gloom with expectations of a brighter scene after death, and I think I have a strong probability that I shall not be deceived' (*GT* (i), pp. 311–12). In fact, Boswell, anxious in case 'some unexpected revolution' in his mind should deprive him of his 'pious faith', even considers applying to Hume, 'telling him that... it would be humane in him to furnish me with reflections by which a man of sense and feeling could support his spirit as an infidel' (*OY*, p. 179).

The important thing, it seems, is in some way to achieve the correct balance between the powers of the imagination and the controlling reason. Only then is it possible to extract the maximum enjoyment from life with the minimum amount of distress. Boswell sometimes manages only grudging deference to reason:

> How powerful is the imagination! What a great Proportion does it bear in this wonderful frame, Man. Happiness and Misery can be alternately the Portion of a human Being according as the Imagination is affected, without the Intervention of any external cause, or any Workings of Reason. Of what infinite consequence is it for us to preserve it clear and bright, unpolluted with the dregs of black Melancholy.... Such an Imagination as mine must be gently soothed and tenderly indulged, tho' at the same time care should be taken that Reason remain its superior. It is more agreable, as well as proper, to have it under direction. (*BP*, I, pp. 66–7)

This, of course, is the youthful Boswell speaking. Only a few years later, in his 'Inviolable Plan', he is quite decisive upon the subject: 'Your great loss', he declares, 'is too much wildness of fancy and ludicrous imagination. These are fine if regulated and given out in moderation' (*Holl.*, p. 377).

Imagery of machines, then, was one way in which Boswell had attempted to regulate and moderate his wild mental processes. From here it is a short step to images with which Boswell attempts to influence his actual behaviour, rather than providing one blanket image for his whole mind, and this is exactly what he seems to be doing when he adopts the image of a soldier.

'Images of fortification and combat', says Paul Fussell, 'are uniformly accessible and very broadly applicable to psychological and polemical circumstances.'[47] In an age, he argues, when 'everybody read epic, everybody read classical history, and everybody read the political and military history of the Civil Wars',[48] it must come as no surprise that military images are well to the fore in the works of major moralists such as Swift, Johnson and Burke. Literary precedents are countless, from St Paul to Shakespeare, Milton and Bunyan. But, in Fussell's thesis, it is the prevalent belief in the eighteenth century 'that life at its centre is a perpetual conflict', first between 'man's inner convictions' and 'the practices of a corrupt "world" outside', and then 'within man himself' between 'the inimical elements of his psychic hierarchy, the will and the flesh', that makes this particular range of metaphor so fitting for the moral rhetoricians of the period. 'What is more "natural" ', he asks, '– that is, permanently meaningful – than that the Augustan humanist should choose to express these unremitting and all-important conflicts in terms of actual warfare?'[49]

Still less should we be surprised, then, that the private writer, preoccupied by the psychological warfare at his own centre, and desperate both to understand and to control the struggles he is experiencing, should similarly have recourse to analogies drawn from battle and the life of the soldier. Fussell cites a prayer adapted by Johnson from the Book of Common Prayer and recorded in 1768:

> Almighty God, who seest that I have no power of myself to help myself; keep me both outwardly in my body and inwardly in my soul, that I may be defended from all adversities that may happen to the body, and from all evil thoughts which may assault and hurt the soul, through Jesus Christ our Lord. Amen.[50]

Boswell seeks precisely this kind of aid from his own use of military imagery: protection from 'evil thoughts', from the distractions of melancholy, and guidance in helping himself in terms of bearing and behaviour. He requires, and to a limited extent finds, both inward and outward regulation.

It is not by coincidence, then, that we find Boswell projecting himself as a soldier, nor that this role begins when he is in fact attempting to keep himself to his rigid system of study while he is in Holland. (There is, of course, the point that Boswell had only just abandoned his intention to be an actual soldier, an officer in the Guards; but that scheme was aimed at the more attractive end of having a gay, easy and showy time in London, with the minimum of duty providing some framework for his pleasures. In such glamorous conditions, melancholy would hardly be expected to present such a problem as to require the mechanical routine of a soldier's life to avoid it.)

From Utrecht, then, Boswell writes in September 1763 to Temple,

> I am grown quite keen that we should both take our posts in the warfare of life. I persuade myself we have spirit enough to make good soldiers. Let us never yield a moment to mental cowardice; if we do, we shall think meanly of ourselves. Let us persist with an unremitting fortitude. (*Holl.*, p. 33)

He will apply a soldier's 'spirit' and 'fortitude' to his system of living, reassured in the knowledge that his best friend is a soldier too. In the same vein, he writes to Zélide that he has 'his *orders* for his conduct during the day with as much exactness as any soldier in any service' (*Holl.*, p. 299). Again, in his ten-line verses for 28 March 1764 he writes,

> The blackest clouds of melancholy hung
> Upon my mind, unwieldy was my tongue.
> And yet (what changes can produce one day!)
> I now am easy, vigorous, and gay;
> And am a bold and generous soldier found
> Resolv'd at all events to stand my ground.
> (p. 196)

And the memorandum for the following day (hence recording the events of the 28th) shows that the image is not *just* figurative:

> You went out to fields, and in view of the tower, drew your sword glittering in the sun, and on your knees swore that if

there is a Fatality, then that was also ordained; but if you had free will as you believed, you swore and called the Great G— to witness that, although you're melancholy, you'll stand it, and for the time before you go to Hague, not own it. (Ibid.)

It is interesting to see Boswell adorning the scene in his recollection of it ('glittering in the sun'), even in the abridged version of the memorandum. If, as here, the image can be translated into actual behaviour, so much greater is its effect. Similarly, in a memorandum written in Geneva we find, 'Swear with drawn sword never *pleasure* but with a woman's aid' (*GT* (i), p. 278).

He is not only a soldier in the warfare of life, then, but, more specifically, a soldier in the battle against melancholy. He will 'stand it, and . . . not own it'. And again, in the memorandum for 22 March 1764: 'This day show that you are Boswell, a true soldier. Take your post. Shake off sloth and spleen, and just proceed. Nobody knows your conflicts. Be fixed as a Christian, and shun vice' (*Holl.*, p. 188). 'A true soldier' in this context is surely the soldier of the Lord, and to 'shun vice' is not merely to refrain from vicious activities but to refuse to submit to the phantasms and fancies of melancholy. The true soldier will 'shake off sloth' and consequently the 'spleen' will have less chance to take over his mind. But, even if the melancholy vision should infiltrate, he will 'stand it', and 'never yield a moment to mental cowardice'. The very idea of being a 'true soldier' can be enough to contain his melancholy, and, in fact, the more he suffers, the more right he has to consider himself a soldier of the Lord. However long Boswell had tried, he could never have turned himself into a machine, but he could earn the right to be, in his own eyes, a soldier.

In a letter to his friend Johnston in April 1764, Boswell speaks of the way he was able to use this idea during his time in Holland. He has just heard of the death of his natural son, Charles, whom he had never seen. This news, he says, has affected him deeply:

I heard of Charles's death. It shocked me. It filled me with gloomy reflections on the uncertainty of life, and that every post might bring me accounts of the departure of those whom I most regarded. I saw all things as so precarious and vain that I had no relish of them, no views to fill my mind, no motives to incite me to action. I groaned under those dismal truths which nothing but a lucky oblivion prevents from weighing down the most vivacious souls. Black melancholy again took dominion over me. All my old dreary and fretful feelings recurred. I was much worse on this account, that after my first severe fit on coming to Utrecht, I really believed that I had conquered spleen for ever, and that I should never again be overcome by it. I lived in this persuasion for four months. I had my dull hours. But I considered myself as a soldier. I endured such hardships; but I kept my post.

You may conceive what I felt on the sad conviction that my hopes were fanciful. Oh, how I was galled! Oh, how did I despise myself. (*Holl.*, p. 206)

Here Boswell is actually describing the effect this particular image had had on his conduct and upon his state of mind during a brief period of his life. He clearly achieved some success in maintaining control over his mind, as well as being able to keep himself to his studies – as, indeed, we know from what remains of his Dutch journal. But the event upon which Boswell reflects in the letter to Johnston really marks the end of his ability to impose order upon himself, and to remain reasonably content, in this particular way. Hereafter, for the next year or so, he is either deeply melancholy, or else, more often, he is keeping his mind occupied in the whirl of living – his courtship of Zélide, visits to the German courts and to Rousseau and Voltaire, his amorous manoeuvres in Italy, and the tour of Corsica. The change is clear from the very beginning of the German tour. Sleeping rough at an inn, Boswell picks out the romantic side of a soldier's life, and is pleased to feel the excitement the image offers:

I was laid upon a table covered with straw, with a blanket and a sheet; and above me I had a sheet and a feather bed. Thus was I just in the situation of a bold officer. Thus did I endure the very hardships of a German campaign which I used to tremble at the thought of when at Auchinleck.

(*GT* (i), p. 9)

This attitude is closer to Boswell's London ideas of a military life. The image of himself as a soldier has already changed from an essential mental prop to a relatively harmless self-romanticising indulgence.

(v)

We have seen Boswell using imagery of machines and imagery of soldiers. Both types were adopted in response to his experience of melancholy, and both, ultimately, proved inadequate to the challenge. Each attempt achieved a partial success, but one foundered on Boswell's pride in his own individuality, his very proper inability to think of his mind, his whole life, as merely mechanical, and the other, it seems, on an event which caught the soldier off guard. This, of course, must have been inevitable. No man so lively and versatile as Boswell, with such a relish of life, with such a zest for experience, could be content for long to adopt one particular role, or to strike only one mental pose. His changeability, which so distressed and confused him, was also a source of great pride. He could never, like Hume, maintain 'a certain posture' to the point of rigidity. He would exercise his freedom to change – whatever, and however painful, the consequences.

And it is the freedom to choose that is the important point about Boswell's imagery of soldiers and machines. A man may be subject to the images of melancholy, to the phantasms and fancies and vain imaginings that slide into his mind uninvited and unwelcomed. But he does not have to submit to whatever, or whomever, is sending these images. He can, after all, exercise his freedom to choose images of his own and fill his mind with these. He does not have to make things easy for the invaders. The mustering of the defences may prove inadequate, the images may eventually shatter and be dispersed by the force of melancholy, but at least he will be proving his independence of spirit and his individuality in choosing for himself.

So melancholy madness, the morbid obsession that has become permanent, may be kept back by constantly choosing, by exercising the right of the individual, for by choosing one retains a sense of identity. That which chooses exists in its own right, while that which is done to becomes merely an object with no will and no rights. The only antidote to the ultimate nothingness of the melancholy vision is a strong sense of *something*, which can only, in the end, be the self. And Boswell always, in the end, comes down to choosing to be himself, 'Boswell of Auchinleck', and, to keep his hold on him, strives to make him 'as fine a fellow as possible' (*GT* (i), p. 28). This task is the work of the imagination.

# 3 Madness and the Role of the Image in Thought

(i)

Imagery, for Boswell, is self-assertion. When he produces an image he is reaffirming his own identity as Boswell the image-producer, and, the more striking the image, then the more satisfying it is to be Boswell. 'Of this week', he says, 'I can observe that my mind has been more lively than usual, more fertile in images, more agreeably sensible of enjoying existence' (*Def*., p. 233). And yet Boswell was not content merely to seek more and more excuses to admire himself. He was, as the existence of his journal makes clear, an essentially honest man, and one, moreover, who was anxious to understand and come to terms with himself. 'Know thyself' *was* his motto, even more than 'enjoy thyself', and we properly regard his journal as one life-long exercise in self-examination. Boswell thoroughly pre-empts the advice of Sir Alexander Crichton, who in 1798, in his *Inquiry into the Nature and Origin of Mental Derangement*, wrote of the need for rigorous self-analysis. The patient, he said,

> should not only be capable of abstracting his own mind from himself, and placing it before him as it were, so as to examine it with the freedom and with the impartiality of a natural historian; but he also should be able to take a calm and clear view of every cause which tends to affect the healthy operations of mind, and to trace their effects.[1]

Yet immediately we should take note of a warning remark from Locke: 'The understanding, like the eye, whilst it makes us see and perceive all other things, takes no notice of itself; and it requires art and pains to set it at a distance, and make it its own object.'² It must be the quality of one's 'art and pains' that is essential to the thorough understanding of one's own mind with 'freedom' and 'impartiality', for, if the method of setting at a distance is faulty or inadequately employed, then one's perspective will be correspondingly distorted. The purpose of this chapter is to consider Boswell's approach to self-analysis, not his method of writing down the events and thoughts of his life, but the fact that he so often chose to analyse what he was feeling and thinking by means of images.

When to be well is to be able to produce 'brilliant fancies' (*GT* (i), p. 52), when self-respect is closely involved with relish of 'the sallies of my luxuriant imagination' (*LJ*, p. 65), and when self-assertion in the activity of image-making is the secret preservative of a sense of identity against the fear of melancholy, then what, we are entitled to ask, is the reaction of the individual when confronted with the image he has produced? Has he been able to control it? And, if not, has he lost his mental hold through exultation, or dejection? Boswell was not always able to govern his behaviour with the rigour he thought appropriate for a man of his rank and principles. How successfully did he control, or even understand, his own mental processes?

(ii)   *The Image and Self-analysis*

In attempting to answer some of these questions, I want first to consider the way Boswell uses imagery in order to look into his own mind. This is often done with a view to assessing his mental and material progress through life, and for this reason can be influential on his future attitude towards himself, and therefore on his future conduct. For example, he is in Edinburgh, comfortably watching a performance of one of his favourite plays, *The Beggar's Opera*:

> I was cheerful and happy, having no pretensions, being very well established as an agreeable companion, and being a married man. Life is like a road, the first part of which is a hill. A man must for a while be constantly pulling that he may get forward, and not run back. When he has got beyond the steep, and on smooth ground – that is, when his

character is fixed – he goes on smoothly upon level ground. I could not help indulging Asiatic ideas as I viewed such a number of pretty women, some of them young gay creatures with their hair dressed with flowers. But thoughts of mortality and change came upon me, and then I was glad to feel indifference.   (*OY*, p. 65)

Here Boswell uses, with his 'road' and 'hill', a fairly commonplace image, but he uses it in a personal way and for a particular reason. The purpose of the image seems to be less as an illustration of the opening statement, pure stylistic elaboration, and more as an attempt at rendering in concrete terms Boswell's personal feelings of maturity and social responsibility. The image is therefore an essential part of the thought itself. The particular opening observations are followed by what *appears* to be a general truth based upon Boswell's individual experience. In fact, the image itself gives expression to the very feelings which were only partially exposed by the attempt at particularity. These feelings would seem to include Boswell's sense of achievement in his social life, satisfaction with his own fixed character after the struggle of 'constantly pulling', and also celebration of hope for the future. The delusion of supposing himself to be a married man of fixed character, however, is quickly revealed (to the reader) by the sensual Boswell's breaking out into 'Asiatic ideas'. To subdue these, he has to rely upon powerful 'thoughts of mortality and change', rather than upon his new constancy and firmness. The basis for his satisfaction has remained unexplored, and Boswell has been celebrating an achievement of which he cannot be certain.

We can see some of the dangers into which Boswell fell in using imagery to persuade himself he was something he was not. The satisfying emotional connotations of the image, unconsciously expressing the feelings of achievement and maturity which mark his state of mind in the theatre, react powerfully with those very feelings, and indulge them at the expense of rational consideration of the reality on which they are supposedly based. As Alexander Smith observed nearly a century later, 'It is often not very easy to say whether the feeling is the parent of the image by which it expresses itself, or whether, on the contrary, the image is the parent of the feeling. The truth seems to be, that they produce and reproduce one another.'³ Boswell's satisfaction is really self-indulgence, and that this is so is obscured from him by, among other things, the image, for it encourages the emotion and prevents genuine self-appraisal, while it masquerades as additional explanation of the opening statement.

As a parallel to this example, it will be useful to consider another from the same year, 1775. Here Boswell is again deliberately looking into himself, and yet in so doing he attempts to provide himself once more with foundation for the same sense of personal responsibility and self-satisfaction. Here he finds a much more striking image:

> I wrote to Temple . . . with great elation, and in high spirits told him that my mind, formerly a wild, had been for some years well enclosed with moral fences; that a storm of passion had lately come and shaken them, but that I found them now firm. I should have added, as I afterwards thought, that as we plant roses and honeysuckles in hedges, and sometimes adorn them at the roots with borders of flowers, so moral hedges should be made pleasing by agreeable circumstances. (*OY*, p. 120)

The implications of this image are important, for Boswell is 'enclosing' his mind, not cultivating it, and probably not really looking into it. To Boswell the fences are the sound principles of behaviour behind which he is trying to subdue his natural passions, but they also become the barriers of imagery he is using to force his mind into recognisable form without having to undergo any real self-examination. The image is the end of the line: what is behind the 'moral fences' and the barriers of imagery remains unexplored – perhaps even unnoticed. In fact, the image arguably constitutes an end in itself, for Boswell is obviously very proud of his 'slight self-pleasing thread'. The hedges are clearly not of the type which surround fields or border roads, but are those planted by a gardener to serve both as enclosure and as ornamentation. Boswell cannot resist decorating them with the colours and scents of flowers, and these further obscure any value the image may have had as a means to self-knowledge. The impression is that Boswell has his eye on the deliberate beauty of his image, rather than on the truth it is supposed to convey. And, just as in the road example Boswell is basing the image upon a self-indulgent feeling, so here he begins his image in 'high spirits', with the clear intention of telling Temple, and himself, that he is indeed Boswell the man of worth. So he is indulging his own feelings of personal satisfaction, as well as his pride in his image-making. In the 'road' example he thinks he is drawing a general truth from his particular experience, and here that he is using imagery to understand himself. In each case he is deluded, for both are really serving the same ends: indulgence and evasion.

Often, then, Boswell is too proud of a striking image to take advantage of any opportunities it offers him of proceeding further in his self-analysis. He fails to recognise the dangers of self-indulgence and delusion encouraged in him by the connotations of the image, and does not realise the possible distortion caused by exaggerated emotional elements. Nor does he see the falsification sometimes resulting from making a state of mind or a situation fit an attractive image. In the words of M. H. Abrams,

> mental events must be talked about metaphorically, in an object-language which was developed to deal literally with the physical world. As a result, our conception of these events is peculiarly amenable to the formative influence of the physical metaphors in which we discuss them, and of the underlying physical analogies from which these metaphors are derived.[4]

Boswell attempts to give coherence to his thoughts and feelings, and to explore his mind, through imagery, but fails to achieve greater self-awareness because he does not seek to examine beyond the figurative.

It may, of course, be argued that an extended simile of the type I have been discussing is only very loosely termed an image, and should certainly not be confused with the mental image. Boswell's use of simile, however, does seem to suggest a particular way of thinking, rather than just a technique of expression; it suggests a mind strongly inclined to seeking pictorial analogies to states of feeling. It is not just the forceful representation to the reader of a portion of experience or a state of mind that we find in the similes of the journals; we find too the only way that Boswell could render the experience or feeling real to himself – certainly the only way he thought he could understand himself. Boswell's use of imagery is indicative of the manner in which he had become accustomed to look at the whole of life. The consciously articulated similes of the journal are merely the written evidence of a mind heavily biased towards the visual, the metaphorical, the poetic – 'my genius for poetry, which ascribes many fanciful properties to everything' (*LJ*, p. 69).

### (iii) *The Role of the Image in Thought*

With this assumption in mind, I should like now to discuss more fully the role of the image in thought: it seems to me to be of supreme importance in any consideration of Boswell's self-portrait in his journals. In order to have available an authoritative account of the workings of the imagination, I shall briefly indicate the central contentions put forward by Jean-Paul Sartre in his book *The Psychology of Imagination*, as they are most relevant to my reading of Boswell.

Sartre first of all draws a contrast between the mental image and language: we cannot learn from the image, he says, in the way we sometimes can from language:

> A simple illustration will clarify this point for us: it often happens that we get to know our own thoughts as we put them into words; language prolongs them, finishes and specifies them; what was a vague 'airy consciousness', a more or less undetermined idea, becomes a clear and precise proposition by being spoken. So that whether our language is overt or 'internal' our thoughts become more and better defined by means of it than we ourselves were able to make them; it *teaches us* something. But the mental image teaches us nothing: this is the principal of quasi-observation. It cannot be said that an image clarifies our knowledge in any manner whatsoever for the very reason that it is the knowledge that constitutes the image. If language then teaches us something, it can do this only because of its externality. It is because the mechanisms

according to which sounds and phrases are arranged are partly independent of our consciousness, that we are able to read our thoughts on the phrases.[5]

So, when Boswell extends his original mental image and formulates it in words, and then completes the externalising process by writing the thought out in his journal as an independent unit, he is merely making more precise something which in fact can have no instructional value.

Sartre continues this line by speaking of the image in relation to judgement:

> An imaginative consciousness includes a knowledge, intentions and can include words and judgments. And by this we do not mean that a judgment can be made *on* the image, but that, in the very structure of the image judgments can enter in a special form, namely, in the imaginative form. . . . What we ordinarily designate as *thinking* is a consciousness which affirms this or that quality of its object but without realizing the qualities *on* the object. The *image*, on the contrary, is a consciousness that aims to produce its object: it is therefore constituted by a certain way of judging or feeling of which we do not become conscious as such, but which we apprehend on the intentional object as this or that of its qualities.[6]

The image can only reaffirm what is known and felt already, yet this reaffirmation is an unconscious one. This is precisely what I have tried to show happening with Boswell.

Next Sartre speaks of the frequent appearance of the image as illustration for thought:

> we arrive at the conclusion that the image as an illustration is produced as the first groping of a lower thought, and that the ambiguities concerning its meaning are due to the uncertainties of a thought which has not yet risen to a clear vision of a concept. . . . The result of these uncertainties is an image which sets itself up for its own sake and also as a step in understanding. . . . From the onset of the image as an illustration, two roads are always possible: one by which thought loses itself in revery as it abandons its first assignment, and another which leads it to understanding as such.[7]

This is the difference between non-reflective and reflective thought. It is with non-reflective thought that the danger lies, for it 'presents itself as *being* itself the essence or the relationship to be determined':

> *Non-reflective thought is a possession.* To think of an essence, a relationship, is on this plane to produce them 'in flesh and bone', to constitute them in their living reality . . . and at the same time to see them, to possess them. But, at the same time, it is to constitute them *under a certain form* and to consider this form as expressing exactly their nature, as *being* their nature. Here thought encloses itself in the image and the image presents itself as adequate to the thought. There follows a warping – possible at any moment – of the further course of consciousness.[8]

And he offers an example of this 'warping':

> 'I would have liked to convince myself of the idea that every oppressed person or every oppressed group draws from the very oppression from which it suffers the strength to destroy it. But I had the clear impression that such a theory was arbitrary and I felt a sort of annoyance. I made a new effort to think: at this very moment there arose the image of a compressed force. At the same time I felt the latent force in my muscles. It was going to break out the more violently the more compressed it was. In a moment I felt to the point of certainty the necessity of the idea of which I could not persuade myself the moment before.'
>
> We see what is involved here: the oppressed *is* the force. But on the other hand, *on* the compressed force we can already read with confidence the strength with which it will be discharged: a compressed force clearly represents potential energy. This potential energy is evidently that of the oppressed, since the oppressed *is* the force. Here we clearly see the contamination between the laws of the image and those of the essence represented. This idea of potential energy which increases in proportion to the force exercised on the object, is the force which *presents* it, it is upon it that it can be apprehended.[9]

## MADNESS AND THE ROLE OF THE IMAGE

The importance of the producing act now becomes apparent (and we may recall Boswell's very conscious pride in his capacity for image-making, and his association of this activity with liveliness of spirits):

> It is not true that unreal objects have more or less power or vivacity depending on the individual. An unreal object cannot be strong since it does not act. But to produce an image of greater or lesser liveliness is to react with greater or lesser liveliness to the producing act, and by the same token to attribute to the imagined object the power of giving birth to these reactions.... At the time of the constitution of the unreal object, knowledge plays the role of perception: it is to it that the feeling is incorporated. Thus is born the unreal object. It is at this point that we should repeat what we constantly maintained: the unreal object exists, it exists as unreal, as inactive, of this there is no doubt; but its existence is undeniable. Feeling, then, behaves in the face of the unreal as in that of the real. It seeks to blend with it, to adapt itself to its contours, to feed on it. Only this unreal, so well specified and so well defined, pertains *to the void*; or, if one prefers, it is the simple reflection of the feeling. This feeling therefore feeds on its own reflection.[10]

So, for instance, in the example of Boswell's 'road', the feeling of achievement upon which the image is based and which the image feeds, is reinforced by the feeling of achievement at the actual production of the image. So the possibility of constructive 'reflective' thought becomes more remote.

This process is particularly important where it can be seen to influence Boswell's actual conduct and his relations with other people. Certain incidents stand out as exceptionally clear examples of image-induced behaviour. Concerning his choice between the final two candidates for the position of Mrs Boswell, the Irish heiress, Marianne, is projected as 'my charming seraph' with her 'little bosom' (*Wife*, p. 215), while his cousin, Margaret, is pictured in a more earthy style: 'Her most desirable person, like a heathen goddess painted alfresco on the ceiling of a palace at Rome, was compared with the delicate little Miss' (p. 227). Boswell allows his emotional attitudes (particularly, as his words suggest, sexual appetite) towards the two women to dictate the type of image fitting to each, and then attempts to make his choice of the more appealing image. While the actual result probably had as much to do with the determination of Margaret herself, Boswell's own mental process towards reaching some conclusion is still revealing.

Of less moment, but equally revealing, are three incidents in which Boswell is confronted with the choice of whether or not to adopt a certain course of action or type of behaviour. At the end of the Louisa affair, having just written to her in terms of coldness, he asks himself, 'Am I not too vindictive? It appears so; but upon better consideration I am only sacrificing at the shrine of Justice; and sure I have chosen a victim that deserves it' (*LJ*, p. 199). Not only is Louisa distanced by being seen as a 'victim' at the 'shrine of Justice', but Boswell's feelings of injured innocence are allowed to direct the constitution of the image in which he is to play the combined role of judicial executioner and priest. Similarly, in Italy, with the courtesan Susette, he tells himself, 'I sacrificed to the graces. I think I did no harm' (*GT* (ii), p. 255). Again, he allows his image to carry persuasive overtones of having fulfilled a sacred duty. This is important as far as future liaisons are concerned. And, in justification of his conduct in Italy as a whole, he writes to Rousseau that 'a being who has had so sad an existence as mine would do badly ... if he did not drink from the stream of pleasure as long as Heaven caused it to flow' (*GT* (ii), p. 20). Here Boswell is the suffering, sensitive man on whom heaven has at last smiled; consequently to deny himself enjoyment is not only unnecessary, but impious. This, surely, is cant!

Perhaps of greatest importance, though, are the glimpses we are given of Boswell's image of Johnson. Here, too, the pictures frequently have overt religious significance. Travelling to meet Johnson at Ashbourne in 1777, Boswell writes that 'I was like one going upon a pilgrimage to some sacred place' (*Ex.*, p. 143). Similarly, in 1776 he writes from Edinburgh 'to Dr. Johnson thanking him for his letters on the great question and entreating to be encouraged by him to come to London this spring. I could scarcely suppose that I should not, but I wished for a *viaticum*, as I was somewhat irresolute' (*OY*, p. 237). But the 'warping' effect of this attitude is brought out most clearly by a letter from Boswell to Johnson in 1774.

## MADNESS AND THE ROLE OF THE IMAGE

Johnson's reply in particular points straight to the fallacy at the centre of Boswell's use of imagery in this way:

> I wrote to him . . . requesting his counsel whether I should this spring come to London. I stated to him on the one hand some pecuniary embarrassments which, together with my wife's situation at that time, made me hesitate; and on the other the pleasure and improvement which my annual visit to the metropolis always afforded me; and particularly mentioned a peculiar satisfaction which I experienced in celebrating the festival of Easter in St. Paul's Cathedral; that to my fancy it appeared like going up to Jerusalem at the feast of the Passover, and that the strong devotion which I felt on that occasion diffused its influence on my mind through the rest of the year.

Johnson replies,

> I think there is no great difficulty in resolving your doubts. The reasons for which you are inclined to visit London are, I think, not of sufficient strength to answer the objections. . . . Your last reason is so serious that I am unwilling to oppose it. Yet you must remember that your image of worshipping once a year in a certain place in imitation of the Jews is but a comparison, and *simile non est idem*. If the annual resort to Jerusalem was a duty to the Jews, it was a duty because it was commanded; and you have no such command, therefore no such duty. (*Def.*, pp. 213–14)

This is the reflective mind at work on the non-reflective.

It is interesting, too, in the light of Boswell's early wish for a military career, to glance at two remarks made during his stay in Prussia:

> My ideas of the value of men are altered since I came to this country. I see such numbers of fine fellows bred to be slaughtered that human beings seem like herrings in a plentiful season. One thinks nothing of a few barrels of herring, nor can I think much of a few regiments of men. (*GT* (i), p. 24)

The soldiers seemed in terror. For the least fault they were beat like dogs. I am, however, doubtful if such fellows don't make the best soldiers. Machines are surer instruments than men. Were I to knock down a scoundrel, I would rather take a stick than a child by the heels to give him a blow with.

(*GT* (i), p. 80)

Certainly, these images do not lead Boswell into any reproachable conduct, but they become more ominous when we remember that, had Boswell succeeded in his scheme of entering the Guards as an officer, he might easily have been responsible for sending similar 'numbers of fine fellows... to be slaughtered'. It is evident that belief in the reality of other people – that is, the awareness that each individual has thoughts, feelings and a unique sense of identity in exactly the same way as oneself – is made almost impossible when they are automatically projected in terms of something else. This is particularly the case when they can be seen as a mob rather than as individuals: characteristically, Boswell gave money to one soldier who had been beaten like a dog (ibid., n. 1).

Boswell, though, actively encourages this way of looking at life. He seems to find it a comforting escape from reality. To his friend Dempster he writes asking for advice over his choice of wife, but adds, 'whatever is the drawing of your reason, pray let me have it agreeably coloured by your fancy' (*Wife*, p. 227). And he similarly requests of Johnston, 'Write soon and give me full advices and put my future life in Britain in agreeable colours. I have need of your assistance' (*Corr.* I, p. 125). Boswell's own version of the world is potentially so much more pleasing than the actual world that he would not willingly have it effaced. What he is really asking Dempster and Johnston is 'tell me what I want to know – reassure me that my image of life is the true one'. In particular, Boswell's image of the world is nicely arranged with himself at the centre. Why, then, exchange it for a situation in which every individual has an equal claim to reality – or at least an equal claim to the central position? So, he is especially pleased to receive 'an excellent letter from my friend Temple, which made me think favourably of myself, without which I am never happy' (*BP*, XIII, p. 170). Boswell's requests to Dempster and Johnston might almost have been made as deliberate illustrations of

Johnson's assertion about the imagination in Rasselas: 'The mind dances from scene to scene, unites all pleasures in all combinations, and riots in delights which nature and fortune, with all their bounty, cannot bestow.'[11]

(iv)  *The Role of the Image in Madness*

Our discussion, then, is moving towards recognition of the point where an excessive freedom of the imagination may more properly be termed madness. Michel Foucault is illuminating on the role of the image in madness:

> just as the consciousness of truth is not carried away by the mere presence of the image, but in the act which limits, confronts, unifies, or dissociates the image, so madness will begin only in the act which gives the value of truth to the image. There is an original innocence of the imagination: 'The imagination itself does not err, since it neither denies nor affirms but is fixed to so great a degree on the simple contemplation of an image'; and only the mind can turn what is given in the image into abusive truth, in other words, into error, or acknowledged error, that is, into truth: 'A drunk man thinks he sees two candles where there is but one; a man who has a strabismus and whose mind is cultivated immediately acknowledges his error and accustoms himself to see but one.' Madness is thus beyond imagination, and yet it is profoundly rooted in it; for it consists merely in allowing the image a spontaneous value, total and absolute truth. The act of the reasonable man who, rightly or wrongly, judges an image to be true or false, is beyond this image, transcends and measures it by what is not itself; the act of the madman never oversteps the image presented, but surrenders to its immediacy, and affirms it only insofar as it is enveloped by it.[12]

Johnson makes a similar point in *Rasselas*, and argues, as Foucault implies, that there are degrees of madness:

> All power of fancy over reason is a degree of insanity; but while this power is such as we can control and repress, it is

not visible to others, nor considered as any depravation of the mental faculties: it is not pronounced madness but when it comes ungovernable, and apparently influences speech or action.[13]

The more completely one surrenders to one's image, and the less one seeks to refer back to the truth of reality, then with greater justice may one be described as mad:

> Veritable madnesses, then, are all the derangements of our mind, all the illusions of self-love, and all the passions when they are carried to the point of blindness; for blindness is the distinctive characteristic of madness.[14]

> Madness occurs when the images, which are so close to the dream, receive the affirmation or negation that constitutes error.... If it is true that on one hand the madman's mind is led on by the oneiric arbitrariness of images, on the other, and at the same time, he imprisons himself in the circle of an erroneous consciousness.[15]

(With reference to this, we may recall Johnson's insistence that both parts of a metaphor should be true, or else be considered as absurd,[16] and Dryden's remark that one should be 'pleased with the image without being cozened by the fiction'.[17])

It is this quality of being 'imprisoned' and 'led on' which finds an echo in Sartre when he speaks of the impossibility of ever moving from non-reflective to reflective thought:

> But thought, although we could express ourselves upon it without keeping account of the images in which it reveals itself, is never directly accessible to us, if we have once taken the imaginative attitude in forming it. We will always go from image to image. Comprehension is a movement which is never-ending, it is the reaction of mind to an image by another image, and so on, in a straight line, to infinity. To substitute for this infinite regression the simple intuition of a bare thought calls for a radical change in attitude, a veritable revolution, that is, passing from the non-reflective plane to that of the reflective. On this plane thought presents itself as thought at the very time that it appears: and so

it is completely transparent to itself. But we can never discover any connecting path which permits us to elevate ourselves progressively from non-reflection to reflective thought, that is, from the idea as an image to the idea as idea.[18]

Images are disorderly: although they progress 'in a straight line', they follow their own internal pattern, they are not governable by any exterior logic. They may be chosen, as Boswell chooses the machine and the soldier, but one cannot choose where they will lead. And it is the arbitrariness and uncontrollability of the products of the imagination which, for Johnson, constitute madness:

> Perhaps, if we speak with rigorous exactness, no human mind is in its right state. There is no man whose imagination does not sometimes predominate over his reason, who can regulate his attention wholly by his will, and whose ideas will come and go at his command. No man will be found in whose mind airy notions do not sometimes tyrannise, and force him to hope or fear beyond the limits of sober probability.[19]

Some measure of Boswell's 'degree of insanity' is the frequency with which he complains of being possessed by a confusion of ideas and images:

> I am perplexed by a swarm of ideas which mingle confusedly in my head. (*GT* (i), p. 58)

> ... all my ideas and all my principles are dissolved, are run into one dead mass. Good GOD, my friend, what horrid chimeras. Reason existed, but was overpowered.
> (*Holl.*, p. 274)

> I was sensible at one moment of a sort of confusion of mind which sometimes affects me, either from having too many ideas, or not enough vigour to arrange them and keep back all but those immediately necessary. At such times the mob breaks in upon the regular troops. (*OY*, p. 181)

It is also some measure of his degree of sanity that he can recognise when he is so disordered. The last example above, with its apt use of the term 'mob' to convey through its connotations of civil disturbance the fear of uncontrollable ideas, is a particularly good demonstration of Boswell's ability at times to view his experience with objectivity.[20] We may in this respect compare Boswell favourably against the standard and limit set for madness by Cervantes, for in the person of Don Quixote is combined 'oneiric arbitrariness of images' with 'imprisonment in the circle of an erroneous consciousness' to produce a figure who is totally convinced of the reality of his own unreal world.

For it is its unreality which is the central feature of the world of madness. This is emphasised by Johnson: 'Then fictions begin to operate as realities, false opinions fasten upon the mind, and life passes in dreams of rapture or of anguish.'[21] The pleasing unreal world is essentially an escape:

> We suffer phantoms to rise up before us, and amuse ourselves with the dance of airy images.... All this is a voluntary dream, a temporary recession from the realities of life to airy fictions; and habitual subjection of reason to fancy.[22]

Our images invite us, as Sartre says, to 'a perpetual "elsewhere" ', 'a perpetual evasion':

> But the evasion to which they invite us is not only of the sort which is an escape from actuality, from our preoccupation, our boredom, they offer us an escape from all worldly constraints, they seem to present themselves as a negation of the condition of *being in the world*, as an anti-world.[23]

Again, we find in Boswell a constant swaying between real and unreal: he and Temple 'amused ourselves by building many aerial castles of future felicity', or he is 'building my castle in the air' (*LJ*, pp. 267, 337). The youthful Boswell had been accustomed to living consciously in a make-believe world: of the habit of 'shaving', for example, he says, 'When I get into the Guards and am in real life, I shall give it over' (*BP*, I, p. 131). But the make-believe is not always conscious: soon

## MADNESS AND THE ROLE OF THE IMAGE 61

after arriving in London he observes, 'I had accustomed myself so much to laugh at everything that it required time to render my imagination solid and give me just notions of real life and religion' (*LJ*, pp. 88–9). 'Real life' here, however, means 'to be a Mr. Addison' (in fact to be a mixture of Addison and Steele, with 'the manners of Mr. Digges'). There must be continual reference made to the world of reality in order to maintain sanity: he is consoled by anecdotes – 'I say consoled, for good real ideas dispel the vapours of hypochondria' (*OY*, p. 237). He is impressed by his brother's firmness: 'David had appeared to me yesterday very intelligent and firm. I saw that much of my unhappiness was *mouldy imagination*. I ought therefore to keep my mind clear by *realities* and activity' (*BP*, XIV, p. 101). And of the relief afforded by conversation he writes, 'I felt realities assure by wavering mind' (XVIII, p. 90).

The problem is that the unreality of the world of images, as the dominion of that world becomes more total, reflects back upon the subject himself, and finally incorporates him completely into the unreality which constitutes madness:

> Thought takes the image form when it wishes to be intuitive, when it wants to ground its affirmations on the vision of an object. In that case, it tries to make the object appear before it, or better still, to *possess* it. But this attempt, in which all thought risks being bogged down, is always a defeat: the objects become affected with the character of unreality. This means that our attitude in the face of the image is radically different from our attitude in the face of objects. Love, hate, desire, will, are quasi-love, quasi-hate, etc., since the observation of the unreal object is a quasi-observation.[24]

> For the rest, the object as an image is an unreality. It is no doubt present, but, at the same time, it is out of reach. I cannot touch it, change its place: or rather I can well do so, but on condition that I do it in an unreal way, by not using my own hands but those of some phantom which give this face unreal blows: to act upon these unreal objects I must divide myself, make myself *unreal*. But then none of these objects call upon me to act, to do anything. They are neither weighty, insistent, nor compelling: they are pure passivity,

they wait. The faint breath of life we breathe into them comes from us, from our spontaneity. If we turn away from them they are destroyed.[25]

The unreal cannot be seen, touched, smelled, otherwise than in an unreal way. Conversely, it can act only on an unreal being.[26]

The essence of madness is nothingness – the nothingness of the world of the imagination, the nothingness of blind error:

> Madness is precisely, at the point of contact between the oneiric and the erroneous; it traverses, in its variations, the surface on which they meet, the surface which both joins and separates them. With error, madness shares non-truth, and arbitrariness in affirmation or negation; from the dream, madness borrows the flow of images and the colourful presence of hallucinations. But while error is merely non-truth, while the dream neither affirms nor judges, madness fills the void of error with images, and links hallucinations by affirmation of the false. In a sense, it is thus a plenitude, joining to the figures of night the powers of day, to the forms of fantasy the activity of the waking mind; it links the dark content with the forms of light. But is not such plenitude actually the *culmination of the void*? The presence of images offers no more than night-ringed hallucinations, figures inscribed at the corners of sleep, hence detached from any sensuous reality; however vivid they are, however rigorously established in the body, these images are nothingness, since they represent nothing; as for erroneous judgment, it judges only in appearance: affirming nothing true or real, it does not affirm at all; it is ensnared in the non-being of error.[27]

The madman, then, exists in nothingness: his feelings 'pertain to the void', his world is 'the culmination of the void'. He is himself a manifestation of nothingness: in his person nothingness is made 'real', given life and immediacy. His is the constant presence of unreality within the world, and his person is a reminder that produces a degree of the dizziness which is itself a foretaste of madness.

(v)

Finally, we may draw some conclusions about Boswell's degree of insanity, for the relationship between our two original concerns should now be apparent. The melancholiac's tendency to see 'the nothingness of all things in human life' finds in the world of Boswell's imagination the essential unreality in which it may flourish. It is because he has not surrendered totally to the image world, because there remains some reference from the unreal to the real, that Boswell suffers the shifting uncertainty of the hypochondriac, persuaded sometimes of his own excellence, sometimes of the truth of the 'hideous representations of life' of his 'gloomy imagination', rather than maintaining the self-sufficient firmness of the madman. The images of the type I have been discussing are essential to Boswell's way of thinking, for they constitute the only barrier between himself and the nothingness of incomprehension, between perception and meaninglessness. But they are themselves the 'something which is nothingness',[28] mere reflections of the real world and structured according to Boswell's internal needs. So Boswell tends to live one step away from life, in a limbo where the real world exists in phantom form, and presents him mainly with the reaction he wants to find. (In this respect, perhaps, we may justly say with Johnson that 'no human mind is in its right state'.)

In the light of such evidence of how a way of thinking is transformed into a way of choosing and acting, it is hardly surprising that Boswell was never able to regulate his behaviour as strictly as he thought appropriate, and that the excuses he found for deviation always presented themselves with greater force than the requirements of the moral principles he claimed to uphold. And it is also apparent that the life-long inquiry Boswell conducted into his own character could give him only a limited kind of self-knowledge – a self-portrait more notable for its strong strokes than its subtle shades; for, while he could examine what he did and said, he was quite unable to achieve any more than a passing acquaintance with the way his mind worked.

The unreal self, though, which apprehends its unreal world, is forced to exist in the world of reality. Boswell must earn his living, seek enjoyment, and relate to other people within the context of 'normality'. In my next chapter I shall be concerned with the problems of survival in the real world, and with the relations between melancholy–mania and normality.

# 4 The Pressures of Society

## (i) *Conformity*

One of the most important points in life is decency; which is to do what is proper and where it is proper; for many things are proper at one time, and in one place, that are extremely improper in another.... It is very proper and decent to dance well; but then you must dance only at balls, and places of entertainment; for you would be reckoned a fool, if you were to dance at church, or at a funeral.... By which you see how necessary decency is, to gain the approbation of mankind.[1]

This is the theme of an early letter from Lord Chesterfield to his son, one of the series which is probably the eighteenth century's most comprehensive course in social instruction. Chesterfield, from the very beginning, selects for particular insinuation the concept that the potentially successful man is he who becomes aware that propriety is neither more nor less than the collective opinion of other people – 'you would be reckoned a fool', 'gain the approbation of mankind'. The man who conforms by instinct alone will be an acceptable member of society, but whoever attains to a positive consciousness of this first principle of social morality may manipulate and exploit his knowledge to his own considerable advantage.

George Cheyne lends to the opinion of those 'other people' the weighty support of his medical authority when, in the Preface to his *Essay on Regimen*, he describes common-sense as manifesting itself in

> asserting and conforming to the Truths and Manners agreed upon explicitly or implicitly, in the Community where Providence has placed us ... and he who pretends to be happy, as to his outward Circumstances, out of common

> Life, or wise as to intellectual Endowments, out of common Sense, in Things on a Level with his Occupation and Education; I take him to labour under some undiscover'd chronical nervous Distemper, be the other Appearances what they will, and have been seldom mistaken in a particular Case.²

Chesterfield's 'fool' is harshly emphasised here, and Cheyne threateningly exposes what had been only a dormant relation to disease. The message is clear: conformity or confinement; let your behaviour reflect the health of your mind, or run the risk of our having to cure you. And Cheyne implies both political and divine sanction for his professional opinion.

Chesterfield and Cheyne were writing in the 1730s, and so represent, as far as a consideration of Boswell is concerned, the attitude of an older order. Yet he had received advice of a similar kind from his friend Johnston in 1763: 'The opinion of the World must not be despised. Whenever one Sinks in its esteem, he must be unhappy, and rendered useless to his Country and friends' (*Corr.* I, p. 80). And the sentiments are ones which Boswell feels no compulsion not to endorse. His writings are littered with expressions of the need for conformity, and of the benefit of restraint. In his 'Address as Recorder to the Grand Jury of Carlisle', in 1786, he uses the traditional image of constitutional sickness and health, 'a desperate disease' and its 'violent remedy', when speaking of Charles I and the Civil War; and he proceeds to discuss the importance of religion and submission in government:

> it is of the utmost importance to inculcate the principles of our holy Religion, by which those dispositions which make men loyal subjects are most effectually cherished. 'Fear GOD and honour the King' is a text which cannot be too frequently recalled to our minds. The union of religion with government, – 'Submission for the Lord's sake', – produces that reverence for our rulers, which, if Men have not, they may be restrained, but are not gently governed.
> 
> (*BP*, XVII, pp. 180–1)

In his *Hypochondriack* essay 'On Prudence', Boswell echoes the sentiments of Chesterfield himself:

Prudence in the genuine and large sense of the word, is a capital virtue, being no less than the habitual power of managing to the best advantage all our talents, and adapting our conduct to circumstances in the most effectual manner. (*BC*, p. 229)

Elsewhere he praises 'that system of good manners by which civilised society is raised so far above the rude state of nature' (*BC*, p. 123), and a similar thought occurs early in the *London Journal*:

> The great art of living easy and happy in society is to study proper behaviour, and even with our most intimate friends to observe politeness; otherwise we will insensibly treat each other with a degree of rudeness, and each will find himself despised in some measure by the other. (p. 89)

Clearly, then, the required precision in behaviour calls for a delicate self-control, even by the most equable of men. The problem, therefore, naturally becomes acute for Boswell, the intemperate side of whose personality was frequently liable at short notice to 'take fire', and whose impulsive zest for living inclined him to pursue enjoyment far beyond its decent limits: 'Is it not true philosophy, my friend, to procure as much happiness, to make as much honey in life, as we can? I mean in consistency with all duties' (*Letters*, II, p. 362). Boswell's maniac bias demands that he indulge in the drinking, gambling, and roaring type of activities which in excess (and Boswell rarely does things by halves) produces the censure of society. The man who cannot regulate his desires within the bounds of public decency will always, as Freud makes clear, constitute a serious threat to the credibility of the assumption upon which any community is founded:

> It is equally clear why it is that the violation of certain taboo prohibitions constitutes a social danger which must be punished or atoned for by *all* the members of the community if they are not all to suffer injury.... It lies in the risk of imitation, which would quickly lead to the dissolution of the community. If the violation were not avenged by the other members they would become aware that they wanted to act

in the same way as the transgressor.... This is indeed one of the foundations of the human penal system and it is based, no doubt correctly, on the assumption that the prohibited impulses are present alike in the criminal and in the avenging community. In this, psycho-analysis is no more than confirming the habitual pronouncement of the pious: we are all miserable sinners.[3]

Boswell is constantly aware of the disgrace of being a likely recipient of society's retributive pressure, and consequently his most frequent self-reprovals, particularly, but by no means exclusively, in the earlier journals, are for allowing his zest to endanger his dignity:

> Another shocking fault which I have is my sacrificing almost anything to a laugh, even myself.... This is indeed a fault in the highest degree to be lamented and to be guarded against. I am firmly resolved to amend it. (*LJ*, p. 216)

> Was sensible that my vivacity is not yet enough under regulation. *Why* wish to entertain every body?
> (*BP*, XIV, p. 118)

In a letter to Temple, Boswell takes a step towards linking this social inadequacy with his tendency to hypochondria when he speaks of 'an antipathy at established rules which I have not yet altogether got the better of' (*Letters*, I, p. 25). This is made more specific in *Hypochondriack* 25:

> Wretched is the state of an Hypochondriack whose distempered pride makes him imagine that he is to preserve incessant dignity of decorum in behaviour. A Brahmin who condemns himself to remain perpetually in one posture does not suffer more pain than the Hypochondriack who remains in continual uneasy elevation, and is for ever galled by the fetters of correctness. (*BC*, p. 151)

Already the confusion of the mania of hypochondria is apparent: the 'established rules' are resented in so far as they constrain natural impulses, and yet it is by no means certain that the maniac's idea of those rules is not itself distorted, with

## THE PRESSURES OF SOCIETY

the result that he attributes to them a far greater severity than does the normal man. Boswell points to a further tendency in a memorandum of 1765, when he advises, 'This day pause; swear solemn behaviour. Madness is no excuse, as you can restrain it' (*GT* (ii), p. 37 n. 1). Mania, at times provoking excessive severity, can also be used as a reason for indulgence.

The mania–madness of hypochondria appears to be rooted less in the individual's propensity to behavioural excesses than in an inability to form a just estimation of the scope allowed by society for deviation. He finds it impossible to define an area outside of which indulgence of the passions must not be permitted. Consequent upon this inadequacy is the confused and spasmodic madness which distinguishes at least Boswell's hypochondria, and the grief and guilt which follow his frequent transgressions.

I suggested in Chapter 2 that Boswell's melancholy often arises from feelings of guilt for some particular incident of misconduct. More frequently, though, it simply flows into his conscious mind as an awareness of the emptiness of life and of the vanity of all human activity. (One need search no further than Johnson to discover that in this aspect Boswell is by no means unique.) The journals consistently present observations of this type:

> I was very dreary. I had lost all relish of London. I thought I saw the nothingness of all sublunary enjoyments. I was cold and spiritless.  (*LJ*, p. 237)

> I think gloomily of the vanity and misery of human life. I think that it is not worth while to do anything. Everything is insipid or everything is dark. . . . Happy is the man who can forget that he exists.  (*Holl.*, pp. 192–3)

> Got up in sad Hyp. . . . Was quite in despair. Could not see any good purpose in human life.  (*BP*, XIV, p. 151)

> I wondered if I could ever be at all in spirits again. I had an absolute indifference as to every thing except *immediate* ease. Yet I was *conscious* this was wrong. Lucky are they who can maintain, or in whom is maintained, a constant earnestness about the *delusion* of this World; for a delusion it

certainly is whenever Reason calmly considers it and attempts to investigate it's rationality. (*BP*, XVIII, pp. 174–5)

And the emptiness often becomes mingled with resentment of the society which forces the 'fetters of correctness' upon the unwilling participant, the man of sensitivity:

> But I at present thought of keeping clear of society as disgusting, or at least insipid. I *felt* how easily I could do with very little of it, and wondered how people could be animated to so much exertion in carrying it on.
> (*BP*, XVI, p. 15)

This resentment is sharpened by the pain the sensitive man suffers as a social and practical being:

> When jaded with business or when tormented with the passions of civilized life, I could fly to the woods; nay, I could be the whinstone on the face of a mountain.
> (*Wife*, pp. 23–4)

> Perhaps it is a weakness to be hurt like Heraclitus at observing the faults of human Nature. But I cannot help it. (*BP*, XV, p. 160)

> I hurried into the streets and walked rapidly, shunning to meet people as much as I could, my perceptions being liable to such soreness from even looks and manner that I suffered acute pain on being accosted, and this was augmented by an unhappy imagination that it must appear how inefficient and troubled I was. (*BP*, XVIII, p. 188)

Even one's reaction to the pain can be the cause of a response from society which intensifies the distress. The thirteenth-century friar Bartholomaeus Anglicus observes of hypochondriacs, 'Also suche holden their peas whan they shulde speake, and speake to moche whan they shulde be stylle.'[4] The effect of such unusual taciturnity may be the same as that which John Hill, in his *Hypochondriasis*, says has often resulted from the hypochondriac's symptom of 'unconquerable numbness in the organs of speech':

I have known the temporary silence that follows upon this last sympton become a jest to the common herd; and the unhappy patient, instead of compassion and assistance, receive the reproof of sullenness, from those who should have known and acted better.[5]

This is part of the whole problem of 'hypochondriacal melancholy' in its relations with non-sufferers:

> Meanwhile, as this disease is in reality more distressing than dangerous, and as his looks are not impaired in a degree that corresponds with the account he gives of his distress, he seldom meets with that sympathy which his sensibility requires and his sufferings deserve. To a circumstantial and pathetic history of his complaints, he often receives a careless, and, to him, a cruel answer, importing that they are all imaginary.[6]

So Boswell's melancholy is intimately connected with his relation to the society of which he is a member. Like other men, he outwardly belongs and subscribes to the common illusion, but, like the writer whose profession he discusses in his first *Hypochondriack* essay, his occasional glimpses behind the scenes make him aware of 'the baseless fabric of this vision', and the knowledge lingers on to murmur of how easily the 'insubstantial pageant' may fade.

(ii) *Keeping up Appearances*

There is a pressing social requirement, then, that the melancholy man should be continually striving to keep up appearances. Boswell, the man of family, advocate and socialite, must not, in his role as bastion of society, let Boswell the melancholiac seep through the cracks of his public facade. To his intimate, John Johnston, he advises on melancholy,

> I advise you to study it carefully. Observe its effects, and find out by what methods to render yourself tolerably easy while it lasts. What I want to do is to bring myself to that

aequality of behaviour that whether my spirits are high or low, people may see little odds upon me.

(*Letters*, I, pp. 14–15)

He tells Sir Alexander Dick that he will 'endeavour to act as if I had it not' (Ibid., p. 80), and writes to Johnson that he is keeping up appearances 'like a reduced garrison' (Ibid., II, p. 253) – again, we see Boswell using the familiar image of a military defence. In London, in 1788, he is assisted by the hospitality of John Courtenay:

> It was a comfortable, good, moderate day. I was miserably low and dusky when I went there. I had not tasted fermented liquor since Sunday. The sensation of it today was grateful, and I soon formed external good spirits, as a stratum of fertile earth is spread on the surface of a rugged rock. (*BP*, XVII, p. 80)

(This, too, is an interesting image. As in the remark, 'I could be the whinstone on the face of a mountain' – *Wife*, p. 24 – Boswell is using the sublime associations of one type of natural scenery to give expression to the 'Byronic' side of his character – the side which idealises the role of melancholy man.) Of a similar gathering in 1790 he reports, 'We were very cheerful; at least the company was, and I appeared to be so' (*BP*, XVIII, p. 93). In Cornwall, with Temple, the battle continues: 'I *acted a part* with so much address that Temple told me I appeared a most lively and happy man. . . . I took the aid of wine today in my colloquial warfare, and of Brandy and water at night, so *kept it up*' (*BP*, XVIII, p. 154). Tricks of mind also prove useful, particularly one of Boswell's conceptions of 'philosophy':

> Philosophy teacheth us to be moderate, to be patient, to expect a gradual progress to refinement and felicity. In that hope I look up to the Lord of the Universe, with a grateful remembrance of the grand and mysterious propitiation which Christanity hath announced. (*Wife*, p. 24)

All this day I ruminated on my nocturnal uneasiness. I found the enamel of philosophy which I had upon my mind, broke, worn off, or worn very thin, and fretfulness corroding it. (*Hebr.*, p. 290)

The mind, it would seem, is not so very different from the body:

There is doubtless a knack of carrying our 'load of life' with more ease than common, without any remarkable strength of shoulders. It may be a kind of suppleness like the poles of English and Irish chairmen. (*OY*, p. 202)

It is interesting that until early middle age Boswell occasionally has sufficient detachment and self-sufficiency actually to enjoy seeing into the emptiness of life and remarking his difference from other men. In 1762 he writes 'I glowed with fancy and was convinced that life is to be altogether despised' (*BP*, I, p. 136). Two months later, in January 1763, he notes, 'Indeed, my ease proceeds not from the good sense it might be imputed to, but from a carelessness of fame and a happy indifference, from a thorough conviction of the vanity of all things' (*LJ*, p. 174). In 1775 he finds himself arguing in favour of indulging hypochondria: 'As I would not wish to have my body of stone, so I would not wish to have my mind insensible' (*OY*, p. 54). And even as late as 1783 he can observe, 'Felt all at once in the Court of Session a happy state of mind which made me view it with complacency instead of disgust. I wondered, while I experienced how little reality there is in external things' (*BP*, XV, p. 157).

This ability is probably owing to Boswell's continuing confidence in his future success and social standing. The buoyancy gradually disappears with his growing belief in his own failure and as the hypochondriac's imagined personal insignificance becomes, for Boswell, a very real thing:

Awaked with the first *image* my mind has produced for a long time. 'My spirits', thought I, 'are worse now than ever. Formerly I could appear gay, though inwardly sad. Now I cannot. The garrison now is so weak that not only is there not a sufficient complement of Men within it, but it cannot even furnish as many as to make a shew upon the walls.' (*BP*, XVI p. 57)

> A number of vexing thoughts crowded upon me. I recalled all the ambitious flutterings which I had experienced from my youth, notwithstanding miserable occasional depressions of spirit. I figured myself retired to the Country without having attained any one object of advancement, and brooding over that consideration; fancying myself despised by others, and undoubtedly being so in my own eyes. In that frame, how could I bear to drag on a life of vexation, and while inwardly gnawed by mortification, how could I entertain company and make any creditable appearance? No, I should never do this. Rather let me hide myself in London, or go to some distant corner of the globe. It made me sick when I imagined myself returned to Edinburgh no better than when I left it, after the enjoyment of London society.
> (*BP*, XVIII, pp. 62–3)

The sense of failure drives Boswell to be constantly making comparisons between himself and the appearances of others, in order to gauge both how far he is actually unique in leading a life of dejection, and how successfully he is concealing this from the world:

> Why should I be vexed that I am not superiour to the generality of men, who really do not pass their time more rationally than I did this day. (*BP*, XIV, p. 62)

> I attended bodily. But my mind was quite feeble. I thought every body had more force of mind than I had. I could have cried for weak, painful dejection. (*BP*, XIV, p. 44)

> My Faith and Piety were quiet and constant, though not vigorous. I suppose I am too nicely anxious for a dignified course of existence. Mine is, I dare say, better than most of those of my rank. (*BP*, XVI, p. 73)

Or else he lists his achievements and causes for satisfaction, yet concludes with a sad note upon the reality of his failure as a lawyer:

> Recollecting my worthy friend Grange and many former ideas connected with this Place, how wonderfully well I am

tonight. The very wish of my heart in early years, when I used to read 'The Spectator' with Temple, is realised. I am now a Barrister at Law of the Inner Temple, have a house in London, am one of the distinguished Literary Men of my age. And at the same time, have an extensive estate, a number of tenants all depending upon me; in short, have, when I please, the POTENTIALITY of a Prince. Yet persevere in attending the Essex Sessions. (*BP*, XVII, p. 46 n. 1)

Melancholy, then, is clearly aggravated by the *fear* of society's punishment of failure; but beyond this, society does react with hostility towards the man who, whether from a sense of his own inadequacy or from a particularly delicate nature, is afflicted with a depression so overwhelming that he is unable to conceal his disaffection with his immediate environment. One of the reasons for this provides a parallel to Freud's explanation of the punishment accorded to uncontrolled passion. The man who appears to see through society's charade is a threat to its continued existence simply because dejection is infectious.[7] He undermines the cohesive sanity of the community – where sanity consists in being more blind less noticeably than the next man, in visibly upholding Cheyne's definition of common-sense. The eighteenth century was well aware of the precarious line between madness and sanity, and warnings against the complacency of reason are frequent. Thomas Fitzgerald in his poem 'Bedlam' provides strong Kiplingesque admonishment:

> If strong Desires thy reasoning Pow'rs control;
> If arbitrary Passions sway thy Soul,
> If Pride, if Envy, if the Lust of Gain,
> If wild ambition in thy Bosom reign,
> Alas! thou vaunt'st thy sober Sense in vain.
> In these poor Bedlamites thy Self survey,
> Thy Self, less innocently mad than They.[8]

Michel Foucault offers a further example:

Matthey, a Geneva physician very close to Rousseau's influence, formulates the prospect for all men of reason: 'Do not glory in your state, if you are wise and civilised men;

an instant suffices to disturb and annihilate that supposed wisdom of which you are so proud; an unexpected event, a sharp and sudden emotion of the soul will abruptly change the most reasonable and intelligent man into a raving idiot.'[9]

Society cannot, therefore, tolerate in its midst one who constitutes an inert source of infection. The unfortunate member must be treated with reserve or confinement depending upon the acuteness of his condition.

As important, though, is the fact that the melancholy man actually represents, and is subconsciously felt to represent, a living indictment of his society. In the first place, his disaffection is an accusation of hypocrisy against those who continue to act when all the words and all the gestures ultimately signify nothing. As Laing has recently put it, 'They are playing a game. They are playing at not playing a game. If I show them I see they are, I shall break the rules and they will punish me. I must play their game, of not seeing I see the game.'[10]

But, further, the melancholy man draws attention to the whole life-style of a society, and its guilt in being the root cause of madness. In any community, there will inevitably exist a certain proportion of members whose physical and psychical structure does not dispose them easily to conform to the general rule. However their dissent manifests itself, it remains the inadequacy of the society which is culpable. Hunter and Macalpine describe the beginnings of conscious awareness of this fact when they consider the emergence of what must have been an underlying trend of attitudes towards the phenomenon of madness during the classical period in England:

> In the early decades of the nineteenth century there developed an interest in what is today called social psychiatry – the influence of society, its culture and organisation, institutions, beliefs, habits, deprivations and calamities on the mental ease and disease of its members.[11]

Foucault takes the argument an interesting stage further when he emphasises, as Fitzgerald's 'Bedlam' implied, the moral character the proposition now assumes:

> From now on one fell ill from too much feeling; one suffered from an excessive solidarity with all the beings around one. One was no longer compelled by one's secret nature, one was the victim of everything which, on the surface of the world, solicited the body and the soul.
> And as a result, one was both more innocent and more guilty. More innocent, because one was swept by the total irritation of the nervous system into an unconsciousness great in proportion to one's disease. But more guilty, much more guilty, because everything to which one was attached in the world, the life one had led, the affections one had had, the passions and the imaginations one had cultivated too complacently – all combined in the irritation of the nerves, finding there both their natural effect and their moral punishment.[12]

But even in Boswell it is possible to find remarks which bear an unmistakable moral slant. For example, in Tunis in 1765 he writes, 'I have too much warmth ever to have the cunning necessary for a general commerce with the corrupted human race' (*GT* (ii), p. 36). And in one of his 'Sienese Reflections' of the same year there is considerable elaboration:

> It is true that a society cannot exist without general rules. I agree. Let us therefore have laws, and let those laws be the general rules. But I want no others. The laws which are really necessary for public happiness are beyond all question very few. Men have many unwritten laws, and this is exactly the evil against which I am trying to argue. These are the laws of fashion, of custom and of so many other particular sorts, that those who live 'in the world', as the phrase goes, are little better than slaves. I wish everyone to live naturally, as he himself pleases, and then possibly we might not hear so many people complaining of this evil world. To me these lamentations seem like the cries of animals in chains or in cages. (*GT* (ii), p. 126)

This sharpens the edges of Boswell's marked emotional ambivalence towards society in general, alternating as he does between the theme of emptiness of previous examples, and the positive relish of human company and the tide of life:

> I love a large society, where men do not come close so as to be rubbed, but are packed with a deal of interjacent circumstances, as hay or wool, to keep them safe.
> (*Ex.*, p. 240)

> We had a pleasing conviction of the commodiousness of civilization, and heartily laughed at the raving of those absurd visionaries who have attempted to persuade us of the superior advantages of a *state of nature*. (*Hebr.*, p. 362)

But, if Boswell is arguably aware of the moral guilt of society concerning his hypochondria, he is in no doubt over the blame to be accorded to his education for the shaping of his character in its problematic form.[13] As Locke argues, 'Nine parts of ten are what they are, good or evil, useful or not, by their education. It is this which makes the great difference in mankind.'[14] I have already spoken of Boswell's traumatic religious upbringing, the shadows of which hung over him for the rest of his life. This is clearly of considerable importance. In addition, one of the most frequent complaints of the journals and letters is the effect which 'the narrowness' of his education has had, concerning which, he tells Temple, 'it was wonderful I had made myself the man I was' (*BP*, XVIII, p. 144). Details of Boswell's education are very scarce.[15] The frequency of his adverse remarks upon his upbringing, however, clearly shows that he himself considered that he emerged from his childhood with a considerable disadvantage. But education is also important to our investigation in so far as it provides a link between the blame attributable to society and the blame upon the immediate family, and in particular upon the father. Lord Chesterfield demonstrates the connection when he directs his son concerning his tutor,

> Again, as I am sure you desire to gain Mr. Mattaire's approbation, without which you will never have mine; I dare say you will mind and give attention to whatever he says to you, and behave yourself seriously and decently, while you are with him.[16]

I shall be returning to this point a little later when discussing Boswell's relationship with his father.

### (iii) *The Hypochondriac in Society*

It is now time to consider the ways in which Boswell sought to cope with this whole problem in so far as his everyday life was concerned. It may straight away be said that none of them could possibly solve adequately all or most of the hopelessly tangled emotional issues involved. Each remedy necessarily simplifies the problem, and is effective only to the extent that Boswell is able to synthetise an average response to any set of events and to ignore contradictory evidence from certain emotions during the time that he is making use of a particular remedy. Only in this way can he be successful in maintaining an attitude. Each, therefore, can operate in the same way as Boswell's analytic use of the image was seen to do in the last chapter, and the result, as there, represents a partial response to a situation which has been falsified by the polish of imagination.

The first method is an aspect of Boswell's activity that has been much discussed by other critics, and will therefore require little comment. As implied in several previous quotations, he regards acting a part as an effective way of inducing himself to present the correct response to society:

> Since I came up, I have begun to acquire a composed genteel character very different from a rattling uncultivated one which for some time past I have been fond of. I have discovered that we may be in some degree whatever character we choose. Besides, practice forms a man to anything. (*LJ*, p. 74)

That this character is essentially a deceit is made clear in *Hypochondriack* 38:

> A much more intimate acquaintance is formed in the country than in the town. In town we see each other only during fragments of our existence, and may more easily assume what character we please. But in the country we have whole days together; and each day is a life, as Shakespeare says in Macbeth; so that it is exceedingly difficult to disguise our real tempers and dispositions. (*BC*, p. 206)

This is closely linked with the next method, which is the emulation of the specific examples of other people whom Boswell considers to be particularly polished in their reaction to society. One of his early exemplars is West Digges – who was, of course, himself an actor:

> Indeed, I must say that Digges has more or as much of the deportment of a man of fashion as anybody I ever saw; and he keeps up this so well that he never once lessened upon me even on an intimate acquaintance, although he is now and then somewhat melancholy, under which it is very difficult to preserve dignity; and this I think is particularly to be admired in Mr. Digges. (*LJ*, p. 89)

Again, so much paper has been profitably covered in exploration of Boswell's role-playing that I shall content myself with emphasising through my examples that it is the public adroitness of his models that he finds admirable. Paoli, for instance, displays a most just balance between familiarity and reserve (*GT* (ii), p. 196) and the French general on Corsica – surely a type of the ideal soldier figure – has his 'fire of youth properly tempered' (*GT* (ii), p. 209). Some patterns, certainly, are chosen for their sensational qualities. This is particularly true of the fictional ones. And Johnson has an unusual place in that he seems to be the man who is permitted, to a certain extent, to break through the barriers of social conformity and politeness. This is one of the remarkable aspects of Boswell's reporting of Johnson's conversation. I shall, however, be devoting a later chapter to the *Life of Johnson*.

It is Edmund Burke, though, who above all seems to represent for Boswell the man most able to blend himself perfectly to the texture of his society and yet retain the integrity of his actual response:

> Still in wonderful spirits. Felt myself easy and *above* the Court of Session. Why cannot such spirits allways last? For I now have as full satisfaction in my own existence as Mr. Burke has, only that I wish for greater objects.
> (*BP*, XV, p. 88)

Burke, moreover, is supremely conscious of his own talents as an orator:

It was astonishing how all kinds of figures of speech crowded upon him. He was like a man in an orchard where boughs loaded with fruit hung around him, and he pulled apples as fast as he pleased and pelted the Ministry.
(*Def.*, p. 169)[17]

Johnson is reported to have observed of Burke's conversation, 'Burke is the only man whose common conversation corresponds with the general fame which he has in the world' (*Life*, IV, pp. 19–20). And Boswell goes to excessive lengths in a footnote to the published Hebrides journal to demonstrate, in opposition to Johnson, the quality and propriety of Burke's wit (*Life*, V, pp. 32–4). Furthermore, Burke knows when to be lively and when subdued:

Found Burke. For a little (for the first time I ever found it) he did not burst forth; his genius was not impatient of restraint like a strong spring from a rock. And he was somewhat flat. But he was shaving, and might have cut himself had he not been quiet. (*Ex.*, p. 267)

A. J. Tillinghast has referred to 'the product of a kind of mental sleight-of-hand on Boswell's part whereby he saw various individuals as repositories of particular sets of virtues'.[18] The reason for this is that Boswell's purpose is not to assess his models, but to inspire himself to similar behaviour. In this way, what he seeks in them is the same as the assistance he looks for in religion and in some of his luxurious images. All represent a short-cut to analysis, and offer an easy solution to the problem of action. They are just some of the countless little ways in which a man, with the best will in the world, is able to conceal himself from himself. Boswell is unique in that his way of attempting to examine his failings was to record them.

This question of emulation is complicated, however, by Boswell's emotional ambivalence to some of his own exemplars. The behaviour of his brother David, for example, evokes different responses from Boswell depending upon his own state of mind at the time. One day he writes that he 'became sensible of the good effects of habitual composure; though what is nature with him is restraint with me', yet only three days later he complains, 'I was not pleased with his inanimate appearance. But it is his *manner*, I suppose from long habits of living in restraint among the Spaniards' (*BP*, XIV, pp. 103, 104). David is a representative of both society in general and of the immediate family, and, moreover, he possesses a considerable degree of their father's emotional coldness. And it is in fact towards Lord Auchinleck that Boswell feels his most conflicting emotions. His father is always seen as the 'worthy' public and family man of the Edinburgh legal world, and hence presents an obvious model for Boswell:

> I am lost when I think intensely of the course of things, and especially of the operations of my own mind. But I avoid that kind of thinking, and have some notion of the kind of existence which my Father had all his life till his faculties decayed. I now prayed for him with delicate awe, that in case he was not yet received into a state of happiness he might be soon received. (*BP*, XV, p. 130)

Boswell frequently measures himself against his father: 'Yet I envied the steady, regular, prudent conduct he had maintained through life, and did not think with any pleasure of the superiour warmth of enjoyment which had been my lot' (*BP*, XIII, p. 202). And he often attempts to disregard Lord Auchinleck's lack of affection: 'He was cold as usual, but I liked to contemplate his uniform steady character in general, though in politics he had been misled by the President' (*OY*, p. 36). Yet Lord Auchinleck also bears the responsibility for Boswell's 'narrow education', both generally and as regards religion, and, like Lord Chesterfield, stands for society in his judgement upon his son. He shaped Boswell in his own image, and is thus entitled to pass continual sentence upon the likeness. Moreover, Lord Auchinleck takes few pains to disguise his feeling that Boswell is already a failure. Hence one of Boswell's major reasons for seeking some government office is to impress his father with his ability to succeed without parental help. He wants to be treated as an equal, not as an irresponsible child. Yet Boswell also wants to gratify him, as he observes in a letter to Johnston:

> The great point will be to begin properly when I return, and get My Father to see me as I realy am. Come, my good

freind, encourage me. Who knows but I may yet rejoice my Father's heart. I call God to witness that I wish most earnestly to do so. (*Corr.* I, p. 165)

Over the whole of Boswell's life there hovers the sardonic presence of Lord Auchinleck, a potential source of warmth, and at the same time a constant figure of censure:

My father seemed to be really kinder of late. I had real happiness in being well with him, and I wished him long life, feeling also a sort of discouraging apprehension that the Family of Auchinleck would not be properly supported by me. (*OY*, p. 188)

But the father also has a psychological role as representative of reason and restraint against anarchic natural impulses. Michel Foucault observes,

Henceforth, and for a period of time the end of which it is not yet possible to predict, the discourse of unreason will be indissociably linked with the half-real, half-imaginary dialectic of the Family. So that what, in their violence, it was once obligatory to interpret as profanations or blasphemies, it would henceforth be necessary to see as an incessant attack against the Father. Thus in the modern world, what had been the great, irreparable confrontation of reason and unreason became the secret thrust of instincts against the solidity of the family institution and against its most archaic symbols.[19]

The Boswells' proximity to this pattern may be estimated by their respective attitudes to John, the second son of the house, who spent a large part of his life actually confined in an asylum. Boswell himself was consistently thoughtful for his brother, and regarded his situation with distress. He often visited him, or had him as a guest at his own home despite John's invariable ill-tempered sullenness. Lord Auchinleck, however, was anxious only to forget his son's existence:

Walked out to father and talked of John. Found him for continuing him in confinement. (*Ex.*, p. 201)

> ... it gave me some degree of tender uneasiness to think that his father was unwilling that he should return home, though he was now wonderfully recovered from his insanity. But my father was formerly so fretted with poor John's disagreeable behaviour that there is no wonder he should decline putting himself in the way of it again in his old age, especially as John's state of mind is very uncertain, and also as bearing with his sickly temper does not make him easier. (*Ex.*, p. 218)

(Even in this Boswell is doing his best to excuse his father's attitude.)

> I came to my father's, and being much affected spoke against sending John to Musselburgh. My father seemed to have no other concern than to be free of trouble by him, and of a kind of *reproach*, as he called it, from having a relation in such a state. (*OY*, p. 44)

Lord Auchinleck demonstrates the man of society's reaction to madness and to nonconformity of any kind: it is not to be comprehended, it will be a reflection upon you in the eyes of other people, it is a 'reproach', therefore shut it away. This above all, I think, highlights the difference between Boswell and his 'worthy' father, and the nature of the relationship which existed between them.

It will be useful to remain a little longer with the subject of family, and to consider Boswell's relations with his wife. Here, too, from our post-Freudian vantage-point, we shall not be surprised to find evidence of emotional ambivalence:

> In almost every case where there is an intense emotional attachment to a particular person we find that behind the tender love there is a concealed hostility in the unconscious. This is the classical example, the prototype, of the ambivalence of human emotions. This ambivalence is present to a greater or less amount in the innate disposition of everyone.[20]

Attention should be directed less at Boswell's more obvious marital failings of drinking, whoring and gambling, than towards his quite conscious references to his wife as a dampener upon *all* of the activities and passions close to his heart:

> My Wife disliked Fielding's turn for low life, as I have observed yesterday. But it is human nature. She has nothing of that english juiciness of mind of which I have a great deal, which makes me delight in humour. But what hurts me more, she has nothing of that warmth of imagination which produces the pleasures of vanity and many others, and which is even a considerable cause of religious fervour. *Family*, which is a high *principle* in my mind, and Genealogy, which is to me an interesting amusement, have no effect upon her. It is impossible not to be both uneasy and a little angry at such defects (or call them differences); and at times they make me think that I have been unlucky in uniting myself with one, who, instead of cherishing my genius, is perpetually checking it. (*BP*, XV, p. 93)

> At night my dear Wife talked seriously of our state in this world; that we ought to be submissive and trust in GOD, and not inquire eagerly into futurity. This seemed sensible, but humbling to an aspiring philosophical curiosity. It however pleased me at the time. (*BP*, XV, p. 24)

This latent hostility surfaces most frequently during Mrs Boswell's last illness. Boswell sometimes seems to treat her almost with malice:

> Some days ago she was in dismal low spirits, and mournfully exclaimed, with death before her eyes, 'O I am terrified for the dark passage.' My heart was most tenderly touched, but I could do her no good, for all my consolatory pious suggestions were not congenial to her too rational mind. I was in charming spirits today and said I could die easily. She said she could not, but she was not in the melancholy frame which I have described. (*BP*, XVII, pp. 97-8)

At best, his desire is to forget her and the increased restraint under which her condition places him, and to be out enjoying the social life of London. And it is largely the response that his behaviour will evoke from this immediate society that worries him: 'Was sorry I staid out till it was, I believe, past eleven. It appeared unkind to my wife, yet I was fully conscious of affection for her' (*BP*, XVII, p. 104).

Apart from this, he can find many ways to satisfy his own conscience:

> My Wife was rather better, but recovering very slowly, and my being so much abroad appeared very unkind to her, though I was *conscious* of sincere regard. At the same time let me fairly mark the modifications of feeling by time and circumstances. I certainly had not that tenderness and anxiety which I once had, and could look with my mind's eye upon the event of her being removed by death with much more composure than formerly. This I considered as humanely ordered by Providence; yet I was not without some upbraidings as if I were too selfish, from leading what may be called a life of pleasure. (*BP*, XVII, p. 87)

> I was inwardly shocked at my rage for pleasure, which made me leave a distressed Wife, who never would have left me, even in the slightest illness. But I braved all tender checks, and truly I came to be satisfied that I had done right; for I added to my stock of pleasing subjects for recollection, and had I staid at home, should have fretted, and done my wife more harm than good.  (*BP*, XVII, p. 107)

The general impression from the journal immediately following her death is one of relief from an overbearing pressure. Although Boswell frequently, and no doubt sincerely, pays tribute to his wife's many good qualities, she does seem to have exercised a particularly strong emotional restraint which, because of its emotional nature, and because of the feelings of guilt it inevitably induced following deviations, was half-consciously resented.

Family, then, is demonstrably an important influence on the way Boswell conducted himself through life. Of more immediate effect, though, is the restraint found in the company of certain people:

> I really feel myself happier in the company of those of whom I stand in awe than in any other company.... It

composes the uneasy tumult of my spirits, and gives me the pleasure of contemplating something at least comparatively great. (*BP*, XIII, p. 41)

This is another way in which Boswell may seek to overcome the problems of appearing in society – to be often in the company of awesome individuals. As might be expected, Lord Auchinleck's presence is usually a restraining influence:

> Was really in a comfortable frame, and felt more agreeably when under parental awe than when unrestrained. It put a lid on my mind and kept it from boiling vehemently. Being thus kept quiet, I was happier than when agitated with ebullitions. (*Ex.*, p. 34)

Such restraint is sometimes seen as beneficial: 'It was a storm of wind and rain. My Mind was quite sound; and what is curious, the restraint here did me good. The coldness checked fretful fancies as frost kills weeds' (*BP*, XIII, p. 173). As often, though, it is resented and complained of as being unpleasant and tedious. At Lord Galloway's Boswell observes, 'I did not find myself happy here. I was under restraint and my Genius was cramped' (*BP*, I, p. 78). With Lord Eglintoune he is uncomfortable because, 'as we are not of congenial tempers, I am under restraint' (*BP*, XIV, p. 24); and of his own brother David he reports, 'Was glad he was not at home, he is such a restraint on me' (*BP*, XVI, p. 179). It can only be concluded that restraint is good or bad depending on Boswell's general attitude to the person concerned, together with his own state of mind at the time.

Corresponding to the government of conduct by emulation of certain individuals is a rather more subtle process which Boswell occasionally finds both helpful and reassuring, and that is comparison with persons who are *not* to be emulated but who nevertheless bear some resemblance to Boswell himself. Foucault's observations on 'Recognition by Mirror' provide an interesting comparison here. The madman suffering from delusions of grandeur, says Foucault, may sometimes be brought to an awareness of his own madness by observation of an identical condition in another:

> Thus madness, in the spectacle of itself as unreason humiliated, was able to find its salvation, when, imprisoned in the absolute subjectivity of its delirium, it surprised the absurd and objective image of that delirium in the identical madman. Truth insinuated itself, as if by surprise . . . in this play of reciprocal observations where it never saw anything but itself. . . . [It] became responsible for what it knew of its truth; it imprisoned itself in an infinitely self-referring observation; it was finally chained to the humiliation of being its own object. Awareness was now linked to the shame of being identical to that other, of being compromised in him, and of already despising oneself before being able to recognize or to know oneself.[21]

This, in a diluted form, seems to be the process by which Boswell, at twenty-two, can observe of the young Mr George Goldie, 'From his having a great degree of liveliness and not much knowledge of the World, his manners might now and then by severe People be construed as forward. But that wears off by time and a longer acquaintance with Society' (*BP*, I, p. 66). Boswell's satisfaction comes from finding someone with the same failings as himself who has not yet attained to his own standard of awareness and control, and hence Goldie becomes a temporary measure by which Boswell may adjust his own behaviour. So too does Houston Stewart. Boswell warns himself, 'Take care. Be firm and shun falling back to Houston Stewart' (*Holl.*, p. 238). The same process is involved in his attitude to Oliver Goldsmith, whose garrulity Boswell recognises as exceeding even his own: 'BOSWELL. "I like very well to hear honest Goldsmith talk away carelessly." JOHNSON. "Why, yes, Sir; but he should not like to hear himself" ' (*Def.*, p. 114). Boswell here condones his own failing in patronising it in Goldsmith, although Johnson's rejoinder indicates that Boswell is in no way sympathising with Goldsmith: he is judging from a purely selfish position.[22]

Andrew Erskine, too, seems to become a kind of standard. He is a hypochondriac whose melancholy is more total than Boswell's, for with Erskine the sense of emptiness embraces everything so as to render serious action impossible:

> On comparing notes, I found he differed from me in this: that he at no time had any ambition or the least inclination

to distinguish himself in active life, having a perpetual consciousness or imagination that he could not go through with it. Whereas I have a restless wish for distinction in England, in short on a great scale. (*BP*, xv, p. 105)

We must not ignore the affection of a lifetime's friendship; but, reasoning upon Swift's principle of 'The Screen remov'd', it is not surprising that Erskine's suicide in 1793 caused Boswell considerable distress – he was not even able to write the name when recording the event in his journal (*BP*, xviii, p. 221).

Finally, in the consideration of Boswell's occasional remedies for the problems created by hypochondria, may be mentioned his use of persuasive imagery. An attractive image can, for example, be at least temporarily effective in the recommendation of restraint: 'I resolved to take London as one takes mercury; to intermit the use of it whenever I should feel it affect my brain, as one intermits the use of mercury when it affects the mouth' (*Ex.*, p. 220). The implication is that London is recognised treatment for a physical condition, but, like mercury, it can itself be the cause of illness if taken in excess. This is straightforward and reasonable, and, in fact, during the London visit of Easter 1778, Boswell does adhere with remarkable consistency to his own code of conduct.

More interesting, though, if also more tenuous, are the implications of Boswell's use of music as a source for a small number of images. He records talking with James Harris: 'I said subordination like music. He said this fine illustration and old one' (*Ex.*, p. 311). And of an afternoon spent with William Nairne and the Solicitor-General he reports,

> The Solicitor was prudent and formal, which I believe procures a kind of respect. Yet why lose the pleasure of gaiety? There should however be *some* restraint. Much of the beauty of which we are agreeably sensible is formed by restraint, by *shapes*, and by *sounds limited by time*.
> (*Ex.*, p. 106)

Clearly music provides a very satisfactory image of the universality of restraint, of the beauty of order, and hence of Boswell's right to a place in the divine scheme provided he is able to exercise sufficient self-control to maintain himself in his proper station in society. Boswell, we know, played the flute and wrote and performed songs. Yet music is also clearly important to him at a subconscious level as an agent which induces harmony and tranquillity, as he makes clear in commenting upon the qualities that attract him to Mrs Rudd:

> Her language was choice and fluent and her voice melodious. The peculiar characteristic of her enchantment seemed to be its delicate imperceptible power. She perfectly concealed her design to charm. There was no meretricious air, no direct attempt upon the heart. It was like hearing the music of the spheres which poets feign, and which produces its effect without the intervention of any instrument, so that the very soul of harmony immediately affects our souls.
> (*OY*, p. 358)

The jaded soul of the hypochondriac is insensibly soothed by music, as two early commentators upon the condition, Bartholomaeus Anglicus and Philip Barrough, recommend: 'And they muste be gladded with instrumentes of Musicke – and some deale be occupied';[23] 'Let them be mery as much as may be, and heare musicall instruments and singing.'[24]

But, for Boswell, all the remedies for his condition, and all the aids to restraint, can be effective only in a temporary capacity, and depend wholly upon the chance of his state of mind at a particular time for the impression they make. They remain mere surface distractions from the underlying social problem of the hypochondriac's inability to maintain a satisfactory relationship with his environment. At best, such a man as Boswell must experience in his public life and private meditation the duality of identity which the writers of *The Mirror* describe in their character-study of Hamlet:

> The melancholy man feels in himself... a sort of double person; one which, covered with the darkness of its imagination, looks not forth onto the world, nor takes any concern in vulgar objects or frivolous pursuits; another, which he lends, as it were, to ordinary men, which can accommodate itself to their tempers and manners and indulge, without

feeling any degradation from the indulgence, a smile with the cheerful, and a laugh with the giddy.[25]

It is to the subject of the 'double person', and its relation to the published 'self' of the printed word, that I wish to turn in my next chapter.

# 5 Freedom and the Pen

## (i) *A Double Life*

Boswell's journals afford many examples of his awareness of the difference between the inner self and the outer, of the gloss necessary for safe participation in social and business life – indeed, in all but the most extraordinary personal intercourse. Of Lord Marchmont he observes without irony, 'He is a true Politician so that the qualities of the heart must be dispensed with' (*BP*, I, p. 106). Johnson in company with Wilkes 'tuned himself up to appear quite as an easy man of the world, who can adapt himself at once to the manners of those whom he may chance to meet' (*OY*, p. 347). Of John Lee's warning that Boswell's *Letter to the People of Scotland on ...Diminishing the Number of Lords of Session* might anger Dundas 'when you are on terms of friendship with him', Boswell says, 'I laughed it off on the difference between one's publick and private attitudes' (*BP*, XVI, p. 96). And in the *Letter* itself he writes 'It is my system to regard, in a publick capacity – measures, and not men; in a private capacity, men, and not measures.'[1]

This dichotomy between public and private is consciously examined in the second essay 'On the Profession of a Player':

> The double feeling which I have mentioned is experienced by many men in the common intercourse of life. Were nothing but the real character to appear, society would not be half so safe and agreeable as we find it. Did we discover to our companions what we really think of them, frequent quarrels would ensue; and did we not express more regard for them than we really feel, the pleasure of social intercourse would be very contracted.... This double feeling is of various kinds and various degrees; some minds receiving a colour from the objects around them, like the effects of

the sunbeams playing through a prism; and others, like the cameleon, having no colours of their own, take just the colours of what chances to be nearest them.

(*Player*, pp. 19–20)

The line of discussion continues in *Hypochondriack* 8 with reference to the way in which people act up to their clothes:

> Every one has felt himself more disposed to decorum and propriety and courtesy, and other good qualities, when genteelly dressed, than when in slovenly apparel. Perhaps there is a general propensity in our faculties to assimilate themselves to that circumstance about us, which is most perceptible of whatever sort it is, as matter takes a form from whatever mould is applied to it. (*BC*, p. 59)

This theme was, of course, an extremely common one in eighteenth-century literature. Attitudes to clothes are an important part of the satire in *A Tale of a Tub*; Pope in the *Essay on Man* and the *Moral Essays* discusses the problem of self-love and social, and the distinction between public and private character: 'But grant, in public, men sometimes are shown, / A woman's seen in private life alone.'[2] And Pope even uses the image of the chameleon to suggest the changing characters of women.[3] Boswell is exploring a personal problem, but he is doing so through well-established modes of thought.

In consequence of this knowledge, Boswell is careful to remind himself of the dangers of probing too rashly beneath the surface appearance. One such warning merits a place in the 'Boswelliana':

> Few characters will bear the examination of reason. You may examine them for curiosity, as you examine bodies with a microscope. But you will be as much disgusted with their gross qualities. You will see them as Swift makes Gulliver see the skins of the ladies of Brobdingnag. (*Bosw.*, p. 286)

The same allusion to Swift occurs in a *Hypochondriack* essay of the same year, 1779, upon the subject of censure:

> *Swift* has shown us to a degree of exquisite disgust the consequence of prying, when we ought to be satisfied with

external beauty of person and dress. If we will set ourselves to investigate in his manner, we all know what nauseous ideas will be excited; yet happily for us how very seldom are we disturbed by them as our views skim pleasingly along the surface. (*BC*, p. 148)

Boswell concludes the essay,

> I believe upon the whole, that he who would pass his life comfortably should not only abstain from censure, but habituate himself to take things in the most agreeable view; and by no means to search for faults. I have observed that no persons are less happy themselves, or more disliked by others than those who are continually examining and inquiring with a nice keenness; and instead of being satisfied with good plain general enjoyment of society, are upon every occasion analysing people's characters. (Ibid.)

There is, though, a more private argument against close examination, if an equally important one for the health of one's social relations:

> Maclaurin observed very well, when he was last with me, that thinking metaphysically destroys the principles of morality; and indeed when a man analyses virtues and vices as a chemist does material substances, they lose their value as well as their odiousness. (*OY*, p. 217)

And elsewhere Boswell considers how analysis may often have a detrimental effect upon religious faith, glancing reproachfully as he does so at his profession, which, he thinks, encourages this:

> But perhaps I considered as weakness that meek submission of Reason to divine faith which Religion requires, and from which I am too much estranged by being accustomed, as a practical Lawyer, to continual close controversial reasoning. (*BP*, XIII, p. 179)

So Boswell is aware of the element of deceit essential in the face a man presents to the world, and yet alongside this necessity treads the constant danger of actual confusion in thinking. It is an easy step from imposing upon others to imposing upon oneself. In a world in which, as Chesterfield implied, decency consists in the opinions of other people, responsibility is only a superficial virtue, and, mad or sane, the inner man may be allowed, or even encouraged, to expire. Foucault describes how, within the asylum, this forms the basis of one kind of therapy:

> under observation madness is constantly required, at the surface of itself, to deny its dissimulation. It is judged only by its acts; it is not accused of intentions, nor are its secrets to be fathomed. Madness is responsible only for that part of itself which is visible. All the rest is reduced to silence. Madness no longer exists except as *seen*.[4]

This may be useful for the man whose madness is extreme and antisocial enough to warrant confinement and professional treatment, but for the partial insanity with which we are all, to a certain extent, afflicted it can only result in the further deterioration of the accuracy of one's image of the world, and a further enfeeblement of the ability to distinguish between forms and reality. This is precisely what Johnson means when he advises Boswell to clear his mind of 'cant': 'don't *think* foolishly' (*Life*, IV, p. 221).

From this position we may move to understand Boswell's problem of his own identity – why he needed continually to examine himself in different social and private situations, and why he placed such importance upon written evidence of his character. (This latter point will be discussed at greater length in a later chapter.) Between the various lines which need to be drawn to enclose a man's persona, will the true Boswell be found within the area described?[5] And when he thinks, and judges his actions, is it Boswell who is in control, or Boswell's adoption of his own image reflected in society? As Yeats asks,

> How in the name of Heaven can he escape
> That defiling and disfigured shape
> The mirror of malicious eyes
> Casts upon his eyes until at last
> He thinks that shape must be his shape?[6]

*The Mirror* agrees with this sentiment, though expressing it in less forceful terms:

> In the present state of society, we have few opportunities of exhibiting our true characters by our actions; and the habits of the world soon throw upon our manners a veil that is inpenetrable to others, and nearly so to ourselves.[7]

Geoffrey Scott relates the problem to Boswell in considering his role-playing:

> To be James Boswell was a hopeless, almost an unmeaning, aim till he could fix that wavering image in the glass, which even till death remains so doubtful. This absence of inward fixity gave more zest and a kind of pathetic eagerness to his histrionic temper. He enacted each momentary role with the desperation of a man who had no identity to which he could confidently return, and in the fear that there were no features behind his assayed mask. (*BP*, V, pp. 7–8)

Certainly, this is a point which Boswell himself makes in his second essay 'On the Profession of a Player':

> And it must be observed, that the greater degree a man is accustomed to assume of artificial feeling, the more probability is there that he has no character of his own on which we can depend, unless indeed he be born of an uncommon degree of firmness. (*Player*, pp. 20–1)

As Johnson observes, the nicest judgement is necessary in the consideration of a man's true identity:

> He cautioned me against trusting to impressions. Said there was a middle state of mind between conviction and hypocrisy, of which many were unconscious (a fine remark), and that by being subject to impressions a Man was not a free agent. (*BP*, XIV, p. 243)

And this difficulty in maintaining the perception of a consistent real identity, says Boswell, is particularly acute for the hypochondriac:

> Nothing is more disagreeable than for a man to find himself unstable and changeful. An Hypochondriack is very liable to this uneasy imperfection, in so much that sometimes there remains only a mere consciousness of identity. His inclinations, his tastes, his friendships, even his principles, he with regret feels, or imagines he feels are all shifted, he knows not how. This is owing to a want of firmness of mind. (*BC*, p. 325)

A series of journal entries between 25 November and 8 December 1776 presents a practical instance of Boswell's behaving and thinking as a private individual, sharing a world only with his journal, and shows how this inner Boswell is sharply jerked back to 'reality' by the intrusion of society in the form of his wife. On Monday the 25th, he 'met a young slender slut with a red cloak in the street and went with her to Barefoots Parks and madly ventured coition. It was a short and almost insensible gratification of lewdness.' On Wednesday the 27th, he 'met a plump hussy who called herself Peggy Grant' and 'went with her to a field behind the Register Office, and boldly lay with her'. On Thursday he seeks out Peggy Grant for further activity, but he cannot find her, and instead feels the proddings of conscience. These, however, are successfully put down: 'I was shocked that the father of a family should go amongst strumpets; but there was rather an insensibility about me to virtue, I was so sensual. Perhaps I should not write all this. I soothed myself with Old Testament manners.'

On Sunday 1 December, he plans 'full enjoyment' with Peggy, resolutely inquires for her, and is able to 'lay with her twice' 'in a mason's shed in St Andrew's Square'. At home the same night, however, his wife is suspicious and Boswell confesses his 'mischief': 'She was very uneasy, and I was ashamed and vexed at my licentiousness. Yet my conscience was not alarmed; so much had I accustomed my mind to think such indulgence permitted.'

Boswell, despite his wife's discovery, remains private in his knowledge of the extent and details of his 'mischief', and of his confidential mental extenuations. The inner sanctum survives inviolate, and the furtive relief from constraining public standards can still be remembered with pleasure. All these events are recorded either on or before Tuesday 3 December. But on Sunday 8 December, 'my wife insisted to read this journal', and thus is revealed everything up to the evening of Monday 2 December. Naturally, 'finding in it such explicit instances of licentiousness, she was much affected and told me that she had come to a resolution never again to consider herself as my *wife*'. The secret Boswell is (temporarily) dissolved, and he is forced to regard himself from the viewpoint of an outsider: 'I was awaked from my dream of licentiousness, and saw my bad conduct in a shocking light. I was really agitated, and in a degree of despair' (*Ex.*, pp. 61–5).

The only lesson, apart from continence, that Boswell might have learnt from this, however, is to reveal less in his journal. The cleft between internal and external reality remains as wide as ever, as it must for any man living in a society where only a small part of himself is considered fit to be seen. Consequently, Boswell's sense of identity simply becomes more strained. There is no real answer to this. Very few men are able to govern their public life by the standards of their private. Not many more are really aware of how far the difference extends – into their behaviour, their conversation, and even into their thinking.

Boswell at least recognises the problem, and is concerned enough to discuss it. In *Hypochondriack* 33, for example, he wonders about the effect drink has upon a man's character:

> An opinion has been generally entertained that the real character of a man is best shown when he is drunk, for that then he is without disguise. I cannot admit the truth of this opinion. On the contrary I am persuaded that Drunkenness frequently alters a man's real character, and creates one totally different, so that instead of being without disguise, he is, according to the common phrase, 'disguised in liquor'. (*BC*, p. 184)

He also recognises that other people must have just the same difficulty concerning public and private identity, and finds this a reassurance when feeling doubtful about the quality of his own character:

> It however hurt me to be sensible that I was deficient in vigour of mind, was not enough a *Man*. But then I could not

tell but others, who appeared to me sufficiently manly, might feel as I did. Upon the whole, I had no just reason to complain. (*BP*, XIII, p. 262)

I prayed to GOD that now my much respected freind was gone, I might be a follower of Him who I trusted was now by faith and patience inheriting the promises. But it gave me concern that I was conscious of a deadness in spiritual feeling, and indeed a cold indifference as to the aweful subject of Religion, having just a sort of superficial speculation that I might take my chance with a careless hope of mercy. This, I beleive, is the state of most people, even of those who have had the ordinary religious education.
(*BP*, XVI, p. 66)

As David Passler observes, 'Whatever his situation', Boswell 'almost always attempts to show its connection with common behaviour rather than to seek what is unique in the experience.'[8]

With the same view in mind, Boswell searches for a consistent identity beneath the appearance of people he knows, or of whom he is told, like the rake-turned-soldier-turned-Methodist Mr Stockdale,

What a curious creature is man! how changeable is he! how inconsistent! Where is the resemblance between Stockdale the Buck, drinking, whoring and giving a loose to whim, and Stockdale the Parson, in his gown and cassoc, showing an example of Sobriety and austere virtue and preaching with vehement warmth against the horrid nature of Sin and Iniquity? Is there any identity of Person here? Yes, there is. They are both in reality the same Person. (*BP*, I, p. 94)

Even upon the death of Lord Covington he can make a similarly encouraging reflection: 'I felt myself quite reconciled to the course of nature, without any gloom; but by looking forward was sensible that Mr. Alexander Lockhart was in his progress of being, and had only made a great move' (*BP*, XV, p. 134). And in his *Hypochondriack* essay 'On Youth and Age' he comments more generally,

> I think that young men and old may by habitual efforts of reflection attain to a constant impression of this truth, that they are the same beings in age as in youth, with only the difference of circumstances attendant upon these several states of existence. . . . The transition from youth to age is so imperceptible, that the notion of our identity is never broken. It seems strange then, that there should be the idea of so wide a distinction between the two states.
>
> (*BC*, pp. 63–4)

As early as 1764, when only twenty-four, and shortly after his meetings with Rousseau and Voltaire, Boswell feels that his careful observations of mankind have given him

> a remarkable knowledge of human nature. This is different from a knowledge of the world as much as is the knowledge of a florist, who understands perfectly the works of Nature, from that of him who understands flowers formed by art. The florist perceives in general that the artificial flowers are not natural, but whether they are made of gummed linen, or china, or of copper, he cannot tell. So I know in general your men of the world to be artificial, but am not able to develop their different qualities. What is really Man I think I know pretty well. (*GT* (i), p. 296)

And fifteen years later, in the *Hypochondriack*, when speaking of the caution necessary in reconciling dignity with amusement, he adds, 'there are very few who can distinguish the substantial general character itself from the occasional appearances which it assumes' (*BC*, p. 152).

The realisation that not only himself but most men are in reality different from what their social images would suggest is an essential one for Boswell. As he observes in *Hypochondriack* 23, the hypochondriac is particularly prone to the desire to expose 'the faults of those with whom he happens to be in company':

> By giving attention to the different characters of our companions we soon come to know what circumstances about themselves they consider to be unfavourable; and these we should shun to mention, if we wish to have them easy and to

possess their good will. An Hypochondriack ought to be chiefly upon his guard. For though he is not cruel, there is an irritation in his frame which makes him rather pleased with seeing the slighter sort of uneasiness which is produced by raillery. (*BC*, p. 143)

The very earliest journal contains a warning of this type:

> Raillery is indeed a very dangerous weapon, and it requires both a penetrating insight into the characters of our friends and Companions and a delicate masterly hand to use it without hurting. What is very slight at first may in the heat of contention come to be very rough. And therefore he who plays with so keen a sword had need to possess the greatest caution. (*BP*, I, p. 68)

Simply, one must always remember that others have feelings in the same way as oneself, and one should study to respect these. So Boswell is very impressed by Johnson's consideration with regard to Beauclerk's relations with the Duke of Marlborough, his brother-in-law, whose seat at Blenheim Johnson 'would be very glad to see if properly invited':

> He had a prudent and delicate resolution against asking Beauclerk to carry him there, which I should not have thought of, but have asked him slapdash. 'I doubt', said he, 'if Beauclerk be on that footing with the Duke as to carry anybody there; and I would not give him the uneasiness to see that I knew it, or even to put himself in mind of it.' I must study to have more of this kind of delicacy. It is the same to many men with regard to the mind as to the body. I would not strip myself naked before every one, and would be shocked to occasion another being so exposed. Mental nakedness should be avoided with equal scrupulousness.
> (*Hebr.*, p. 288)

Nevertheless, two years later Boswell notes that 'For some time past I have indulged coarse raillery and abuse by far too much.' He reminds himself, 'If people have faults, one would not wish to be the hangman to them. If reputations may be stained, one would not wish to throw the dirt' (*OY*, p. 176). At the same time, he points out what is implied in *Hypochondriack* 23, that 'there is a kind of mischievous gratification in such indulgence'. In fact, one *would* like to throw the dirt, and one *does* enjoy seeing another completely exposed to the view of the world. There is a guilty fascination in showing the secrets of others, particularly their vices. This is partly because we are reassured that others, too, have inevitably a more furtive self than their appearances would indicate, and also because there is a not unpleasant thrill in being reminded of the possibility of our own humiliation by public exposure.[9]

(ii) *Communications*

It would be unfair to assume, though, that Boswell's interest is to uncover how much hypocrisy is hidden under the best honoured type of contemporary morality. He is far more concerned to achieve some degree of genuine communication with people. As Freud suggests,

> Psycho-analysis has shown us that everyone possesses in his unconscious mental activity an apparatus which enables him to interpret other people's reaction, that is, to undo the distortions which other people have imposed on the expression of their feelings.[10]

Boswell is particularly proud of his ability to be well with people as individuals: 'Am I not fortunate in having something about me that interests most people at first sight in my favour?' (*Letters*, II, p. 285) He considers he has divined, for example, the true Voltaire: 'I touched the keys in unison with his imagination. I wish you had heard the music. He was all brilliance. He gave me continued flashes of wit' (*GT* (i), p. 285). Again we see the recurring theme of music used in imagery describing an activity of enhanced spiritual quality, though turned here to self-flattery, for it is Boswell himself whose skill has brought forth the brilliant display.

Yet it is not only great men upon whom Boswell expends his talents: 'I can tune myself so to the tone of any bearable man that I am with that he is as much at freedom as with another self, and, till I am gone, cannot imagine me a stranger' (*GT* (i),

p. 296). True communication is a relief because to some extent it allows a freedom from the constraint of normal social life. This is what Boswell feels with the soldiers and peasants of Corsica when, for example, they ask him to play his flute:

> To have told my honest natural visitants, 'Really, gentlemen, I play very ill', and put on such airs as we do in our genteel companies, would have been highly ridiculous. I therefore immediately complied with their request. . . . The pathetic simplicity and pastoral gaiety of the Scots music will always please those who have the genuine feelings of nature. (*GT* (ii), p. 185)

Such direct relations – indeed his whole life-style on the island – genuinely make the Corsican trip seem like 'just being for a little while one of the "prisca gens mortalium"' (*GT* (ii), p. 69). 'Nature', says Foucault,

> as the concrete form of the immediate, has an even more fundamental power in the suppression of madness. . . . In nature . . . man is doubtless liberated from social constraints (those which force him 'to calculate and draw up the balance sheet of his imaginary pleasures which bear that name but are none') and from the uncontrollable movement of the passions.[11]

Genuine, felt communication is, for Boswell, an effective equivalent to a return to the freedom of nature.

On top of this, there is the very real pleasure of an exchange of ideas. As Cowper testifies in a letter to the Rev. William Unwin,

> There is a pleasure annexed to the communication of one's ideas, whether by word of mouth, or by letter, which nothing earthly can supply the place of, and it is the delight we find in this mutual intercourse, that not only proves us to be creatures intended for social life, but more than anything else perhaps fits us for it.[12]

The hypochondriac in particular (and it is worth pointing out that Cowper was himself a hypochondriac) feels this need, and is always gratified to find a fellow sufferer with whom he may share melancholy confidences in the security of a clearly defined relationship. Boswell is frequently seen 'comparing notes' with hypochondriacs he discovers, such as the Hon. A. E. (*BP*, XVI, p. 155), and Bennet Langton, with whom he agrees on the 'deceitfulness of all our hopes of enjoyment on earth' (*BP*, XVI, p. 203). This security of relationship serves a very deep-rooted desire in the hypochondriac: it counters to some extent his obsessive sense of inferiority and rejection, so often marked by Boswell,[13] and obviates, at the same time, the necessity of continually attending to conventional propriety. So Robert James in his *Medicinal Dictionary* notes how such patients enjoy the attention of their doctors:

> No disease is more troublesome, either to the Patient or Physician, than hypochondriac Disorders; and it often happens, that, thro' the Fault of both, the Cure is either unnecessarily protracted, or totally frustrated; for the Patients are so delighted, not only with a Variety of Medicines, but also of Physicians.[14]

The patient's delight in this stable relationship provides one link with the modern conception of hypochondria.

Boswell, however, is not remarkable for his seeking the services of the medical profession in a psychological capacity. Rather, he prefers a more varied field in which to make his disclosures, and consequently he lays himself open, through unwise confidences, to that very ridicule and censure which was earlier distinguished as one of the aggravations of hypochondria. In London in 1786, he talks of his failures and low spirits to his fellow bar counsel: 'This was imprudent. But mental pain could not be endured quietly. I had talked in the same way to Mrs. Strange' (*BP*, XVI, p. 202). Similarly, he feels he has been too open even with Seward, himself a hypochondriac: 'Breakfasted with Seward, and was a little relieved by talking of melancholy and hearing how often he was afflicted with it. I was sensible it was wrong to speak of it. But the torment was such that I could not conceal it' (*BP*, XVI, p. 146). As Johnson observes, 'though it must be allowed that he suffers most like a hero that hides his grief in silence ... yet it cannot be denied, that he who complains acts like a man, like a social being, who looks for help from his fellow-creatures'.[15]

Clearly, though, a vicious circle can easily develop: the

strain of covering melancholy by the appearance of normality is an extra burden upon the disordered spirits, and one which increases the natural desire to communicate and to seek for understanding and sympathy; yet such communication, once one succumbs, may provoke a reaction which will itself add to the original derangement. So Boswell regrets the 'very great misfortune to be one of those people, who may be said to have no fanners in their minds with which they can winnow the grain from the chaff, so that all their thoughts of every sort are brought forth whatever may be the consequence' (*BC*, p. 139).

He is clearly fighting against his natural tendency: 'I am too open and have a desire to let all my affairs be known' (*LJ*, p. 136); 'But really I have a kind of strange feeling as if I wished nothing to be secret that concerns myself' (*OY*, p. 214). Again this is important not only for Boswell's own reputation, but also regarding his relations with others. He may see that another man wears a mask, but he must not make his knowledge public. The man may not himself be aware that he has another face beneath his worldly one, and even if he is he will not be happy to know that it is perceived and broadcast. Boswell, while seeking the reassurance of discerning the gap within another's identity, must guard against rashly exposing others as often as he does himself.

With regard to the need for communication, and the dangers of conversational impropriety, we may appreciate the high estimation of letters. A private letter by its nature allows a less inhibited expression of one's true self than is normally advisable. Indeed, as Locke points out, it is inevitable:

> the writing of letters has so much to do in all the occurrences of human life, that no Gentleman can avoid shewing himself in this kind of writing. Occasions will daily force him to make use of his Pen, which ... always lays him open to a severer Examination of his Breeding, Sense, and Abilities, than oral Discourses.[16]

In a letter, one may impart with relative freedom in the confidence that no publication will be made without one's express permission.[17] Perhaps Boswell's life-long correspondence with Temple is ample demonstration of how highly he valued the opportunity for frank exchange of mind. And, of course, Boswell's letters to Temple are the vehicle for enthusiastic declarations of friendship. A letter is a substitute for conversation between friends, as Cowper remarks: 'A letter is written as a conversation is maintained.... If a man may talk without thinking, why may he not write upon the same terms?'[18] In this respect, the writing of a letter may be a useful aid against 'Antiquity', as Boswell advises Johnston:

> Indeed it is very hard to have no friend to whom we can lay open our dejected minds, and by tender sympathy obtain relief. But pray my friend do this in your letters. Whenever you are in low spirits sit down and write to me all your thoughts, tho' never so gloomy: freely and without Study. This will do you good and by imagining that you are talking to your absent friend you will insensibly feel yourself lightened of the dreary burthen under which your fancy labours. (*Corr.* I, p. 30)

There is the additional advantage of a letter that one is able to choose one's words with more care than is possible in a conversation in order to provoke a specific effect upon the recipient. While this is not quite true open communication, nor does it necessarily constitute dishonesty. In the *London Journal*, Boswell lists the men to whom he has just written, each in an appropriate style, and concludes: 'I have touched every man on the proper key, and yet have used no deceit' (p. 353). Some of his epistles to Zélide, his introduction of himself to Rousseau, and his begging letter to Sir Andrew Mitchell on behalf of Temple, all show Boswell's considerable skill in concocting a suitable approach to each. And it is notable, concerning his regard for written evidence, that he requests M de Zuylen to return his proposal of marriage to his daughter Zélide, 'for I shall always be curious to recall how I expressed myself in an affair of this consequence' (*Holl.*, p. 341). Boswell's ability in this field demonstrates how, with thought, he is able to use his perception of men's true characters with propriety and to his own advantage.

Boswell's attitude to letters, though, is also indicative of the way he regards writing in general. He likes, as a reader, to be carried along by the personality of his author, and to feel that he is experiencing more than the verbal communication of an actual relationship. Of Francis Osborne's works, for example, he is pleased that he has 'found much shrewd and lively sense, expressed indeed in a style somewhat quaint, which, however, I do not dislike. His book has an air of originality. We figure to ourselves an ancient gentleman talking to us' (*Life*, II, pp. 193–4).

Elsewhere, he makes this quality his supreme test of a piece of literature:

> I know not if I can explain what I have felt, but I think the high test of great writing is when we do not consider the writer, and say, 'Here Mr. Johnson has done nobly'; but when what we read does so fill and expand our mind that the writer is admired by us instantaneously as a being directly impressing us, as the soul of that writing, so that for a while we forget his personality, and, by a reflex operation, perceive that it is Mr. Johnson who is speaking to us.
> (*OY*, p. 80)

Part of his dislike for *The Decline and Fall of the Roman Empire* is owing to Gibbon's subverting this relationship:

> I said the style was beautiful, quite mellifluous, but that there was poison conveyed in it, and it was a strange thing to meet with infidelity in a history. That it was not fair to attack us thus unexpectedly, and that he should have warned us of our danger, before we entered his garden of flowers of eloquence, by an advertisement: 'Springs and traps set here.' (*OY*, p. 282)

As a writer, too, Boswell is careful to inform his own readers that he is aware of their presence. He begins the *Hypochondriack* series by discussing essays:

> This invention therefore is I hope proved to be for the mutual benefit of writers and readers: and I cannot help thinking that readers are but too little considered by writers.... Writers should remember that they would make but a sorry figure were it not for readers. (*BC*, p. 22)

Taking his leave in the last number, he summarises his

attitude, 'a writer though unknown, is always personified with sufficient distinctness by the imagination, so as to be the object of affection of one kind or other' (*BC*, p. 356).

Yet Boswell is under no delusion concerning an author's actual character. He knows that the 'I' with whom the reader sympathises is probably either a hoax, or else totally imaginary, built out of one's own desire for the impression of true communication. (Indeed, Boswell would have been very insensitive not to have recognised the difference between an author and a persona in the eighteenth century.) In this sense, the therapeutic effect of a relationship with a favourite authorial 'voice' is based upon a lie. Boswell warns his readers of this in *The Hypochondriack*, using as illustration the idea of an actor assuming a role:

> But, there must not be too positive expectations entertained of finding a similarity between an author's conversation and his writing.... He may be an imposter, so as to have been assuming the appearance of virtuous or amiable qualities, which he no more possesses, than a player does many of the characters which he represents upon the stage with a vivacity of deception.... Indeed, there is nothing more delusive than the supposed character of an author, from reading his compositions. (*BC*, pp. 356–7)

He mentions in a letter to Temple that the quality of a man's conversation does not necessarily indicate ability to write well (*Letters*, II, p. 232), and, conversely, wonders that the dramatist John Hoole has written tragedies 'when I perceived so little fire in his conversation, and indeed so little imagery or genius of any kind' (*OY*, p. 332). Against this view, it should be observed that Johnson's literary character is identical to the picture Boswell gives of his actual character, and that Boswell was able to write his letter to Rousseau with the experience only of his writings and reputation. But then Johnson and Rousseau were hardly ordinary men. And Johnson himself begins *The Rambler* 14 by speaking of the 'manifest and striking contrariety between the life of an author and his writings'; those who seek a 'nearer knowledge' of the writer himself often find that 'the phantom of perfection has vanished when they wished to press it to their bosom'.[19]

## (iii) *The Published Word: Being in Print*

Even the dichotomy between a man and his writings, though, can be turned to advantage in a partial solution to Boswell's hypochondriacal problems. For a clever writer may construct for himself an impeccable public character which will impress many hundreds of readers who will never know the failings of the man. Whatever the individual may do in his immediate social sphere, and whatever bruises may be inflicted upon him through his own inadequacy, he will always remember the consolation of having erected a fixed image of himself which remains secure and untarnished. Boswell makes this point in the preface to his *Account of Corsica* (pp. 131-3), and tells Temple that he even hopes to live up to the character he is establishing for himself (*Wife*, p. 112).

It is *The Hypochondriack* which brings all these issues into focus. The key to the series is not the therapeutic value of actually putting ideas onto paper (this after all could be quite adequately accomplished through his journal and letters), nor is it the pleasure and benevolence of giving advice to others. And, as Boswell declares in the first number (*BC*, p. 25) that he is no longer a sufferer, it is unlikely that he wrote them, at least to start with, to divert his own melancholy. Rather, the benefit derives from the opportunity for the freedom of open communication of the same kind as may be indulged in letters and the best kind of conversation: 'And still I would have it kept in view, that being in print is not so very different from expressing our thoughts in conversation, or in letters to our friends, that we should be so very much afraid of it' (*BC*, pp. 158-9).

Success in this design will assure Boswell of the acceptability, by a large number of people, of a less restrained and so of a more genuine self.[20] And he knows that all that this stance embodies will constitute its appeal to the readers to whom he addresses himself. He is a hypochondriac speaking in his own voice to hypochondriacs. Again and again Boswell emphasises his attitude towards his readers:

> my sincere wish is, and I pretend to nothing higher, only to be their companion and friend.... [The Hypochondriack] wishes without affectation to accost them in the true spirit of

> those good primitive authors, who have prefaced their works with such phrases as these, 'Gentle Reader, Worthy Reader, Christian Reader.' (*BC*, p. 54)

> I do not impose upon myself the task of regular system or exact order; but just throw out what thoughts occur to me, as if I were sitting with a friend. (*BC*, p. 74)

> Here again I am anxious to have it understood, that *The Hypochondriack* does not pretend to the wisdom and influence of a teacher.... As I am only the companion of my readers, I have no scruple to write freely, as they will judge for themselves. (*BC*, p. 169)

In the final essay is an assurance that he has used no deceit in his presentation of himself:

> For myself, I cannot perfectly judge of my manner, which I have no doubt must vary with the fluctuation of my spirits. Nor can I boast that my practice is uniformly what it should be. But I am absolutely certain that in these papers my principles are most sincerely expressed. (*BC*, p. 357)

And he suggests that his pose as a friend has been no mere literary device:

> Yet it is an interesting fancy that there may be some of my readers so habituated to sympathize with the soul of the HYPOCHONDRIACK, that the instant of our being personally known to each other there would be a cordial friendship between us. (*BC*, p. 356)

John Hill draws his treatise, *Hypochondriasis*, to a conclusion in a way which similarly suggests an awareness of the hypochondriac's need for sympathetic identification with the writer – here reinforced by the comfort of the doctor–patient relationship:

> Let him who takes the medicine, say whether anything here be exaggerated. Let him, if he pleases to give himself the trouble, talk over with me, or write to me, this gradual

decrease of his complaints, as he proceeds in his cure. My uncertain state of health does not permit me to practise physic in the usual way, but I am very desirous to do what good I can, and shall never refuse my advice, such as it may be, to any person rich or poor, in whatever manner he may apply for it.[21]

Boswell, of course, has the considerable advantage of writing within a highly developed tradition of periodical literature. From the *Spectator* onwards, the essayist had adopted as his own the role of adviser to society on social matters. As Alexander Chalmers writes, 'There were innumerable topics, which, though of great importance in promoting regularity and propriety in social life, and securing the happiness of the domestic relations, had been but slightly touched by any of the teachers of wisdom.'[22] Johnson had added a new development to the tradition in *The Rambler* by addressing himself not to society but to the private individual, and by concerning himself with matters of personal morality. Chalmers observes that Johnson's essays represent a departure from what had become the *Spectator* tradition, and that his subjects are totally new in the history of that type of writing.[23] Boswell takes something from both branches by addressing the private individual upon a very personal subject, but concentrating upon the practical aspect of how that subject relates to society. And the voice of the club-man of the *Spectator*, and of the preacher of *The Rambler*, becomes familiarised into the open-hearted tones of a friend and confidant.

The element of the tradition, though, which makes it possible for Boswell to be so unconstrained upon the delicate subject of hypochondria is the privilege of anonymity, granted upon the condition that the individual whom the voice represents is permitted only the most general physical features. Johnson points particularly to this idea in the last *Rambler*:

> The seeming vanity with which I have sometimes spoken of myself, would perhaps require an apology, were it not extenuated by the example of those who have published essays before me, and by the privilege which every nameless

writer has been hitherto allowed. 'A mask', says Castiglione, 'confers a right of acting and speaking with less restraint, even when the wearer happens to be known.' He that is discovered without his own consent, may claim some indulgence, and cannot be rigorously called to justify those sallies or frolicks which his disguise must prove him desirous to conceal.[24]

Boswell, too, notes that 'anonymous publication be a veil sufficient for concealment' (*BC*, p. 158), and he takes full advantage of his freedom. *Hypochondriack* 39, for example, in which Boswell talks himself through an actual attack of melancholy, must surely be one of the frankest pieces of writing published before the end of the eighteenth century. His mistake, as far as the desire to continue living comfortably in society is concerned, occurs when he drops the mask.

With the *Journal of a Tour to the Hebrides*, Boswell attempted to transfer what he had been able to do anonymously within one accepted tradition to another very different tradition, with consequent grave infringements of the rules of social and literary propriety. As one contemporary reviewer remarked, Boswell's *Tour* was 'unprotected by the shield of correctness, and unadorned by the beauty of drapery'.[25] The essayist speaks in generalisations, and if individuals are mentioned they are accorded a veil as properly as the writer himself. The satirist is permitted by tradition to attack and even to name individuals, and indeed is expected to do so. But the writer of a book of travels can look only for censure and resentment should he dare to assume the role of another. The biographer ridicules at his peril those who are still alive to feel the humiliation of public exposure, for society's displeasure will rather be directed at the folly of the transgressor than at his unfortunate victim. Paul Fussell writes about the attitude of the eighteenth century to genres:

> But although the humanist version of this theory of genre is generally flexible, it does carry the implication that, since the ancients were exquisitely aware of the nature of man, the genres they devised to address his central capacities are to be tampered with only at great risk.[26]

And he goes on to speak of Boswell, 'with his apparent sense that it all doesn't matter very much and with his gay misunderstandings of the requirements of the traditional genres'.[27] The fool without his cap is a fool indeed, as well as a danger both to himself and to others.

Boswell, in fact, had shown very early in life an inclination to allow himself greater freedom concerning literary publications than was acceptable to more cautious contemporaries. His dedication of *The Cub at Newmarket* led to a reprimand from his friend Eglinton: 'I was really in a passion for your having brought me into a sad scrape by publishing your *Cub* and dedicating it to the Duke of York without his leave. I can assure you he was very angry' (*LJ*, p. 192). Lord Auchinleck made severe remarks upon the publication in 1763 of the *Letters between the Honourable Andrew Erskine, and James Boswell, Esq.* (*LJ*, p. 362), and even Boswell himself wrote upon this occasion to Johnston that 'Captain Erskine and I have published a Collection of our letters, with the utmost boldness too, as we have printed our names at length' (*Corr.* I, p. 70). Then, in 1767, a paragraph by Boswell in the *London Chronicle*, in which he spoke of the 'unavoidable occupations of a laborious employment', was censured as most unseemly. Ralph Walker records that 'Boswell's pretentiousness in thus venturing to refer in public print to the weight of his legal labours at the end of what was only his first full session of the courts had aroused disapproval in Edinburgh even among his friends' (*Corr.* I, pp. 225–6 n. 7). And it was, in fact, to Boswell's legal reputation that John Lee pointed in commenting on possible damage from the *Journal of a Tour to the Hebrides*: 'There is hardly any Quality more essential to Success in our Profession, than that sort of Prudence, which knows, what is fit to be said, and what ought to [be] concealed (*Corr.* I, p. 306 n. 7).

The published Hebrides journal, then, represents not Boswell's deliberate attempt to free himself from the encumbrances of eighteenth-century literary propriety, but a further miscalculation of the social role of a writer. His failure is that he did not realise how completely contemporary morality governs every activity in which the individual members of a society may choose to engage. What is intolerable in the direct contact of social intercourse does not become any more acceptable when it is written down and published. The distance between a man and what he writes is not so great as to make the one invisible to whoever beholds the other. The 'true' self of the literary publication has, if he is not to outrage the sensibilities of his socially minded readers, just as much need of that 'superficial' social virtue, responsibility, as does the artificial self which acts out the various roles assigned to it in public life. Boswell looked in his writing for a freedom from that insincerity and decorum which made so difficult his commitment to public and business life. The very act of ignoring literary propriety was the result of the pressures of being forced to live within the society which itself constructed the artistic barriers along the lines of its own values. The attempt to conform was, for Boswell, the direct cause of his specific nonconformity.

It is scarcely conceivable that Boswell actually intended to heap humiliation upon those who were offended by his material in the *Tour*. And it is even less acceptable to assume that he voluntarily exposed himself and the memory of Johnson to the type of ridicule Peter Pindar hurled at the triviality and egotism of the account:

> Yet honest praise, I'm sure, thou wouldst not shun,
> Born with a stomach to digest a tun! ...
> Who will not, too, thy pen's *minutiae* bless,
> That gives posterity the Rambler's dress?[28]

A. J. Tillinghast has written concerning the adverse commentary upon the *Tour*,

> The important point was that the *method* suffered few attacks and while a few criticized Boswell's minuteness and lack of grandeur, the majority of unfavourable responses were concerned with Boswell's and Johnson's personalities and what they did and said rather than how these were described.[29]

Certainly, Boswell's purposes for this particular instance of his 'rage for publication' were first to establish his claim upon Johnson and make public his intention to write the biography, and then, as Tillinghast suggested, to test a biographical method. With these foremost in his mind, it is quite probable that the question of the propriety of his exhibition of himself and of others simply did not occur to him. Frederick Pottle's opinion is that much of the polishing and censoring of Boswell's original Hebrides journal may be attributed to the more decorous Malone.[30] Even Boswell, though, was not so indiscreet as, for example, to retain his reference to Macdonald as an 'insect' (*Hebr.*, p. 125), but some of his allusions to 'a very penurious gentleman of our acquaintance' (cf. *Life*, v, pp. 277, 315–16), or to 'a rapacious Highland Chief' (*Life*, v, p. 378), hardly indicate any great dedication to the task of pruning to conformity. Boswell no doubt considered that, even if Macdonald's perceptiveness were sufficient to penetrate the veil, reflection would convince him that the rebukes were well deserved.[31] Similarly, Lord Mondoddo, surely by this time aware of his notoriety as an advocate of extravagant theories, would scarcely object to Boswell's confirmation of the picture the world already saw of him. Nor is there any evidence to suggest that Boswell had ever encountered the 'green goose' type of judgements to which his narrative and interviewing techniques in the *Tour to Corsica* had exposed him.

The conclusion, then, that Boswell did, if not rush, then at least scamper fairly nimbly, into print with his *Journal of a Tour to the Hebrides*, and that he was thus totally unprepared for the reputation it gained him, may be drawn if that work is seen as a continuation of the line of public expressions in which he found some relief from the trials of establishing and preserving a relationship between society and the hypochondriac spirit. In his view, the matter was as simple as his justification to Macdonald: 'In his "Journal of a Tour to the Hebrides" he conceives he was entitled to make and publish such remarks upon men and things as occured, provided they were founded in truth and expressed with decency and propriety' (*BP*, XVI, p. 248). Society's subsequent reserve concerning Boswell's company, though, and the ridicule of the 'shallow or envious cavillers' ('Advertisement to the Third Edition', *Life*, v, p. 3), convinced him of the inescapable responsibility an author owes the world for his productions. Boswell writes of the Macdonald affair, 'What mischief may imprudent publications bring upon even a good man' (*BP*, XVI, p. 142). And

Mrs Piozzi's *Letters to Dr. Johnson* leads him to reflect, 'I felt myself degraded from the consequence of an ancient Baron to the state of an humble attendant on an Author; and what vexed me, thought that my collecting so much of his conversation had made the World shun me as a dangerous companion' (*BP*, XVII, p. 75).

Finally, in the oft-quoted letter to his son Alexander in 1794, Boswell draws from his own experience the moral of which the writers of the essays he there recommends were instinctively aware – in fact, they did more than anyone else to make that moral valid: never forget that the observer is himself observed, the judge judged.

> But you must be very cautious of letting other people know that you are such an *Observer* and such a *censor morum*, as they may be apt to misunderstand and form a wrong notion of you. I speak from experience, because I am certain that there is not in reality a more benevolent man than myself in the World; and yet, from my having indulged myself without reserve in the discriminative delineations of a variety of people, I know I am thought by many to be ill natured; nay, from the specimens which I have given the World of my uncommon recollection of conversations, many foolish persons have been afraid to meet me, vainly apprehending that *their* conversation would be *recorded*. No study, however, is more improving than the study of *Man*; and my friend Courtenay pays me the compliment of having 'imbibed' from Dr. Johnson 'That great art, the art to know Mankind'.
>
> Keep yourself quietly in mind of that admirable maxim *Nullum numen abest si sit Prudentia*, and you will both enjoy your surveys of life with a truer relish and reap substantial improvement, without incurring any disadvantage. I would recommend to you to read again those excellent essays upon life and manners which the Writers of Queen Anne's Reign, the Augustan age of England, have left us in the *Tatler, Spectator*, and *Guardian*. (*BP*, XVIII, p. 319)

Boswell's advice to his son makes interesting comparison with Lord Chesterfield's.

Clearly, then, the total *Hebrides* experience, as I have

sketched it, is a vital influence upon Boswell's attitude to the task of the *Life of Johnson*. This influence is not only the so frequently emphasised technical aspect of Boswell's dramatic biographical method. There is a strong case for seeing the *Tour to the Hebrides* less as a trial-run for the *Life*, than as the crucial experience which made Boswell aware of just how much his acceptance of his final great role was to cost him. I reserve consideration of this, however, for a later chapter, and turn first to discuss how we may see the journals in the light of all that I have been offering.

# 6 'Scribo ergo sum': the World of Boswell's Journals

(i) *Time and Memory*

In his *Hypochondriack* essay 'On Time', Boswell remarks upon the most 'melancholy and discouraging' of the operations of time:

> It is plain then, that we are not only persuaded of the existence of time, but of its existence and powerful activity. Such indeed is its activity, that there is nothing material upon the face of the globe, but what its progressive operation will progressively make as if it had never been. (*BC*, p. 327)

The subject had clearly occupied his mind for some years, for he had brought the idea of annihilation by time into his discussion of actors in the second essay 'On the Profession of a Player' in 1770. The 'talents of the greatest actor', he had noted, 'die with him', and 'it is impossible to give succeeding ages, who have never seen him, an adequate idea of his wonderful powers'. In this respect, he went on, 'the poet and painter have the advantage over him... for the works of a painter and poet are transmitted down from age to age with successive admiration' (*Player*, pp. 16–17). Boswell, of course, was neither poet nor painter, and at the time of expressing these sentiments only the *Account of Corsica* among his publications might with any justification have been regarded by him as a likely preservation of his name and powers. And, even so, one or two artistic relics could hardly be expected to give any real impression to future ages of the whole life, the whole personality of the man who produced them. As Bertrand Bronson points out, it was not enough for Boswell that a few isolated specimens of his creative skill might survive to suggest to futurity that such a man once existed: 'Boswell was so fascinated by the spectacle of life, he had such a zest and relish for it, that he was impelled to try and save as much of it as possible from oblivion.'[1]

One supremely important reason for Boswell's journalising, then, must always be that only by means of such a continuous picture of himself could he hope to preserve from the abyss of time any sizable mass of evidence in proof of his own existence. As F. A. Pottle notes in an introduction to the *Boswell Papers*: 'He wrote it primarily for himself, but he seldom wrote without the feeling that after he was dead and had finished with it, it would still preserve his personality for all time' (*BP*, XIII, p. vi).

Boswell, from the very beginning of his journal, is fully aware that he is 'saving' his life from time's destruction. Opening his *London Journal*, he declares as one advantage of keeping a journal that 'I shall preserve many things that would otherwise be lost in oblivion' (*LJ*, p. 67). Towards the end of his Hebrides journal he remarks that 'I must lament that I was so indolent as to let almost all that passed evaporate into oblivion' (*Hebr.*, p. 388). And he concludes the *Hypochondriack* essay 'On Diaries' with the observation, 'For my own part I have so long accustomed myself to write a Diary, that when I omit it the day seems to be lost, though for the most part I put down nothing but immaterial facts which it can serve no purpose of any value to record' (*BC*, p. 336).

Not that Boswell always seems to enjoy the process of recording. At times he displays an enormous sense of fatigue at the burden of responsibility he has placed upon himself, and of hopelessness at the magnitude of his task: 'I sat up all last night writing letters and bringing up my lagging journal, which, like a stone to be rolled up a hill, must be kept constantly going' (*LJ*, p. 349). And elsewhere he appears as one battling helplessly against the ceaseless flow of time: 'And now on this Wednesday, the 6th of November, I have my journal brought up to the preceding day, according to what I have constantly purposed but seldom fulfilled. I hope henceforth never to let time run over me more than a day unregistered' (*Ex.*, p. 52). Boswell's effort may be exhausting, but his journal remains the only sure way of rescuing at least some of his life from oblivion, however inadequately. 'It is unpleasing,' he says, 'to observe how imperfect a picture of my life this Journal presents. Yet I have certainly much more of *myself* preserved than most people have' (*BP*, XIV, p. 32). The journalist experiences frustration at his own shortcomings as a recorder, but at the same time satisfaction at having preserved anything at all.

It is also noticeable – and noticed by Boswell – that the satisfaction of expecting a situation to be recorded reflects back upon the activities themselves at the time they are experienced, and even upon those to which Boswell's normal reaction is one of distaste: 'I saw that the keeping of books was a great help to make a man like farming; at least it would be so to me, who will go through almost anything with a degree of satisfaction if I am to put an account of it in writing' (*OY*, p. 6). This naturally adds impetus to Boswell's zest for experience: 'My journal will afford materials for a very curious narrative. I assure you I do not live with a view to have surprising incidents, though I own I am desireous that my life should *tell*' (*Letters*, II, p. 372). But it reveals something, too, about the way in which Boswell actually experiences. He is one in whom to experience is to communicate, whose sensations and thoughts are formulated into words as soon as they are realised. Boswell's journal is the product of a combination between a sensibility acutely aware of varieties of sensations, and a powerful need to communicate experiences and thereby to render them more permanent. He lives to enjoy and to record, and he records so that he may be able to live with the knowledge of time.

But keeping a journal not only saves Boswell from the abyss of time to come. It also helps to prevent him from lapsing into awareness of the abyss within time present, for the very habit of regular writing serves partly to fill up the 'empty milieu' of everyday life in which the mind can so easily slide into melancholy: 'I shall find daily employment for myself,' he says at the beginning of his *London Journal*, 'which will save me from indolence and help to keep off the spleen' (*LJ*, p. 67). In the same way, he explains elsewhere, the writing of essays is often highly beneficial:

Men of the greatest parts and application are at times averse to labour for any continuance; and could they not employ their pens on lighter pieces, would at those times remain in total inactivity. Writing such essays therefore may fill up the interstices of their lives, and occupy moments which would otherwise be lost. (*BC*, p. 21)

For the hypochondriac, then, a daily journal is excellent therapy for indolence, and for his sense of waste of time and personal uselessness. The more wholeheartedly he is able to engage himself in such activity, the more satisfying will become his sense of productivity and regularity: 'Who will say that I am not a man of business, I who write my journal with the regularity of the German professor who wrote his folio every year?' (*GT* (i), p. 21).

Moreover, the very act of writing might, he thinks, be therapeutic, and he might even be able to transplant a fit of hypochondria from his mind into his journal: 'I know not if it be right thus to preserve my weakness and woe. Lord Monboddo said on Saturday that writing down hurts the memory. Could I extract the hypochondria from my mind, and deposit it in my journal, writing down would be very valuable' (*OY*, p. 240). At other times, though, he feels that hypochondria would be better left out of the record altogether: 'I really believe that these grievous complaints should not be vented; they should be considered as absurd chimeras, whose reality should not be allowed in words' (*Holl.*, p. 207).

This is not to say that the purpose of Boswell's journal which is more frequently emphasised by commentators, that of analysis of his own character and behaviour, is not of considerable importance. Boswell himself places this very point before all others at the beginning of the *London Journal*:

A man cannot know himself better than by attending to the feelings of his heart and to his external actions, from which he may with tolerable certainty judge 'what manner of person he is'. I have therefore determined to keep a daily journal in which I shall set down my various sentiments and my various conduct, which will not only be useful but very agreeable. It will give me a habit of application and improve me in expression; and knowing that I am forced to record my transactions will make me more careful to do well. Or if I should go wrong, it will assist me in resolutions of doing better. (*LJ*, p. 65)

Early in his journalising career, though, Boswell is brought to realise that his self-portrait must inevitably contain certain disturbing glimpses if it is to retain any validity as a record, and that he can perhaps learn from temporary disillusionment with himself. One instance, in 1763, concerns his thoughts of giving up his Guards scheme, for which he originally came to London, and of returning to Edinburgh to pursue a legal career:

I now see the sickly suggestions of inconsistent fancy with regard to the Scotch bar in their proper colours. Good Heaven! I should by pursuing that plan have deprived myself of felicity when I had it fairly in my power, and brought myself to a worse state than ever. I shudder when I think of it. I am vexed at such a distempered suggestion's being inserted in my journal, which I wished to contain a consistent picture of a young fellow eagerly pushing through life. But it serves to humble me, and it presents a strange and curious view of the unaccountable nature of the human mind. I am now well and gay. Let me consider that the hero of a romance or novel must not go uniformly along in bliss, but the story must be chequered with bad fortune. Aeneas met with many disasters in his voyage to Italy, and must not Boswell have his rubs? Yes, I take them in good part. (*LJ*, p. 229)

If he regards it in the right way, his journal can serve as a means for usefully maintaining his eyes perpetually upon himself with a view to constructive criticism, and, 'as a lady adjusts her dress at a glass, a man adjusts his character by looking at it' (*Ex.*, p. 230).

The crucial point for the self-analytical function of the journal, though, is Boswell's attitude before the mirror – does he use it to 'adjust his character', or does he merely admire his own reflection? When Boswell writes about 'the hero of a romance or novel' and says that 'Aeneas met with many disasters ... and must not Boswell', he seems to have inclined very much towards the second attitude. Yet, if the record really has 'served to humble me', then he has derived some considerable benefit from the journal, though it ought to be noted in this instance that Boswell does in fact change his mind again and return to a Scottish legal career. Self-analysis is, in Boswell's eyes, certainly one reason for journalising, but he does nevertheless often display a remarkable lack of self-knowledge. For example, in September 1769, only a few months after his passionate love-affair with Mrs Dodds, for whom he rented a house in Edinburgh, and who bore him an illegitimate daughter, Boswell writes of his cousin Charles Boswell,

> I knew he had a lady who lived with him for several years. I returned and found her to be a comely, sensible, agreeable woman, with a modesty and decency of behaviour very different from that of a kept mistress.... It gave me concern to think she was not my cousin's wife. It also was out of character for a son of Auchinleck to be living in a licentious style. (*Wife*, p. 310)

Moreover, it is by no means certain that Boswell, when reading over his account of a past event, is ready to judge himself dispassionately:

> According to the humour which I am in when I read it, I judge of my past adventures, and not from what is really recorded. If I am in gay spirits, I read an account of so much existence and I think, 'Sure I have been very happy.' If I am gloomy, I think, 'Sure I have passed much uneasy time, or at best, much insipid time.' Thus I think without regard to the real fact as written. (*GT* (i), p. 140)

We must here take note of a central problem in Boswell's attitude towards his journalising. There are, as he implies, two incompatible world views, the melancholy, with its hopeless indifference to all values and all activities, and its 'swarm of ideas which mingle confusedly' (*GT* (i), p. 58), and the 'normal', which for Boswell means an enormous appetite for stimulation of every kind. Boswell clearly feels that in the act of writing, in allowing its reality in words, he is himself bestowing upon the bleak hypochondriac vision a more convincing claim to existence than if it were merely allowed to fade from his memory into oblivion. Yet, if, as he says, he is anxious to explore and understand himself, he cannot omit what is often a very obtrusive part of his experience. The journal would lose much of its value for Boswell if completely deprived of one half of his personality, for he could neither attempt to 'adjust his character' nor could he have the satisfaction of preserving as faithful a record as his powers allowed.

Understandably, then, his attitude towards his recorded past seems to be extremely unpredictable. Clearly, the journal does at times serve to 'humble' Boswell, does fulfil a useful self-analytical purpose, but equally at other times he is prepared to ignore the 'real fact as written' and to reinterpret his past in the light of the mood of the moment. Is it possible, then, with reference to such varying functions of the journal, to make any clear statement about Boswell's attitude towards memory? How important is the past to Boswell in the present, and how important does he think the present will be to Boswell in the future? And would we be right simply to equate Boswell's memory with Boswell's journal?

In *Hypochondriack* 67, 'On Memory', Boswell quotes from Locke's *Essay on Human Understanding*:

> Memory is as it were the *Storehouse* of our ideas; for the narrow mind of man not being capable of having many ideas under view and consideration at once, it was necessary to have a *Repository* to lay up those ideas which at another time it might have use of. (*BC*, pp. 338–9)

(An editorial note points out that the italics in this passage are Boswell's own.) And in the 'Introduction' to the *London Journal* he declares,

> I shall here put down my thoughts on different subjects at different times, the whims that may seize me and the sallies of my luxuriant imagination. I shall mark the anecdotes and the stories that I hear, the instructive or amusing conversations that I am present at, and the various adventures that I may have. (*LJ*, p. 65)

One function of the journal, it seems, is to serve Boswell as a storehouse for his past thoughts and experiences, and, in particular, for his creativity in the images which are, for him, such an important part of his mental well-being: 'Of this week I can observe that my mind has been more lively than usual, more fertile in images, more agreeably sensible of enjoying existence' (*Def.*, p. 233). Not only is the journal a storehouse for Boswell's *bons mots* of company – 'I described Castle Stewart as a castle impregnable by wine – that could not be *sapped* – that had a deep moat of wine around it' (*Def.*, p. 242) – but all the images he produces to convey his states of mind, his attitudes towards life in general, are given coherence by being formulated there. They are made permanent by their expression in words and their insertion within the journal.

Furthermore, to the hypochondriac Boswell it is some evidence of his own sanity that he is able to order and select from the 'sallies', which sometimes seem 'a sort of confusion of mind' and sometimes a 'high and fine flow of thought' (*OY*, pp. 181, 252). The important thing, as Johnson advises, is to record the state of one's mind (*Def.*, p. 182). Descriptions of incidents are of greater or lesser value in so far as they explain or revive the state of mind which accompanied them. Boswell's view, at one entry, is that, 'though words do but imperfectly preserve the ideas, yet such notes as I write are sufficient to make the impressions revive, with many associated ones' (*Wife*, pp. 149–50). It is perhaps of less importance in this respect to set out events and states of mind with great precision, or to show impeccable personal consistency, for the journal is 'not so much ... a history as ... a reservoir of ideas' (*GT* (i), p. 140). And the mere expression of one's changeability and rush of ideas is some assertion of the controlling power of reason over the mind.

In effect, then, Boswell is creating in his journal what amounts to a second memory. 'An Hypochondriack', he remarks in *Hypochondriack* 67, 'is subject to forgetfulness, which may be owing to another cause; that there is a darkness in his mind, or that its perceptive eye is injured and weak at times' (*BC*, p. 341).[2] A second memory is important in that it is always there: it can be relied upon to supplement the information possessed by the real memory, and, more important, revive the impression of mind. Boswell may not always choose to use it as a reliable source, not regard the 'fact as written', but, for the hypochondriac, the mere presence of the journal may be of infinite value. He is afflicted with melancholy doubts over the value of his past life, and over his ability to learn and improve himself through experience. The more efficient memory of the journal serves as some reminder of the events, impressions and self-assessments of the past, and so can act as a constant guarantee in case of such painful failures on the part of the real memory. Even if the melancholy Boswell is reinterpreting the past in a light of gloom, then the recording of previous lapses will be some reassurance that order can be imposed upon hypochondria, as well as some evidence of how low his spirits have sunk in the past. The current dejection can then be seen alongside earlier levels and, as it were, graded appropriately.

It is likely, then, that having a permanent and accessible version of the past can be of very real value to Boswell in the present. But, while the journal is essential to the ordering, and therefore to the interpretation, of the past, it is also written with an eye on the future. Boswell, when recording, as the question-and-answer device of this extract suggests, frequently has a reader in mind, including himself at a later date:

> At night indolence made me think, why give myself so much labour to write this journal, in which I really do not insert much that can be called useful? Beg your pardon. Does it not contain a faithful register of my variations of mind? Does it not contain many ingenious observations and pleasing strokes which can afterwards be enlarged? Well, but I may die. True, but I may live; and what a rich treasure for my after days will be this my journal.   (*GT* (i), p. 56)

He seems to maintain in his journal a continual temporal restlessness.[3] The focus of attention shifts between the events of the past, the present of himself as recorder, and the reader of the future, either himself, a friend, or else posterity. As he writes in a letter to Temple in 1789, 'You have told me that I was the most *thinking* man you ever knew. It is certainly so as to my *own life*. I am continually *conscious*, continually *looking back* or *looking forward* and wondering how I shall feel in situations which I anticipate in fancy' (*Letters*, II, pp. 371-2). Again, time is seen to be a central concern of Boswell's thinking. He is acutely aware of what it means to have one's existence under the fixed rule of time. (In this light, the image of the soul as a watch stands out in a new freshness.)

An example from the original Hebrides journal shows plainly that Boswell is fully aware of the effect the passing of time may have on his two memories. He describes how he and Johnson discussed their tour in comparison with their previous expectations of it. Boswell then observes,

> It will be curious too, to perceive how the impression made by reading this my journal some years after our roving will affect the mind, when compared with the recollection of what was felt at the time. Mr. Johnson said I should read my Journal about every three years. (*Hebr.*, p. 329)

This seems to be based on the assumption that there will inevitably be a difference between the two memories, and that this difference will certainly increase with the passing of time. Boswell goes on to remark 'that scenes through which a man has gone improve by lying in the memory. They grow mellow' (*Hebr.*, p. 329). It will be the real memory that changes, while the journal memory, of course, remains constant. It follows, then, that the journal, for all its admitted inadequacies of expression, is ultimately the more accurate record. It must be remembered, though, that the accuracy of the journal is in this case only relative. The past in the journal is coloured by Boswell's state of mind at the time of recording, and so the future impression of the account, coloured again by his state of mind at the time of reading, will be at least two stages away from the original reality. And, of course, Boswell may be in a less than sober state when actually experiencing the events he records, and so a third element of bias must be admitted.

At one point in his journal, in fact, Boswell actually discovers an example of his having recorded an exaggerated view of the past. He has made his first visit to Lord Bute's, and has described the occasion in glowing terms, emphasising in particular the splendour of the 'Constellation of laced footmen; all glitter' (*BP*, XIV, p. 213). A few weeks later, however, he makes a second visit, and reports rather shamefacedly,

'Perceived that there was not one bit of lace on the footmen, and that my fervent imagination had gilded them and produced the blaze' (*BP*, XIV, p. 219).

The world of the journal, then, must not be taken as an objective picture of the real world. It is as subjective, as imaginary (in that it is interpretation and impressions colouring the mere recording of facts) as Boswell's own memory of the past. When he writes, 'My imagination preserves beauty and every amiable quality, so that if it has once existed in an object, and touched my senses, it is embalmed for ever' (*Ex.*, p. 101), he implicitly raises several important points about the status of his journal's-eye view of the world, about his recorded imaginative vision. In the first place, of course, he is referring to his desire to save things of value from destruction by time. But the remark also affords other insights into the working of Boswell's mind. For one thing, it is a reminder of the possible distorting effects of the imagination, its capacity to mistake creation for recreation, as in the Bute example. More than this, though, the remark makes quite clear Boswell's own vital position at the focal point of his journal, that it is *his* world we are reading about, not the objective world of facts. His journal, like the 'image' of Chapter 3, can reflect no more than Boswell projects into it. It is an assertion of his interpretation of reality, a personal reality, and of his own importance within that 'reality'. So, in exercising the ability to organise and order a world within a world, the 'reality' of the journal, Boswell is in effect providing constant reassurance of his own sanity, rather than having to let time 'run over' him 'unregistered' and hence uninterpreted.

### (ii)  *A Second Reality*

In creating a second memory in his journal, then, Boswell is in fact creating a second 'reality'. But, in so far as this 'reality' is distant from the factual reality of the everyday world, he is able to reveal himself in it more openly and honestly than he dare do in company, even in the company of friends. We can see how for him the 'reality' of the journal is more true to himself than the reality through which he had lived, for the imaginary world in the journal is one in which Boswell can safely indulge everything which is under restraint in the real everyday world. The privileged position of the journalist allows him free interpretation of past events, unlimited observation upon his own present, and gratifying speculations for the future. He may give expression to minor opinions and flippancies which decorum required should be suppressed during the actual incidents in which they arose – for example, Boswell's idea of a course in concubinage, or his unflattering thoughts about Anna Seward's similarity to a coal-pit (*OY*, pp. 286, 294–5). Or he is able to work out judgements of people, which he cannot often do with the help or knowledge of others. Such estimations require some sort of external expression before they become coherent, and the journal provides the opportunity for the necessary formulation. In this way, for example, Boswell clarifies his ideas on his various friends in London and Scotland:

> And here I must observe that my connexions with Erskine and Dempster are really not those of friendship. We are in the style of companions. It is only fancy that cements us. It is only because we are entertaining to one another that we are so much together. Dempster I do not know thoroughly. Erskine has too much selfishness and too bad a temper to be what I call a friend. Thank heaven! I have some true friends. Johnston is most strictly so. Temple is also one. Honest McQuhae is also one. To these I can unbosom my anxious mind; from these I am sure of sympathy and kindness. Besides, these all agree with me in many things which are of consequence. They all, with me, look forward to another world, which Dempster and Erskine never think of. They have all strong ideas of real life and manners, which Erskine and Dempster see in fanciful and ludicrous lights and are not in earnest about. Such distinctions are very nice and are better felt than explained.   (*LJ*, p. 215)

Even more important, Boswell is able to give in his journal a complete and true portrait of himself. He need conceal nothing of his behaviour and thoughts. (It is notable, though, that he does sometimes censor things which he had originally included: for example, some of the details of his brutal treatment of the dog Jachone – *GT* (ii), pp. 241 n. 1, 243 n. 3.

There are obviously some things which Boswell cannot bear to have continually brought to remembrance.) Not even conversation and letters between friends, and not even the privileged position of the Hypochondriack, are able to confer the freedom granted to the writer of a journal. And the habit of writing for a reader, perhaps arising from Boswell's plan to send his earliest journals to his friends McQuhae and Johnston, has the advantage of instilling a sense of communication of an honest and valuable kind. Boswell's journal has been called his confessional.[4] Even when he is censuring himself for something of which he is ashamed, Boswell is as open as he can be. He allows as much insight into the true identity behind the disguises adopted for society as he possesses himself. Such things as are 'passed by in silence' (*LJ*, p. 67) are those which Boswell cannot bring himself to face. As far as possible, he attempts to follow the advice of *The Rambler* in attending to his own conscience only: 'That every man should regulate his actions by his own conscience, without any regard to the opinions of the rest of the world, is one of the first precepts of moral prudence.'[5] Clearly, to be able to move from social to personal propriety, even within the relatively secluded world of the journal, is a considerable relief from the pressures of actual living.

In this connection, we may consider the particular importance of Boswell's interest in reporting conversations. For one thing, he had a large share of the taste of his age for this form of sociable enjoyment. Naturally, he would want to preserve a great deal of what passed during a favourite activity. But the conversation recorded in the journal has woven into it much that Boswell is unable or unwilling to say in the conversations which actually took place. Boswell in fact recreates what he remembers of a conversation, adding his own views on the subjects under discussion, and often drawing its relevance to his own particular case. To do either in the conversation itself might lay him open to censure or ridicule. For example, Johnson and Boswell, travelling from Derby to Ashbourne, discuss drinking:

> he said General Paoli spoke to him with much concern of my drinking; that it would make me go mad, for madness was in my family. I said drinking moderately was a pleasure which

I was unwilling to give up. 'To be sure,' said he, 'not to drink wine is a great deduction from life, but it may be necessary.' I in my own mind schemed to enjoy the satisfaction of drinking wine. (*Ex.*, p. 165)

Or, again, in London in 1778, they talk about good humour, with Boswell recording privately the criticism of Johnson he was clearly not prepared to voice:

He said a man had from nature a certain portion of mind, the use he made of which depended on the human will. 'That a man has always the same firmness of mind, I do not say, because every man feels his mind less firm at some times than others. But I think a man's being in good or bad humour depends upon his own will.' If this be true, the Doctor is much to blame upon many occasions. But for my part I believe that a man's humour is often irresistible by his will. (*Ex.*, pp. 324–5)

And, if Boswell is unwilling to venture certain opinions in company, it is even less likely that he will point out in any but the most general terms how a particular subject bears upon his own feelings and behaviour. Yet he does often find useful advice in conversation which perhaps affects him in a way quite unforeseen by the speaker:

I called on Sir John Pringle and walked up and down his parlour with him a good while. . . . We got upon religion. He was keen for Socinianism, for Dr. Priestley's kind of Christianity. He talked with vivacity against the Trinity, the satisfaction of Christ, and the eternity of hell's torments, and said that at the Day of Judgement people would be ashamed of having entertained such notions. . . . I drank some small beer with Sir John as a cooling beverage. This kind of conversation relaxed my mind somewhat; and the effect was thus: if churches for ages, if bishops and most learned clergy, if I myself have so grossly erred in *doctrine* as Sir John thinks (and as to which he *may* be right, for I cannot answer him), may not there be as much error as to morals? And I saw no great risk of vice in running after fine girls. In this frame I quitted Sir John; and, having met a beautiful

Devonshire wench in the Strand, was lasciviously fond of her; and dallied for a while, and was restrained from completion by other considerations than religion.
(*OY*, p. 139)

In this way, Boswell creates in his journal something new out of the bare events of his life, by registering the relevance they acquire for him at or around the time when they occur, as well as the occurrences themselves. This is another aspect of his intention to give an impression of his mind rather than just a plain story, for the private writer is able to comment upon both behaviour and motives of the public actor. And all is blended beneath the smooth surface of the single account. So Boswell presents a more complete past, or version of the past, for his own consideration at some future date. The whole mixture of record and comment becomes, in effect, a constant recreation and interpretation of the past.

At one point in his journal, Boswell draws a distinction between two types of conversation, and goes on to compare one type to sailing on a lake, and the other to being out in the open sea. This is important in considering the reasons for Boswell's choice of the conversation to record.

Somebody remarked to me once in conversation, or I have read somewhere, that that conversation is the best of which we recollect nothing but a general impression of happiness. I think otherwise. I think that conversation of which the *memorabilia* can be preserved is most valuable. Witness what I have recorded of Paoli in Corsica. Witness the many hundreds of pages which I have treasured up of Dr. Johnson's effusions of mind. Perhaps the first-mentioned kind of conversation may be most agreeable at the time to an indolent hearer. He is like a man who reclines at ease, sailing on a smooth lake in a fine level country. But there is more enjoyment, surely, in navigating briskly through an agitated sea, and beholding a variety of objects which strike the imagination and of which one can take views in perspective drawing. The first kind of conversation leaves nothing in the mind that can afterwards entertain ourselves or others. The second supplies a store of intellectual enjoyment. (*Ex.*, p. 224)

The 'lake' type of conversation acts like a drug, dulling the senses of the man who becomes addicted to it. He is a being who lives solely in the present, whose existence is static. Boswell's preferred type of conversation, on the other hand, is seen as active and invigorating. As suggested by the metaphor 'take views in perspective drawing', the participant is required to make some evaluative assessment of the 'variety of objects' he has viewed, to grade them in order of size, distance and importance, and to do this not only during the conversation itself, but upon each subsequent recollection, when new experience may necessitate some revaluation. If the meaning of 'perspective' as a telescope is implied (Johnson's first definition of the word), this, too, conveys the idea of being able to see clearly over a considerable distance both of space and of time. Such conversation has relevance for both present and future, for one may always refer back and learn from it, and hence gauge one's progress in relation to it. However one's circumstances or view of life may alter, it will continue to be valuable for the man who is willing to look back and make a renewed effort in order to learn from the past. In this way Boswell's journal really does provide a 'store' for future benefit and enjoyment, and the conversation he gleans is appropriately described in many places as a 'crop': 'It was but a poor crop of conversation, though we were manured with a good dinner' (*OY*, p. 96).

Recorded conversation is also one way in which some balance is achieved in the journal between the ideal Boswell as seen through his own imagination, and the real Boswell of his actual words and actions. If on the one hand he creates a new past out of the conversations at which he has been present, and in so doing perhaps alters the emphasis and relevance of what was actually said and meant, on the other the words and expressions used at the time do, as far as we can tell, remain to give the account a firm basis in reality. The opinion of most critics seems to be that Boswell's reporting of conversation is really quite accurate. James Clifford examines an occasion of which Boswell's record of a conversation may be compared with another account – the diary of Dr Thomas Campbell – and shows that there is surprisingly little variation between the two. Clifford concludes,

One could go on and on citing examples. The main point in each instance is the same, only the peripheral matter is different, and this depends on the narrator's own particular interests and natural desire to put himself into the picture. Thus the comparison does reassure us of the general reliability of Boswell's reporting of Johnson's ideas, and at the same time gives further evidence of his dramatic skill.[6]

It is important, however, to take note of the rider – the narrator's interests and his desire to occupy a noticeable position in the account. Total objectivity is prevented by these considerations, and, while the facts are given, they are naturally coloured by all that constitutes the narrator's personality.

Conversation, though, is not the only factor which tends to make the journal more balanced between Boswell's version of the past and actual naked truth, for Boswell's large and detailed self-portrait includes as one of its elements some of the opinions other men express of him. Frank Stewart, for example, after listening to Boswell's anecdotes, tells him, 'You are an extraordinary man, and have had extraordinary good fortune in meeting with such a singular variety. It has been said that Mr. Johnson is a walking library. You are a walking collection of men' (*Wife*, pp. 165–6). Or Boswell records as 'a very apt illustration' the remark of an English officer in Holland:

> He said that I was like a great stone couched on the slope of a mountain, and while I stayed there, I was lumpish and heavy; but when I was once set in motion, I went with amazing velocity, so that it was impossible to stop me until the projectile force being exhausted, I came again in rest. (*Holl.*, p. 123)

(This in fact is from one of Boswell's French themes: we can only guess as to whether he included it in the lost Holland journal.) Boswell goes on to elaborate upon this observation, and discourses on the qualities of his own conversation: 'a brilliant vivacity, a rapidity of thoughts ... a fire of language'. This example particularly underlines Boswell's tendency to mix fact and interpretation in whatever he writes. As is to be expected, the selective memory of the journalist recalls a larger proportion of favourable opinions than of critical ones. But Boswell has no qualms about writing down, for example, many of Johnson's harsh remarks to him, or some of the censures made by his wife during moments of disharmony. These all enable the reader to form a slightly more objective view of Boswell than would have been afforded by a record consisting entirely of his own opinions.

Finally, as far as the question of balance is concerned, there is one very important factor which is never very far from Boswell's mind. This is the possibility of discovery:

> indeed it is a strange disagreeable thought, that what may be properly enough called so much of one's mind should be in the possession of a stranger, or perhaps of an enemy. This should serve as a lesson not to write any thing in a Diary, the discovery of which may do one essential hurt, unless the person who writes it carries his diary continually about with him, and can take as good care of it as Caesar did of his Commentaries. (*BC*, p. 334)

This pressure is exerted from outside the world of the journal, and the mere consideration of it forces a more objective attitude upon the journalist. Not that the discoveries that were actually made, such as the one by Mrs Boswell described in the previous chapter, or the early ones by Lord Auchinleck and the Rev. George Reid (cf. *LJ*, p. 361 n. 2; *Corr.* I, pp. 55–6), ever led to anything but a temporary increase in Boswell's reticence. And the various security devices he sometimes introduces, such as coding, or foreign words and letters, are always allowed to lapse after a day or two. What does happen is that the idea of his journal's being read by someone not chosen by Boswell, and who is not posterity, draws him instantly from the world of the journal into the world of the illicit reader. This clearly provides a valuable antidote to what must always be a danger of creating an exclusive and personal world, the self-obsession which becomes madness. Boswell is forced to look at himself from the point of view of an outsider, whose attitude may be at least impartial, if not completely hostile.

But the possibility of discovery also acts as a subtle reminder of the shameless pleasure of public nakedness – what must be one motive behind all artistic or autobiographical exertions. This in its turn balances the tendency to discretion which might otherwise be a consequence of the fear of unauthorised prying. Behind Boswell's exposures there is ultimately knowledge of the possibility of discovery, and perhaps even the hope for it. After writing down his sentiments concerning Dempster and Erskine (quoted earlier), for example, Boswell adds,

> Another shocking fault which I have is my sacrificing almost anything for a laugh, even myself; in so much that it is possible if one of these my companions should come in this moment, I might show them as a matter of jocularity the preceding three or four pages, which contain the most sincere sentiments of my heart; and at these would we laugh most immoderately. (*LJ*, p. 216)

The desire for public nakedness may undergo many transformations as it passes into the conscious mind, and by the time it is able to be expressed it will no doubt be disguised as something else.[7] Here it is the wish to excite laughter, even at the expense of self-humiliation.

Despite these balancing elements, however, it must be emphasised that the world of Boswell's journal is inevitably something different from reality, although it is probably a closer approximation to it than the recollection of memory would be. For, as Sartre says, the memory has certain significant limitations, what he calls 'the illusion of immanence': 'if immediate consciousness can distinguish by nature the object as image from the object that is present, memory confuses these two types of existence because real and unreal objects appear before it as memories, that is, as the past'.[8] The journal constitutes Boswell's image of the world, and the image of himself in relation to it. The memory itself needs help in distinguishing between the images and the reality of the past, and this the journal could supply – indeed probably does supply to a certain limited extent. But the very act of formulating and writing down gives validity to the world of the imagination and makes it, too, into a type of reality. And the same act begins the attempt to give coherence and consistency to the various images Boswell has of himself. He is a dictionary-maker (*Holl.*, p. 158), a lover, a lawyer, or he sees himself as a machine, or his mind as a lodging-house (*Wife*, pp. 147–8). Boswell inhabits his created world in a profusion of shapes, each designed to consolidate one aspect of his personality. This many-sided picture is the only way he can hope to give himself a convincing account of what it is to be Boswell. This is a further reason for the unexpected effect of the published *Journal of a Tour to the Hebrides*: not only was Boswell's account of the past in conflict with other people's memories of it, but his images of himself and of other people were in conflict with their own images of him and of themselves. Boswell's journal, while it is able reliably to preserve the past, shares with the real memory its limitations concerning the 'illusion of immanence'.

The journal, then, is not only a record of Boswell's life, but an essential element within it. It is an actual part of Boswell himself. When he discovered that his Dutch diary had been lost, he says he 'felt as if a part of my vitals had been separated from me' (*BC*, p. 334). So important a part of his life is his journal that Boswell would be a completely different man without it:

> I had lately a thought that appeared new to me: that by burning all my journal and all my written traces of former life, I should be like a new being; and how soon may this be done; nay, how soon might all the libraries in Britain be destroyed! Were I just now to go and take up house in any country town in England, it would be just a different existence. Might it not be proper to change one's residence very frequently, so as to be literally a pilgrim upon earth? for death would not be such a violent circumstance, as one would not be strongly fixed.   (*Ex.*, p. 84)

Burning his journal, or changing his residence, would, he feels, relieve him of his responsibility for the past, as well as the burden of recording it, and enable him to live continually in the present. This, clearly, is part of the desire to be free from the many restraints of living in society. But only an animal or a madman can live in a permanent present. Boswell has too powerful a sense of time to be able to limit his mind only to what is now. Moreover, to extinguish knowledge of past and future is to attempt to evade the fallen lot of mankind. The hypochondriac in particular feels the weight of postlapsarian existence, and, while he is therefore most anxious to be free of it, he is also most aware of the futility of any attempt at escape. Boswell must continue to live in time and in the society of other men, and to restrain the tensions of doing so beneath a surface of equanimity. The journal is therefore valuable as a relief from these tensions. It allows the construction of an ideal world as proof of the sanity which is called into question by the pressures of life.

(iii)  *Style: the Down upon the Plum*

But, if Boswell takes pains to render a complete and honest portrait of himself, he is equally concerned over the literary quality of his account, for he is anxious to improve himself in expression (*LJ*, p. 65), to present as flawless a 'reality' as possible. The more perfectly realised the world in the journal is, and the more apparently like the real world, then, in a way, the saner Boswell has proved himself to be. His version of events, the version of a man subject to melancholy, and hence to misinterpretation and to fears for his own sanity, must be seen as feasible by an imagined objective reader, the reader of the future.

In this light may be seen the significance of Boswell's reflections upon the inadequacy of words and of his own powers of expression – reflections which often at the same time add lustre to the account of which they complain. Even if events can be described, says Boswell, it is virtually impossible to convey with any impression of authenticity the states of mind which accompany them or result from them: 'It is impossible to clap the mind upon paper as one does an engraved plate, and to leave the full vivid impression' (*OY*, p. 133), and 'Words cannot describe our feelings. The finer parts are lost, as the down upon a plum; the radiance of light cannot be painted' (*Def.*, p. 108).

It is remarkable that nowhere else in his writings does Boswell achieve so striking a collection of images as he is able to amass in the very passages where he is complaining of the shortcomings of language:

I observe continually how imperfectly, upon most occasions, words preserve our ideas. This interview is but faintly seen in my Journal And all I have said of the Stratford Jubilee is very dim in comparison of the scene itself. In description we omit insensibly many little touches which give life to objects. With how small a speck does a painter give life to an eye! The vivid glances of Garrick's features, which cannot be copied in words, will illuminate an extent of sensation, if that term may be used, as a spark from a flint will throw a lustre in a dark night for a considerable space around it. Certain looks of my dearest life and certain tones of her voice, which I defy all the masters of language to show upon paper, have engaged my soul in an angelic manner. I find my self ready to write unintelligibly when I attempt to give any idea of such subjects. (*Wife*, p. 311)

Boswell's opinions here coincide with those of Johnson: 'Language is scanty and inadequate to express the nice gradations and mixtures of our feelings. We say we are pleased when there is more pleasure than pain, but we do not tell how much there is of one and of t'other' (*BP*, xv, p. 211). This, says Boswell, is a particularly difficult problem when discussing hypochondria:

let any one try to express the most severe pains which he had endured, at any distance of time after they have ceased, and he will find his language quite inadequate; so that he must use those strong indefinite phrases which do not particularly specify anything, convey any distinct meaning, or excite any lively perception. (*BC*, pp. 48–9)

And a certain type of man encounters more than usual hardship in attempting to give a convincing and concise account of himself:

in a thousand instances we are sensible that what we mean, or what we feel, is not expressed by us with sufficient precision, and it is to be observed, that for the most part, men of uncommon fertility of mind, and quickness of fancy, are often at a loss for words. The truth is, they require many more words than other men, and they must also have them more speedily in readiness. (*BC*, p. 271)

But many of Boswell's observations of this nature themselves, in fact, serve as partial counterweights to the problems they point out. He cannot give the picture he would like, but at least he can speak of the defects in a captivating way, and so draw the reader's (and therefore his own) attention away from the very flaws of which he appears to be complaining. Similarly, when he considers that he is writing particularly well, he says so in a manner which directs notice upon his way of saying it, as if to divert critical observation away from the actual piece of good writing he is praising:

> How easily and cleverly do I write just now! I am really pleased with myself; words come skipping to me like lambs upon Moffat Hill; and I turn my periods smoothly and imperceptibly like a skilful wheelwright turning tops in a turning-loom. There's fancy! There's simile! In short, I am at present a genius: in that does my opulence consist, and not in base metal. (*LJ*, p. 211)

It is not that the reader's judgement will necessarily be adverse, but that Boswell, in the liveliness of his writing, seems to be trying to make the reader suspend criticism altogether, and allow himself to be carried along by personality.

So Boswell is actually capturing the mind of the reader, committing him to an endorsement of the account, its coherence, reality and sanity. The impression of the journal will be one of vivacity, rather than of inadequacy, and it will be praised for its originality and its striking qualities, rather than exposed to objective critical attention. A glittering surface is invaluable for distracting the eye from what lies within. The important thing is the way one expresses oneself, for one's ideas will be more easily accepted if their vehicle can first arouse admiration. 'It is amazing,' says Boswell, 'how much of sentiment consists in expression. Nothing but hard science remains the same when put in different words' (*Wife*, p. 293).

In the same way, Boswell is concerned to present his actual behaviour in an arresting manner. This may not consciously be to avert censure, but the effect, nevertheless, is often to dazzle the perception of a disapproving eye. Boswell, for example, describes a night of indecorous behaviour: 'at supper I drank more and increased the heat and intoxication, and talked a great deal in an idle, jocular, impolite strain. Little did I apprehend that my honoured Father was then lying on his deathbed!' (*BP*, xv, p. 120). This is one of the few instances in the whole journal in which Boswell deliberately allows his later knowledge to intrude into his description of an event, and the effect is considerable. It is a particularly clear case of his recreating the past. Boswell presents himself as behaving shamefully, in a manner unsuited to the son of the 'worthy' Lord Auchinleck; he then underlines the sense of shame by superimposing his later feelings upon learning about his father's condition. The result is that the scene is given the emotional colouring which it will always retain in Boswell's own memory, and the description involves a real and effective shift in the reader's attitude in mid-paragraph. Boswell at supper is suddenly frozen, and an after-image of the scene remains shimmering behind the narrative voice. This tends, however, not to diminish Boswell's stature, but to increase it, and he becomes not a shameful figure deserving censure, but a grief-stricken one imbued with a certain amount of nobility. The impression is that this vivid scene will remain in the memory to render him a changed man, and so produce a complete reformation. (No doubt Boswell hoped that it might.) The reader's attitude towards Boswell, then, is deftly turned to a combination of sympathy and admiration. This is assisted, perhaps, by the familiarity of an ever-central protagonist, and by a certain distaste for Lord Auchinleck personally. But Boswell's artistry has made it virtually impossible for the reader to be anything but impressed by his portrait, and he has therefore secured endorsement of his personality, and of his whole created world.

A similar technique is evident in the description of a scene of less consequence which occurs after his move to London, and after the death of Mrs Boswell and the publication of the *Life of Johnson*. Boswell is sauntering through the city in the mood of modified dejection which is common at this period of his life. He is without an invitation to dine but is still hoping to meet somebody who would ask me. But all in vain. I stood dejected in the Court of St. James's Palace, and heard half-past four strike. I could no longer expect an invitation. The evening was dusky and dull. As I was walking up St. James's Street, I heard a voice saying, 'I cannot let an old friend pass without speaking to him.' It was Lord Eardley who had observed me.... When hurrying home, I felt a wonderful elation. After a dreary despair, here was not only a dinner, but a capital dinner. 'There is no place but London', I exclaimed, 'where this could have happened.' (*BP*, XVIII, pp. 231–2)

Here the reader's sympathies remain with Boswell as he saunters around with fading hopes, when he is surprised by the voice, and as he hurries home in elation. As his attitude changes, so does the reader's. It is only realised in retrospect that Boswell knows the result all the time he is writing (as in the much-praised 'Louisa' episode in the *London Journal*). This leads to an appreciation of the artistry which has filled in the details of mood – the striking clock, the dusky evening – and delayed the 'voice' until the last possible moment. The initial eeriness of the disembodied 'voice' is a final contrast to the exultation following Lord Eardley's identification and his offer of dinner. The scene is truly dramatic, and is pleasing on two levels, both the factual and the artistic. Admiration for Boswell is added to sympathy, and once again endorsement of his world is secured.

Boswell, then, is all the time striving to achieve the most complete involvement of the reader in his journal, and thereby the fullest possible appreciation of his own mind. This involvement and appreciation will then act as a guarantee both of Boswell's sanity and of the preservation of his life. And, although this entails some warping of the truth (to express even the simplest incident in words must inevitably require some selection and presentation), it would be unfair to assume that Boswell is consciously deceiving. He is merely rendering Boswell of Auchinleck 'as fine a fellow as possible' (*GT* (i), p. 28), and expressing in the most convincing way the ideas and events of his life. As he observes to Temple, 'I certainly have the art of making the most of what I have' (*Letters*, II, p. 380). Naturally, as success eludes him in life,

Boswell's journal comes to present a more consistently dark picture, while his self-doubts are more insistent. But to the very end the reader is kept completely absorbed in Boswell's state of mind.

Boswell's journal, then, served for him an extremely complex purpose, for not only was he saving his life from oblivion, making it 'tell', but the very act of doing this in itself seems to have made it easier for him to live at all. It gave him a second reality, a world in which Boswell could be Aeneas, or at least could be 'as fine a fellow as possible', and receive from his imagined readers praise for the achievement, praise that really meant an affirmation of the melancholy man's sanity, and a full acceptance of Boswell's volatile personality.

### (iv) *The Hypochondriac and the Countryside*

It was no doubt of value to Boswell to see accounts of his waywardness actually set down before him, although it must be remembered – the reminder is hardly necessary – that he never reformed his whoring, drinking and gambling habits, and scarcely even showed any lasting contrition at his inability to mend his ways. My argument, however, is tending against the view that the journal is an essential tool in Boswell's efficient self-analysing kit. His self-analysis was often less than efficient. And the journal, while it is useful in that it allows Boswell to proceed to a certain descriptive level of self-exploration, does not, as I have tried to show throughout this study, assist further progress to the thorough understanding displayed by a Johnson – perhaps in fact makes such progress impossible. What, then, is the true value of Boswell's journal? To answer this, we must return to one of the fundamental causes of hypochondria – the individual's isolation in the face of the pressures of society, and the guilt feelings which, partly as a consequence, are associated with this.

Boswell, like the majority of his civilised contemporaries, was essentially a townsman. With Johnson, he believed that for 'the intellectual man' London comprehends 'the whole of human life in all its variety, the contemplation of which is inexhaustible' (*Life*, I, p. 422). The occasional country jaunt might provide an amusing diversion, and, in fact, staying in

Cornwall with his friend Temple in 1792, Boswell in one journal entry is full of praise for rural retreat:

> The retirement of it, a small congregation of vulgar, only the view of Falmouth bay from the Windows, the Old fashioned appearance, in short the *tout ensemble*, soothed my mind, and I romantically speculated on living out of the World – at Bewdoc. As my friend and I rode calmly between his Churches, I observed that he held a creditable actual station in Society, whereas I held none.
> (*BP*, XVIII, p. 153)

Within only twenty-four hours, however, he is complaining of the monotony of country existence: 'The dampness of the climate and the want of variety of objects to engage and agitate, and a certain unfortunate association of melancholy with the Country, especially about the fall of the leaf, now affected me sadly' (*BP*, XVIII, p. 154).

And it is this attitude that Boswell most consistently expresses towards the country life: discomfort, tedium, and, for the hypochondriac, decay and reminders of death. 'My mind', he says, '*rusts* very soon in the Country, especially in damp weather' (*BP*, XVIII, p. 145); and 'There is indeed in the country the variety of seasons to contemplate; but the circling year moves too slowly for him whose blood bounds with rapidity, and he is apt to grow impatient and fretful' (*BC*, p. 199). Boswell proved himself to be a conscientious and humane landlord when he finally succeeded to the family estates,[9] but he sometimes displays considerable contempt for rural inhabitants:

> I had amused myself during this jaunt with the remarks on the inhabitants of the County, whom I called Cornish *Clouts*, from Spenser's *Colin Clout*. I talked of them as wild animals; and that droves of them might be seen running about with bare legs, some with shoes, some without. One of them yesterday gaped and laughed like a fool when I said to F. Temple, 'There's one that is *shod*. But he must have been *worked*.' They truly reminded me of Yahoos.
> (*BP*, XVIII, p. 149)

Elsewhere he goes so far as to say that books written in retirement are not a true picture of life (*Bosw.*, pp. 237–8).

*The Hypochondriack* has three entire essays, 'On Living in the Country', devoted to this subject. But even here, where Boswell sets out to state objectively the respective advantages of country and town life, there is an underlying contempt for those who are suited for the former, coupled with overt admiration for devotees of the latter:

> The innocent pleasures of the senses, and mere tranquillity of mind, may be enjoyed more perfectly in the country than in the town; and therefore they, who are satiated and jaded, and sigh for *repose*, delight their fancies with rural felicity. But animated intellectual pleasure must be sought in cities; that is amongst numbers of people assembled together, and having their powers and faculties excited by the vivifying motives of gain, ambition, emulation, and every thing else, by which we find man urged on to extraordinary exertions and attainments. (*BC*, p. 194)

To be able to survive contentedly in the country, the mind must be already worn out, and of little further use in the real activities of life:

> I may be wrong. But I do confess, it appears to me at present that a man cannot be happy in the country whose mind is not tolerably sedate, either naturally, or from having seen and enjoyed a great deal, and exhausted his curiosity and eager desires. (*BC*, p. 199)

And a certain type of man (no doubt the type of man Boswell judged himself to be) would do particularly well to keep away from the country for the greater part of his time:

> Let not then a man of exuberant vivacity, keen sensations, and a perpetual rage for variety, attempt to live in the country. If he does, it is more than probable that he will be miserable himself, and the scorn, perhaps the scourge of those around him. Let the edge of his mind be blunted in the world, and his spirits be reduced to a temperate state before he settles in a situation where the greatest part of his

time must pass without vivid consciousness of any kind, and at best in uniform serenity. (*BC*, p. 200)

The basic occupations of human existence are, quite simply, boring and must be seen as means to some more civilised end, such as making money, to be even moderately bearable: 'A man of vivacity, unless his views are kept steady, by a constant golden prospect of gain, cannot long be pleased in looking at the operations of ploughing, dunging, harrowing, reaping, or threshing.' No real man of spirit could 'prefer ploughing to a play-house' (*BC*, pp. 199–200).

For the hypochondriac, of course, boredom is fatal, as writers from Burton to Johnson insisted, and consequently some diversion, be it a course in rope-dancing or, for Boswell, a course in concubinage, is essential to ward off gloom and despondency. So Boswell, not surprisingly, strongly advises that hypochondriacs should not allow themselves to drift into the stagnancy of a country existence:

> Even if the occupations of agriculture could give lively minds pleasure, we must consider what dull intervals there are. When a field is completely sown, and left to itself, we cannot actually perceive the crop springing. Even plantations, the rearing of which is by much the highest rural enjoyment, advance so imperceptibly; that a Hypochondriac proprietor is sick and sick again and again with *ennui*, and is tempted with wild wishes to hang himself on one of his own trees long before they are able to bear his weight.
> (*BC*, p. 200)

Boswell, in fact, very clearly differentiates between the rural life and the pastoral, between the actuality of living in the country and the idealised conception of it. While many classical and eighteenth-century writers felt a strong attraction to a life of placid contentment at a country retreat, Boswell's position is unashamedly one of down-to-earth common-sense: 'The truth is that the happiness of a country life has been pictured by those who have not always enjoyed it; and I have a notion is not so much in the country itself as in change and by comparison' (*BC*, p. 194).

But Boswell is not able to manage totally without some

accommodation of the basic instincts which lie behind the pull felt by many townsmen towards the country and its traditional activities. He might look down upon the rural life, and laugh with Johnson at the philosophy of primitivism (*Hebr.*, p. 362), but he cannot divorce himself entirely from nature, as an examination of a selection of his own imagery in his journal makes clear. For example, one of the most common types of imagery Boswell uses when referring to his journal itself is drawn from that very style of life for which he displays such distaste. The whole range of country affairs and natural processes is opened up by Boswell as he searches for images which express how he feels towards his journal. When he is ill and confined to his room in London, he will not be able to cultivate the soil of his journal and its fertility will be wasted: 'What will become of my journal for some time? It must be a barren desert, a mere blank' (*LJ*, p. 190). And of the minutiae of journalising he says that he will not 'take the trouble to gather what grows on every hedge' just because he has 'collected such fruits as the *Nonpareil* and the BON CHRETIEN' of Johnson's conversation (*Life*, V, p. 414); that, of a particular meeting, he does not 'recollect much that can bear being bottled' (*OY*, p. 243); and, writing up his journal, that he will pause to 'glean a little of past days' (*OY*, p. 329). He speaks, too, of the course of his life as it will be recorded in the journal:

> The life of every man, take it day by day, is pretty much a series of uniformity; at least a series of repeated alternations. It is like a journal of the weather: rainy – fair – fair – rainy, etc. It is seldom that a great storm or an abundant harvest occurs in the life of man or in the progress of years. (*Def.*, p. 233)

However, images from nature and country life are by no means confined to Boswell's remarks about his journal: a chance thought about the practice of law is 'a bud which would have an excellent appearance if fully and beautifully blown' (*Def.*, p. 33); and learning is to the mind 'like manure to the earth' (*BC*, p. 258). Other types of writing, too, are described in terms of growth, fruitfulness and preservation. Just before leaving for his tour of Europe, Boswell writes to his friend Johnston from London,

> Your receiving a letter every third day must be another diverting circumstance. It is very wonderful to think that all these great matters are of this year's growth. But it is grievous to think that the crop will not continue. The fertile Tree itself is to be transported into other climates where it may perhaps bear as well, but from whence the fruit cannot be so easily transported. However, you may depend upon it, they shall be preserved. (*Corr.* I, p. 105)

Here again Boswell is seeing the events of his life as a crop worth harvesting, first into his letters home, and then into his journal.

These instincts for preserving and using what he has produced may be traced, too, in Boswell's images drawn from food and culinary processes: his journal is 'in the larder, only to be sent to the kitchen, or perhaps trussed and larded a little' (*Bosw.*, p. 299); by marking down references and his own observations while reading, he will be able to build up 'a rich stock for composition' (*OY*, p. 216); and the notes he writes in his journal are 'like portable soup, of which a little bit by being dissolved in water will make a good large dish; for their substance by being expanded in words would fill a volume' (*BC*, p. 332).

Such imagery, while almost as traditional as the activities from which it is taken, does seem to have a particular personal relevance for Boswell, and to serve a very real and precise purpose. This is best seen in one of several comparisons between his own life and a harvest: 'I am fallen sadly behind in my journal', he says. 'I should live no more than I can record, as one should not have more corn growing than one can get in. There is a waste of good if it be not preserved' (*OY*, p. 265). Boswell repeats this image in more or less the same words in his *Hypochondriack* essay 'On Diaries' (*BC*, p. 332): for him it constitutes in itself one of the good things that ought to be preserved. More than this, though, we can deduce that Boswell's whole life was rendered productive and useful in his own eyes, not merely by having interesting experiences and ideas, but by recording them in his journal. The diligent farmer gathers into his storehouse a portion of existence, saves it from the decay of passing time, and preserves it for the benefit of himself and of posterity. He is engaging in one of the most basic of human activities, and brings himself into a tradition which is nearly as old as man, and into contact with the perpetual rhythms of nature. The feelings of satisfaction and the sense of belonging produced by this can be opposed to the isolation and the uselessness which characterise the state of mind of the melancholy man.

Boswell seems to derive similar satisfaction from seeing himself as a tree, something which literally has its roots embedded in the soil of the ages. He is able to feel either fruitful or noble, depending upon the type of tree he chooses to be. In the letter to Johnston quoted earlier he was a 'fertile Tree'. To Rousseau he writes, 'My Lord Marischal is old. That illustrious Scottish oak-tree must soon fall. You love that ancient country. Preserve a sapling from it' (*GT* (i), pp. 227–8). Or, elsewhere, he is 'a tree which produces much fruit' (*BP*, xv, p. 198).

Access to feelings of belonging and of productivity is clearly of the greatest importance to the man with a tendency towards hypochondria. For Boswell, going back to nature was not a literal return to the soil, but rather a matter of earning the right to place himself firmly within the great natural cycles of growth and fruitfulness. A contemporary of Boswell's, though, John Hill, thought that an actual, if limited, return to nature might be beneficial to hypochondriacs. In his treatise *Hypochondriasis*, published in 1766, he tells his suffering readers, 'For me, I should advise above all other things the study of nature.'[10] And he goes on to offer particular examples of natural life which might repay careful study – mosses, weeds, fungi, or insects.[11] The advantage of such study seems to be that ultimately the patient will be able to appreciate how everything is ordered, each element fulfilling itself by playing its rightful and natural part within the order:

> The poorest moss that is trampled under foot, has its important uses: is it at the bottom of a wood we find it? why there it shelters the fallen seeds; hides them from birds, and covers them from frost; and thus becomes the foster father of another forest! creeps it along the surface of a rock? even there its good is infinite! its small roots run into the stone, and the rains make their way after them; the moss having lived its time dies; it rots and with the mouldered fragments

of the stone forms earth; wherein, after a few successions, useful plants may grow, and feed more useful cattle.[12]

Everything has a use, everything is valuable. Hill's implication seems to be that the hypochondriac, too, has his part to play in the natural order of things. The obvious treatment for the man who fears himself cut off from the rest of life is to lead him into renewed contact with the soothing processes of nature, into acceptance of the idea of an ordered creation that includes himself as an essential part of the order. Boswell himself in *The Hypochondriack* tell his own fellow sufferers: 'A learned and ingenious physician gave me a very pretty similitude.... Said he "You are like one who has forgotten nature, and tries all the sounds of a flute till his ear acknowledges its old acquaintance"' (*BC*, p. 341).

But for Boswell the *Hypochondriack* essays and his journal provided a more long-term therapy, for they earned him his place in the order of nature. They gave the lie to his hypochondriac's view of a life of waste and indolence, and prevented him from remaining, in his words from his Dutch journal, 'a poor blasted tree that cannot bear' (*Holl.*, p. 188). Christ's curse of fruitlessness[13] could be averted by the therapy of serious and sustained hard work, by, in fact, those 'extraordinary exertions and attainments' that Boswell had associated with the diversions and excitements of life in the city.

(v)

One effect of Boswell's sense of satisfaction at the achievement of keeping a journal may be to blur even more the vision of himself, and render the image in the mirror even less useful for an adjustment of his character. Satisfaction, particularly if one is only half conscious of it, does not make for objective self-analysis. So some of Boswell's declared reasons for beginning a journal risk being frustrated by one unforeseen result of the very effort which was to fulfil them. This, however, is not ultimately of great importance. The value of the journal lies chiefly in the activity of keeping it. All the elements within it, including Boswell's own initial motives, belong, in the last analysis, to the world of the hypochondriac. They are signs of and struggles against madness. But only the continuing process of recording, the effort involved, and the satisfaction afforded, could rescue Boswell from the kind of mental derangement observed in Chapter 2. It is therefore of less importance that the account may be inaccurate, or self-indulgent, or delusive (though of course it matters for the critic to be aware of this when discussing Boswell: it is not difficult to be lured by his striking personality into the very errors which he unconsciously committed). What is of real consequence is that Boswell owed his sanity to his journal.

This, however, is not to say that we should not also value Boswell's integrity and honesty. As W. K. Wimsatt writes,

> Boswell and his *Journal* sometimes today do encounter the criticism that it is difficult to like Boswell. The question is hardly more relevant than a question whether we can *like* Hamlet or Heathcliff. Boswell writes a true story – beyond question – and this, as we have observed, is one undoubted source of its peculiar power.... If we know what we are about as we read and respond to this extraordinary saga of self-portrayal, we shall hardly stop to wonder whether we do like Boswell, whether we ought to like him.... At the same time there will doubtless be many respects in which we find it very difficult to like him. Why should we not admit this? What kind of purity, of whitewash, do we look for in the protagonists of our most impressive stories? The correct response to Boswell is to *value* the man through the artist, the artist in the man.[14]

Boswell gives, by and large, only his true, naked response. He follows the advice of Jeremy Taylor (as recalled by Johnson): 'Never lie in your prayers; never confess more than you really believe' (*Life*, IV, p. 295). Indeed, writing in *The Hypochondriack*, Boswell himself praises the diary of Dr John Rutty for these same qualities, and values him on this account: 'His Diary is written with an honest simplicity and conscientious self-examination which are rarely to be found, so that while we cannot but laugh, we must feel a charitable regard for him' (*BC*, p. 336). Boswell is equally frank. He is more sincere and more himself than the ordinary man can be. He falsifies only unconsciously. His truth, by Johnson's definition, is 'moral truth':

> Physical truth, is, when you tell a thing as it actually is. Moral truth, is, when you tell a thing sincerely and precisely as it appears to you. I say such a one walked across the street; if he really did so, I told a physical truth. If I thought so, though I should have been mistaken, I told a moral truth. (*Life*, IV, p. 6)

And this, finally, must remain Boswell's appeal as a journalist to posterity. He offers himself as he sees himself, as honestly as he can, and artistically as well as he can, unaware that honesty and artistry are not necessarily compatible. To accept Boswell in this way is to endorse his journal and its world at a higher level than he, from the centre of the picture, could have understood.

# 7 Balancing the Accounts: the *Life of Johnson*

(i)

I have argued in an earlier chapter that the importance of the publication of the *Journal of a Tour to the Hebrides* became for Boswell less the knowledge of the success of a biographical method than that he was made aware of the insoluble social problem of decorum with which he would be faced when he came to write the *Life of Johnson*. The most striking public reaction was to the material itself – a reaction combining relish and outrage – and not to Boswell's artistic presentation of that material. The effect of this was, I believe, to force Boswell, the writer of anonymous puffs and occasional paragraphs in the newspapers, to face up to his responsibility as an author. He realised that a writer is answerable for what he publishes, and that the first step to artistic integrity involves the recognition of this fact. Unlike the private materials on which, particularly in Boswell's case, it is based, a biographical work does not begin and end with its author. Every published word will be taken by the reader to be a result of a deliberate choice and representative of a deliberate purpose. Only in the *Life of Johnson* does Boswell clearly have such a purpose, and write with the full awareness of what he is doing. As William Siebenschuh observes,

> Perhaps the most important conclusion to be drawn from the difference between Boswell's treatment of his material about Johnson in the *Life* as compared with the *Tour* is that his great achievement in the *Life* was clearly a conscious one, and clearly an interpretative act. It was not at all simply the result of the dramatization of a greater amount of material about Johnson in the manner of the *Tour to the Hebrides*.[1]

The narrator of the *Life of Johnson* is more serious and rather wiser than he was in the *Tour*, and his voice bears traces of bitterness.

At the end of the *Life*, Boswell writes on the subject of Johnson's sense of sin and his constant moral upbraidings, and concludes,

> I am conscious that this is the most difficult and dangerous part of my biographical work, and I cannot but be very anxious concerning it. I trust that I have got through it, preserving at once my regard to truth, – to my friend, – and to the interests of virtue and religion. Nor can I apprehend that more harm can ensue from the knowledge of the irregularity of Johnson, guarded as I have stated it, than from knowing that Addison and Parnell were intemperate in the use of wine. (IV, p. 398)

To maintain such a delicate sense of balance was Boswell's task throughout the *Life*. Not only had he to bear in mind the interests of truth, of virtue, and of religion, but also his responsibility to himself and to the society in which he lived.

### (ii) The Image of Johnson

Boswell's primary motive in writing the *Life* was, as Johnson wrote of his Corsican journal, to 'express images which operated strongly upon yourself' and to impress them 'with great force upon your readers' (II, p. 70). Now, though, the image is of Johnson himself. In Ralph Rader's words,

> Boswell had not to record dead memories but to construct a re-enactment of Johnson which would be concretely adequate in itself to reproduce and release in the reader the emotion which the living man had once produced in him.... Boswell's image of Johnson is the selective, constructive, and controlling principle of the *Life*, the Omnipresent element which vivifies and is made vivid in the whole.[2]

In discussing just what Johnson meant to Boswell, it is necessary to distinguish between two aspects of his influence – his social character and his private one. Boswell's task was to convey both sides of Johnson, and show how they combined in the physical reality of the man himself. The first was the easier, for Johnson had long been a famous public figure and, in particular, notorious as a vigorous conversationalist. The privileges Johnson assumed regarding conversational propriety had, in the eyes of many people, made him one of those who 'alienate the world by neglect of the common forms of civility, and breach of the established laws of conversation'.[3] In 1762, Charles Churchill had attacked him for his want of social decency: Johnson is a man

> Who scorns those common wares to trade in,
> *Reas'ning, Convincing*, and *Persuading*,
> But makes each Sentence current pass
> With *Puppy, Coxcomb, Scoundrel, Ass*;
> For 'tis with *him* a certain rule,
> The Folly's proved when he calls Fool; ...
> Who 'bove the vulgar dares to rise,
> And sense of *Decency* defies,
> For this same *Decency* is made
> Only for Bunglers in the trade;
> And, like the *Cobweb Laws*, is still
> Broke thro' by *Great ones* when they will.[4]

And Lord Chesterfield's 'respectable Hottentot' (if, indeed, it was ever intended as a portrait of Johnson) is similarly oblivious to the requirements of polite society:

> He disputes with heat, and indiscriminately, mindless of the rank, character, and situation of them with whom he disputes: absolutely ignorant of the several gradations of familiarity and respect, he is exactly the same to his superiors, his equals, and his inferiors; and therefore, by a necessary consequence, absurd to two of the three.[5]

For Boswell, however, Johnson's disregard of polite behaviour was an inspiration – not to do likewise, but as evidence that one could exist in society and yet not be bound by it. To the melancholy man, suffering from the frustrations imposed by propriety, Johnson's example calls not for condemnation but for reverence. In the *Life*, Boswell makes it clear that it is Johnson's genius that gives him the right to behave with such singularity, and not simply his genius, but the fact that it is directed towards the public good. His conversation is not only blameless, but tends towards the deliberate dissemination of virtue and religion, and sets an example of truthfulness:

> Johnson gave a very earnest recommendation of what he himself practised with the utmost conscientiousness: I mean a strict attention to truth, even in the most minute particulars. 'Accustom your children (said he) constantly to this... you do not know where deviation from truth will end.' (III, p. 228)

The way he says a thing is justified by the value of what he says. Boswell may, in the *Life*, drop cryptic hints about Johnson's torments of passion and his doubtful behaviour with Savage (e.g. I, p. 64; IV, pp. 395–6), but his conversation is without blemish. Whatever might be misconstrued is suppressed, as, for example, the discussion on conjugal infidelity (III, p. 406 n),[6] and Boswell insists upon the purity of both Johnson's own language and the language of those in his presence. He even finds an opportunity of raising this whole question with Johnson himself:

> While we were upon the road, I had the resolution to ask Johnson whether he thought that the roughness of his manner had been an advantage or not, and if he would not have done more good if he had been more gentle. I proceeded to answer myself thus: 'Perhaps it has been of advantage, as it has given weight to what you said: you could not, perhaps, have talked with such authority without it.' JOHNSON. 'No, Sir; I have done more good as I am. Obscenity and impiety have always been repressed in my company.' (IV, p. 295)

Moreover, Boswell uses Johnson's notoriety as part of his argument for Johnson's good nature. He gives several examples of Johnson's seeking to pacify those he has offended in conversation, including an apology to Goldsmith (II, p. 256), and a reconciliation with Boswell himself. The latter instance provides an opportunity for him to make the specific point:

> This little incidental quarrel and reconciliation, which, perhaps, I may be thought to have detailed too minutely, must be esteemed as one of many proofs which his friends had, that though he might be charged with *bad humour* at times, he was always a *good-natured* man. (II, p. 109)

Johnson as conversationalist becomes, in Boswell's hands, an example of moral rather than merely social excellence, and, at the same time, in Professor Rader's words, 'a token of the simultaneous freedom and commitment which is possible to human beings'.[7] He upholds both the dignity and the virtue of human nature.

This would be of little use, though, if Boswell had not also realised that he had to give a convincing account of Johnson's inner self, his worth as a private man. Johnson must be seen as neither affecting a virtue he does not possess, nor as being complacently unaware of the temptations and struggles of others. His wisdom must be that of a man who knows himself, and who is always able to face, if not to overcome, his personal weaknesses. Here Boswell is able to make good use of Johnson's *Prayers and Meditations*, which had been recently published by Strahan. Quotations from these provide a new side to the image of Johnson, and, in particular, allow Boswell to emphasise the essential quality of sincerity: 'Such was the distress of mind, such the penitence of Johnson, in his hours of privacy, and in his devout approaches to his Maker. His *sincerity*, therefore, must appear to every candid mind unquestionable' (IV, p. 398).

This side of Johnson provides his qualification for acceptance as a teacher of wisdom, and allows Boswell to reveal some of their private consultations upon such tender subjects as melancholy and the fear of death. That he does this often at the risk of appearing to have been thoughtlessly pushing is an indication of how important Johnson's role of 'mental physician' was to Boswell. Our sympathy with Boswell at the death, for example, is reduced by his series of letters insisting that Johnson should recognise as real his tendency to melancholy:

> Having conjured him not to do me the injustice of charging me with affectation, I was with much regret long silent. His last letter to me then came, and affected me very tenderly. ... Yet it was not a little painful to me to find, that in a paragraph of this letter . . . he still persevered in arraigning me as before, which was strange in him who had so much experience of what I suffered. (IV, p. 380)

Clearly Boswell was anxious for Johnson to provide written evidence of his belief in the genuineness of Boswell's affliction before he died. If we lose sympathy with Boswell, though, our respect for Johnson's common-sense and humanity is correspondingly increased, and he becomes even more a suitable object for Bosewell's veneration: 'I cannot help worshipping him, he is so much superiour to other men' (III, p. 331). It is Boswell's portrayal of Johnson's inner worth which makes the *Life* more than just a collection of memorabilia, and Boswell himself more than a mere idolater.

Boswell's biography has for so long been the standard work on Johnson that it is easy to forget that his was only one of a very large number of publications concerning the life and sayings of Johnson, both during his life and after his death. As Boswell himself says,

> As Johnson had abundant homage paid to him during his life, so no writer in this nation ever had such an accumulation of literary honours after his death. ... The Lives, the Memoirs, the Essays, both in prose and verse, which have been published concerning him, would make many volumes. The numerous attacks too upon him, I consider as part of his consequence, upon the principle which he himself so well knew and asserted. (IV, pp. 421–2)[8]

In fact Boswell at times felt 'great despondency as to *Life of Johnson*' (*Corr.* II, p. lxxiii), fearing that the market might already be saturated with Johnsoniana. Boswell also realised, though, that since his death the world's image of Johnson had been altered, and was still being altered, by the influence of this welter of critical and anecdotal material, including, it must be remembered, Boswell's own *Tour to the Hebrides* and the publicity which surrounded it. A large part of his task, then, was to refute what he considered to be damaging misinterpretations of Johnson's character, not only by his traducers, but also by such false friends as Sir John Hawkins and Mrs Piozzi: Boswell had to make his image of Johnson more convincing than the collective images of his rivals.

Boswell's defence of Johnson is both general and specific. He makes wholesale assaults on those other writers who have spread lies about Johnson's character:

> I am desirous that my work should be, as much as is consistent with the strictest truth, an antidote to the false and injurious notions of his character, which have been given by others, and therefore I infuse every drop of genuine sweetness into my biographical cup. (*Life*, III, p. 391)

They have waited until after his death before making their cowardly attacks (*Life*, IV, p. 422). And they have insisted 'with very unfair aggravation' upon such delicate subjects as Johnson's fear of insanity (I, p. 66).

In particular, Boswell takes it upon himself to correct allegations made by Hawkins and Mrs Piozzi. Sometimes he opposes without indication that he is doing so. When, for example, Boswell mentions that Johnson 'accepted of a guinea from Mr Robert Dodsley, for writing the introduction to "The London Chronicle"', and describes it as 'one of those little occasional advantages which he did not disdain to take by his pen, as a man whose profession was literature' (I, p. 317), his remarks are given extra significance when compared with those of Sir John Hawkins on a similar subject:

> But there is another, and less criminal sense of the word prostitution, in which, in common with all who are called authors by profession, he may be said to stand in need of an excuse.... Under this notion of works written with a view to gain, and those that owe their existence to a more liberal motive, a distinction of literary productions arises which Johnson would never allow; on the contrary, to the astonishment of myself who have heard him, and many others, he has frequently declared, that the only true and genuine motive to the writing of books was the assurance of pecuniary profit.[9]

Elsewhere, Hawkins is specifically charged with misrepresentation, as when Boswell writes of the Essex Head Club (IV, p. 254), or with remarkable 'carelessness to ascertain facts' (IV, p. 327 n. 5) over, for example, the authorship of the letter to Lord Thurlow concerning Johnson's trip to Italy. The final blow to Hawkins is the assertion that Sir John's theft of Johnson's private diary threw him into such agitation that it 'probably made him hastily burn those precious records which must ever be regretted' (IV, p. 406 n. 1).

Mrs Piozzi emerges even less well than Hawkins. She is accused of profiteering over Johnson's letters to her (II, p. 43 n. 1), and her split with Johnson is cast in the least favourable light, with suggestions of her previous hypocrisy and present vanity (IV, pp. 157–8). Boswell even says of a remark in her *Anecdotes*, 'I wish the lady had not committed it to writing' (IV, p. 318) – precisely the charge that was made against his own *Tour to the Hebrides*. Boswell may have been frank, but Mrs Piozzi is indecent! She is more than once condemned for carelessness through the mouth of Johnson himself: 'It is amazing, Sir, what deviations there are from precise truth, in the account which is given of almost every thing. I told Mrs. Thrale, "You have so little anxiety about truth, that you never tax your memory with the exact thing"' (III, pp. 403–4). Finally, as the culmination of a clever attack, Boswell mounts a full assault on the authenticity of her *Anecdotes*, pointing out inaccuracies and inconsistencies. 'It is amazing', he says, 'that one who had such opportunities of knowing Dr. Johnson, should appear so little acquainted with his real character' (IV, p. 344). He concludes with a paragraph which, while complaining of his own distaste for this type of infighting, serves to bolster Boswell's fidelity to truth and his suitability as the biographer of Johnson in the eyes of the reader:

> It is with concern that I find myself obliged to animadvert on the inaccuracies of Mrs. Piozzi's 'Anecdotes', and perhaps I may be felt to have dwelt too long upon her little collection. But as from Johnson's long residence under Mr. Thrale's roof, and his intimacy with her, the account which she has given of him may have made an unfavourable and unjust impression, my duty, as a faithful biographer, has obliged me reluctantly to perform this unpleasing task.
> (IV, p. 347)

The net result of these attacks might have been to load the *Life of Johnson* with so much petty quibbling as to lose sight of its hero beneath the quarrelsome vanity of the biographer. But Boswell never forgot that, while he was part of a debate, he was not merely to answer his chosen antagonists, but to obscure them. The amount of space given to refutation is, by means of silent corrections, made to appear smaller than it is, and Boswell continues to maintain the impression that he is writing out of his sense of love and duty to Johnson, not in order to assert his rights over the biographical remains. And this, in its turn, conveys a favourable idea of Boswell's own moderation and consistency of purpose. All is submerged beneath the controlling image of Johnson.

A further factor to be taken into account by Boswell in the balancing-act of the *Life of Johnson* was the image he had already conveyed in his *Journal of a Tour to the Hebrides*. As William Siebenschuh argues,[10] Boswell in the *Tour* confirmed the image the public already had of Johnson soon after his death – the bear, the Tory, the Rambler – and drew contrasts with his unusual physical situation. Johnson in the Hebrides is essentially a localised Johnson. The image is effective largely because he *is* in the Hebrides, and not in London. By the time of the *Life*, however, not only had the public's image of Johnson been reshaped by the calumnious material which had been exposed, but Boswell himself had undergone an important experience in so far as his role as an author was concerned. Yet, in providing what he intended to be the definitive image of Johnson, Boswell had to take care not to make the Johnson of the *Life* inconsistent with the 'innocent' portrait in the *Tour to the Hebrides*. A noticeably different attitude towards his material would seriously undermine both works.

Boswell prepares for this difficulty when he speaks of the restraints which have been forced upon him by the reactions to the *Tour* (I, pp. 2–4). Any differences may be put down to Boswell's needing to be rather more careful in his communications. He is careful to point out, too, despite a number of alterations, that the 'character' of Johnson that he gives at the end of the *Life* is in 'the greatest part' taken from the *Tour to the Hebrides*: Boswell sees no 'reason to give a different character of my illustrious friend now, from what I formerly gave'

(IV, p. 425 n. 1). Certainly, the space devoted to the 'character' is roughly the same in the *Life* as in the *Tour*, yet almost half of the earlier sketch had been taken up with remarks upon Johnson's prejudice against Scotland (suitably placed to whet the reader's appetite for Johnson's actually living among Scots, but hardly relevant, and therefore omitted, in the *Life* portrait), and with a description of the clothes he wore while travelling (V, pp. 19–20). In the *Tour*, Johnson's principles and intellectual powers are dealt with first, and Boswell then proceeds to his manners and appearance, for it is upon this aspect of the image of Johnson that Boswell must primarily rely for the effect of his book. Between remarks about Milton's shoes and Johnson's oak stick, and the paragraphs on Johnson's anti-Scottish prejudices, however, is sandwiched a reference to 'that Wonderful Man, whom I venerated and loved while in this world, and after whom I gaze with humble hope, now that it has pleased ALMIGHTY GOD to call him to a better world' (V, p. 19). Boswell's worship is not, in this context, easy to understand.

The *Life* sketch, however, opens with a brief physical description, frankly mentioning Johnson's infirmities, yet Boswell uses his example of longevity as 'a proof that an inherent *vivida vis* is a powerful preservative of the human frame' (IV, p. 425) – in contrast to the *Tour*, the purely physical is never allowed to dominate. The rest of the 'character' is concerned with showing how Johnson's virtues and defects, principles and prejudices, are aspects of one consistent dynamic personality. In fact, Boswell actually emphasises (as he had not done in the *Tour* sketch) that Johnson's apparent contradictions are not evidence of shallowness or inconsistency:

> Man is, in general, made up of contradictory qualities; and these will ever shew themselves in strange succession, where a consistency in appearance at least, if not in reality, has not been attained by long habits of philosophical discipline... and, therefore, we are not to wonder, that Johnson exhibited an eminent example of this remark which I have made upon human nature. At different times, he seemed a different man, in some respects; not, however, in any great or essential article, upon which he had fully employed his mind, and settled certain principles of duty, but only in his

manners, and in the display of argument and fancy in his talk. (IV, p. 426)

Yet Boswell is acute enough to present the appearance of similarity between the two sketches by lifting phrases and sentences from the *Tour* and distributing them (not necessarily in the same order) through the *Life* version:

> He was a sincere and zealous Christian, of high Church-of-England and monarchical principles, which he would not tamely suffer to be questioned. (IV, p. 426; V, p. 17)

> He had a constitutional melancholy, the clouds of which darkened the brightness of his fancy, and gave a gloomy cast to his whole course of thinking. (IV, p. 427; V, p. 17)

Boswell clearly paid careful attention to his *Life* sketch of Johnson's character, and in it he is able to summarise his considered assessment of Johnson, and at the same time to present the appearance of his own consistency in his attitude towards his subject.

Johnson's conversation, too, is one very obvious point of similarity between the two books. Boswell had long been adept at recording Johnson's talk 'in an authentick and lively manner' (I, p. 2); there is little danger that Johnson at Dilly's or Sir Joshua Reynolds's will sound very different from the conversationalist of St Andrews. Here Boswell is reporting fact, and a little polishing or editing is all that is required of him.

Less obvious, though probably no less decisive in governing the reader's emotional attitude towards Johnson, is the way Boswell uses descriptive imagery. Beneath all the facts and opinions about Johnson is an undercurrent of metaphorical description which runs through both the *Tour to the Hebrides* and the *Life*, as it had through Boswell's journals, and it is in the use of these individual images that Boswell is often at his most skilful. For, while in the *Life* imagery is used in the same *way* as it had been in the *Tour*, each image is now much more controlled, and clearly designed to have a more specific effect upon the reader. The striking fancy has become the literary image, yet has lost none of its freshness and vitality. And, what is particularly important, because the type of imagery has not changed – the images of the *Life* and the *Tour* are equally striking, equally 'Boswellian' – Boswell need not fear that his attitude to Johnson will seem at all inconsistent.

Not surprisingly, some of the images in the *Tour* arise from the surroundings in which Johnson is placed. For example, Johnson sitting on the stern of Rasay's 'carriage' is 'like a magnificent Triton' (*Life*, V, p. 162), or reading on the mountainside in Coll he has 'a most eremitical appearance' (V, p. 302). But other images could be expected in either book with equal likelihood. The image of the organ is a common one, with its suggestions of religious dignity and awesome grandeur:

> The *Messiah*, played upon the *Canterbury organ*, is more sublime than when played upon an inferior instrument: but very slight musick will seem grand when conveyed to the ear through that majestick medium. (V, p. 18)

> Tastes may differ as to the violin, the flute, the hautboy, in short, all the lesser instruments: but who can be insensible to the powerful impressions of the majestick organ?
> (II, p. 335)

As neither of these examples was part of the original journals,[11] we may assume that in both Boswell is pursuing a deliberate policy of description. (William Siebenschuh makes a similar point about Boswell's use of the image of the monument with reference to the *Life*.[12]) Yet a closer comparison reveals that the *Tour* image is used, slightly ludicrously, to describe Johnson's manner of speaking, his '*bow-wow way*'. In the *Life*, its terms of reference have far wider implications, for Boswell is talking about 'his energy of diction', 'his splendour of images, and comprehension of thought' – in fact, about Johnson's whole intellectual and moral character. The image is fully exploited, and its 'majestick' associations are completely appropriate.

Sometimes an image succinctly conveys Boswell's emotional reaction to Johnson in a particular circumstance – for example, his elation at having been 'able to entice such a man' to Scotland: 'I compared myself to a dog who has got hold of a large piece of meat, and runs away with it to a corner, where he may devour it in peace, without any fear of others taking it from him' (v, p. 215). Or, on a particular evening in company, Johnson is like 'a warm West-Indian climate, where you have a bright sun, quick vegetation, luxuriant foliage, luscious fruits; but where the same heat sometimes produces thunder, lightning, and earthquakes, in a terrible degree' (III, p. 300).[13] And, after having pushed a conversation on death beyond Johnson's patience, Boswell says, 'I seemed to myself like the man who had put his head into the lion's mouth a great many times with perfect safety, but at last had it bit off' (II, p. 107).

Part of the emotional effect of the images in the *Life* is from the reader's catching some of Boswell's delight in the creative process. The image of the West Indian climate has this quality. Similarly, Boswell observes of regional accents, 'A small intermixture of provincial pecularities may, perhaps, have an agreeable effect, as the notes of different birds concur in the harmony of the grove, and please more than if they were all exactly alike' (II, p. 160). And of the indiscriminate grouping together of a year's Johnsonian conversation he excuses himself, 'To know of what vintage our wine is, enables us to judge of its value, and to drink it with more relish: but to have the produce of each vine of one vineyard, in the same year, kept separate, would serve no purpose' (III, p. 52). One can sometimes almost feel Boswell reaching out for images of sufficiently immense associations in order to describe his feelings for Johnson. Between Johnson and Paoli, 'I compared myself to an isthmus which joins two great continents' (II, p. 80). Or at the 'great works of Mr. Bolton' near Birmingham he observes, 'I wish that Johnson had been with us: for it was a scene which I should have been glad to contemplate by his light. The vastness and contrivance of some of the machinery would have "matched his mighty mind" ' (II, p. 459). (It is notable that Boswell did not find this particular man–machine equation distressing, for he certainly did so on other occasions.)

But Boswell also uses imagery of animals in his descriptions. The main purpose of this is clearly to give some idea of the physical reality of Johnson:

> Generally when he had concluded a period, in the course of a dispute, by which time he was a good deal exhausted by

violence and vociferation, he used to blow out his breath like a Whale. This I suppose was a relief to his lungs; and seemed in him to be a contemptuous mode of expression, as if he had made the arguments of his opponent fly like chaff before the wind. (I, pp. 485–6)

It will be noticed, though, that Boswell is careful here not to let the whale image dominate what he is saying. It is turned to include Johnson's intellectual as well as his bodily vastness, and the effect of the chaff image (as far as one can judge its effect on a reader living in what was still a predominantly agricultural society) is to leave a less distinct picture in the mind. The two ideas are sufficiently dissimilar to require a conscious mental effort to appreciate their points of likeness. And, in case this is insufficient, Boswell then adds a warning paragraph:

I am fully aware how very obvious an occasion I here give for the sneering jocularity of such as have no relish of an exact likeness; which, to render complete, he who draws it must not disdain the slightest strokes. But if witlings should be inclined to attack this account, let them have the candour to quote what I have offered in my defence. (I, p. 486)

For Boswell clearly knew that he was approaching a dangerous frontier. A common theme among Johnson's slanderers was his ungainliness and his uncouth behaviour, and this was often expressed in imagery of animals – or at least of brutish strength and appetite. James Clifford notes, in fact, that following the publication of the *Tour to the Hebrides* 'Johnson was compared to a dead whale cast up on the sands at Leith, and made a show of by his younger Scots friend'.[14] And Peter Pindar's *Epistle to James Boswell* contains such remarks as 'The pilot of our literary whale', 'lion Johnson', and 'the Rambler, on a large bay mare, / Just like a Centaur'.[15] Charles Churchill saw Johnson as 'Not quite a *Beast*, nor quite a *Man*'.[16] To Robert Potter, Johnson's mind was, 'in some respects, as narrow as a crane's neck',[17] and in his *Lives of the Poets* 'he introduces Gray with his knotted club to knock down the gentle Shenstone, to be himself knocked down at last by our blind Polypheme in the wantonness of his might'.[18] Potter even uses the reputation of Johnson's bodily character to explain his 'deficiencies' of mind:

> But the coarseness of his constitution, his vigorous mind being perhaps vitiated or degraded by the grossness of his body, vibrated not to the delicate touches of a Shenstone and a Hammond, nor even to the stronger hand of a Gray, but gravitated by the weight of that in which it was inclosed to the earth.[19]

And there runs through Potter's conclusion the suggestion of eating and food – 'good morsels of criticism', 'literary butchery', and 'the food of the soul'.[20]

Part of Boswell's defence against misinterpretation of Johnson, then, involves adopting the weapons of his enemies. He will not, as the faithful biographer, seek to suppress any side of his subject's character, and certainly not so well-known a feature as Johnson's physical distinctiveness. He has, for example, 'tossed and gored several persons' (*Life*, II, p. 66); but on the same page Boswell discusses the epithet 'bear', quoting 'a just and happy saying of my friend Goldsmith, who knew him well: "Johnson, to be sure, has a roughness in his manner; but no man alive has a more tender heart. He has nothing of the bear but his skin." ' A balance is achieved between what makes Johnson appear an animal, and what distinguishes him as a man. This same balance may be observed when Boswell discusses Johnson's early progress of mind:

> He might, perhaps, have studied more assiduously; but it may be doubted, whether such a mind as his was not more enriched by roaming at large in the fields of literature, than if it had been confined to any single spot. The analogy between body and mind is very general, and the parallel will hold as to their food, as well as any other particular. The flesh of animals who feed excursively, is allowed to have a higher flavour than that of those who are cooped up. May there not be the same difference between men who read as their taste prompts, and men who are confined in cells and colleges to stated tasks.   (I, pp. 57–8)

Here Boswell is a little less successful, but his intended effect is clear. Mind and body are so mingled, and the image made at the end so general, that the passage cannot confidently be read as suggesting Johnson as a fattening bullock. The concluding idea of the monastery is introduced in order to deflect finally any such inclination in the reader, and the contrast is made into one between the man of health and the pale scholar.

A dinner at Dilly's in 1778 provides a further interesting example of Boswell's technique over a longer stretch of writing. There, Johnson before dinner 'seized upon Mr. Charles Sheridan's "Account of the Late Revolution in Sweden", and seemed to read it ravenously, as if he devoured it, which was to all appearance his method of studying' (III, p. 284). Boswell is already mingling body and mind inextricably, and suggesting the danger of relying only on appearances. He continues by quoting the remark of one of the company, Mrs Knowles, 'the ingenious Quaker lady': 'He knows how to read better than any one (said Mrs. Knowles;) he gets at the substance of a book directly; he tears out the heart of it' (III, pp. 284–5). By showing Mrs Knowles's imagery as being consistent with his own (though independent of it: Boswell's 'ravenously' appears as description in the journal entry – *Ex.*, p. 282 – not as conversation), Boswell recruits her as a respectable witness who demonstrates such a balanced view of Johnson as he himself is putting forward. There follows a more daring image, Boswell even drawing attention to his own coarseness; he continues on the book,

> He kept it wrapt up in the tablecloth in his lap during the time of dinner, from an avidity to have one entertainment in readiness when he should have finished another; resembling (if I may use so coarse a simile) a dog who holds a bone in his paws in reserve, while he eats something else which has been thrown to him. (*Life*, III, p. 285)

Even here, it is interesting that Boswell has toned down his image, for the original journal record compared Johnson to 'a dog who folds a bone in his paws while he licks broth' (*Ex.*, p. 282), with the alternative suggestion 'while eating' (ibid., n. 5). Immediately after this, though, the *Life* has Johnson discussing cookery – a subject introduced, it is implied, by someone else (in the journal Boswell does not know how it came to be mentioned – *Ex.*, p. 283) – and declaring his intention to write a book on it 'upon philosophical principles'; he speaks of the science and skill of cookery, compares it with pharmacy, and digresses incidentally on the inaccuracy and method of writing in a previous manual. The final impression is not that of Johnson the gourmand, but of his immense range of interest and his ability to assume a detachment from what Boswell freely admits was one of the delights of his life.

Ralph Rader remarks on one effect of Boswell's honesty about Johnson's faults:

> Boswell knew that without the blemishes the portrait would not be true and concretely convincing. Unless the reader were to see an image which in its basic structure corresponded to his own imperfect nature, he would not recognise either the paradigmatic likeness or the particular otherness that are the essence of biographical portraiture; he would not admire because he would not believe.... But Boswell had an artistic motive even higher than verisimilitude for his honesty. He can make Johnson even more admirable by showing that he was so in *spite* of his faults and ugliness.[21]

More than this, though, Boswell's animal images are part of the long careful process of the presentation of Johnson. Not only do they become less noticeable in the context of the great variety of imagery Boswell uses in the course of his Odyssey, but the total impression is of Johnson as a man who is quite above all attempts at description. Not only is he greater than each individual image: he is greater than the sum of all the images. From Boswell's point of view, this is one of the salutary effects of Johnson's acquaintance, for the imagery in the journals which distorts and misleads when applied to lesser subjects finds its power rendered ineffectual when it is matched against the firmness and permanence of Johnson. He will never be overwhelmed by any image that Boswell can use of him, for Johnson is always beyond explanation. He has set up his own image, and it needs all of Boswell's skill to mirror it faithfully in the *Life*. And, even then, Boswell has to concede defeat, for Johnson's image cannot be confined. There is always more to be revealed. He is 'so extraordinary, that the more his character is considered, the more he will be regarded by the present age, and by posterity, with admiration and reverence' (IV, p. 430).

### (iii) *The Image of Boswell*

Yet Boswell was also aware that it was only a part of 'the present age' who could be expected to regard Johnson with 'admiration and reverence'. For many writers, Johnson was inescapably identified, both in literature and in politics, with an earlier and more despotic age. As Joseph Towers wrote,

> Indeed, one of the great features of Johnson's character, was a degree of bigotry, both in politics and in religion, which is now seldom to be met with in persons of a cultivated understanding. Few other men could have been found, in the present age, whose political bigotry would have led them to style the celebrated JOHN HAMPDEN 'the zealot of rebellion'; and the religious bigotry of the man, who, when at Edinburgh, would not go to hear Dr. Robertson preach, because he would not be present at a Presbyterian assembly, is not easily to be paralleled in this age, and in this country.[22]

Later writers, too, like Hazlitt and Coleridge, felt that by attacking Johnson they were attacking all the values of an era which was antithetical to their own. In this respect, part of Boswell's task was to steer a careful course between the appearance of total commitment to the attitudes of either party. So, politically, for example, he stresses his position as an unashamed Tory, and his noble pedigree, yet frankly dissociates himself from the views expressed in Johnson's pamphlets. Boswell wanted to be identified on the whole with the values of the Johnsonian era – hence he cites the approval of the 'many and various persons eminent for their rank' (I, p. 13), men whose position in society would associate them with those values – yet at the same time to be distinguished as one who selected and assessed what was admirable and worthy of preservation, both in the values themselves, and in the character of the man who strove to maintain them.

For it would be a mistake to assume that Boswell's only concern in the *Life* was to give an image of Johnson. He was also very much interested in the image he was to present of himself, and not only in order to give added force to the portrait of Johnson, but from the motive of vanity. He wanted to be sure of there being a reasonably true idea of James Boswell presented for the readers of his time, and preserved like the self of the journal from the oblivion of the past. But, here too, Boswell had to contend with the legacy of the *Tour to the Hebrides*, for he had suffered too much from both public and private censure to wish to lay himself open once more to whoever cared to be scathing or witty at the expense of 'Jemmie Boswell'.[23] While recognising that this would inevitably happen, Boswell saw no reason to make things easy for potential Peter Pindars, and he begins the *Life* to this effect:

> In one respect, this Work will, in some passages, be different from the former. In my 'Tour', I was almost unboundedly open in my communications; and from my eagerness to display the wonderful fertility and readiness of Johnson's wit, freely shewed to the world its dexterity, even when I was myself the object of it. I trusted that I should be liberally understood, as knowing very well what I was about, and by no means as simply unconscious of the pointed effects of the satire. I own, indeed, that I was arrogant enough to suppose that the tenour of the rest of the book would sufficiently guard me against such a strange imputation. But it seems I judged too well of the world; for, though I could scarcely believe it, I have been undoubtedly informed, that many persons, especially in distant quarters, not penetrating enough into Johnson's character, so as to understand his mode of treating his friends, have arraigned my judgement, instead of seeing that I was sensible of all that they could observe. (I, p. 3)

The reference to 'distant quarters' and 'not penetrating enough' are the first shots in Boswell's campaign against his own traducers, and the immediately following story of Dr Clarke and Beau Nash is a clear invitation to the reader to choose his side, even though there is no real choice. Boswell always tries to imply that it is he and his readers against 'others'. Whenever he enters into a defence of himself, he is skilful enough to draw the reader to his side and so add another link in their alliance against those outsiders who exclude themselves from the fraternity of admirers of Johnson and virtue.

> I cannot allow any fragment whatever that floats in my memory concerning the great subject of this work to be lost. Though a small particular may appear trifling to some, it will be relished by others; while every little spark adds something to the general blaze: and to please the true, candid, warm admirers of Johnson, and in any degree increase the splendour of his reputation, I bid defiance to the shafts of ridicule, or even of malignity. Showers of them have been discharged at my 'Journal of a Tour to the Hebrides'; yet it still sails unhurt along the stream of time, and, as an attendant of Johnson, 'Pursues the triumph, and partakes the gale.' (III, p. 190)

Boswell's minuteness may be ridiculed 'by men of superficial understanding and ludicrous fancy' (I, p. 33), but he remains 'firm and confident in [his] opinion'. Johnson's prayer on beginning the study of Greek and Italian 'must impress all the thinking part of my readers with a consolatory confidence in habitual devotion' (III, p. 90). And Boswell, referring to the 'feeble though shrill outcry which had been raised' by the *Lives of the Poets* in 'narrow circles' of 'resentment and prejudice', quotes Johnson as 'nobly' declaring, 'Sir, I considered myself as entrusted with a certain portion of truth. I have given my opinion sincerely; let them shew where they think me wrong' (*Life*, IV, p. 65). The similarity between their situations is only implied, but it is clear from Boswell's language that their enemies are of the same species. And the final suggestion of the good nature of the Johnsonian school is Johnson's remark, 'I wonder how I should have any enemies; for I do harm to nobody' (IV, p. 168). To this Boswell adds the footnote, 'This reflection was very natural in a man of good heart, who was not conscious of any ill-will to mankind.' Against this background of companionship and virtue, Boswell's evidence of the unsociability of Sir John Hawkins (e.g. I, pp. 479–80) is quite damning.

Boswell, then, attempts to create an atmosphere in which his readers will feel an instinctive sympathy with him, and which he can use to instil the feeling of respect for him which was lacking in much of the reaction to his self-portrait in the *Tour to the Hebrides*. What he had considered a true likeness had, in the eyes of 'many persons', been distorted into the picture of a fool. The image of himself in the *Life* had, by various devices, to be made more true. He shows that he is aware that, in the words of Warburton, 'Almost all the life-writers we have had before Toland and Desmaiseaux, are indeed strange insipid creatures' (I, p. 29), and he knows, too, that an omnipresent narrator will inevitably sound an egotist. As he had written in *Hypochondriack* 21, 'Thus a speaker or writer who would not have his hearers or readers weary, should not continue long to address them in his own person, but should break his discourse, by occasionally calling in other persons, by Quotation' (*BC*, p. 126). The introduction in the *Life* of other voices, such as Langton, Adams, and Johnson himself, and the changing of tone in his own voice from narrator to participant, help to solve the problem. Yet these techniques could not in themselves provide a complete solution, for Boswell had also to convey a well-balanced image of himself in those portions of the *Life* which could be narrated in no other way but in his own person.

One essential was to release enough information about himself to allow his readers to identify with a recognisable figure. As Paul Alkon says,

> He portrays himself as sufficiently close to the average reader so that the narrator functions as Everyman reacting to the unique Johnson while nevertheless remaining close enough to the Sage in outlook and disposition so that readers will accept the biographer as a fit guide.[24]

This also serves to gratify Boswell's own vanity and his desire to preserve his own memory for posterity. In the 'Advertisement to the Second Edition' he makes just such a point:

> There are some men, I believe, who have, or think they have, a very small share of vanity. Such may speak of their literary fame in a decorous style of diffidence. But I confess,

that I am so formed by nature and by habit, that to restrain the effusion of delight, on having obtained such fame, to me would be truly painful. Why then should I suppress it? Why 'out of the abundance of the heart' should I not speak? Let me then mention with a warm, but no insolent exultation, that I have been regaled with spontaneous praise of my work by many and various persons eminent for their rank, learning, talents and accomplishments; much of which praise I have under their hands to be reposited in my archives at Auchinleck. (I, pp. 12–13)

Yet personal information, notwithstanding Boswell's shameless imparting of his glee in this passage, must not normally be conveyed quite so blatantly. His own character-sketch, for example, which had appeared at the beginning of the *Tour* (V, pp. 51–2), is omitted, and his self-flattery at being 'completely a citizen of the world' (V, p. 20) is introduced with rather more subtlety during an encomium upon Scotland (II, p. 306), where Boswell's purpose is intended to appear more altruistic.

Boswell does contrive, however, that a great deal of information about himself, his family and friends, and his opinions, should be given to the reader during the course of the narrative. We are told, in conversation with Johnson, of Boswell's European travels, and of a possible future publication based upon them (III, p. 301); of the education of his sons, during a discussion on the great schools (III, p. 12); of his interest in the Douglas cause and the pamphlet he wrote on it, during a conversation on the publication of other people's letters (II, p. 230 n. 1); and, in a letter to Johnson introducing him to Boswell's brother David, of the oath of allegiance which David swore before leaving Auchinleck (III, p. 433). We are reminded of Boswell's book on Corsica (II, pp. 59, 69 n. 3), and of his 1785 *Letter to the People of Scotland* (III, pp. 16–17 n. 1); and we learn within two paragraphs of his close friendship with Samuel Derrick, John Home and the Earl of Eglintoune (I, pp. 456–7). Only occasionally does Boswell's Boswell become excessive, as with the defence of his Latin in his civil-law thesis (II, pp. 23–4), or his tedious opinion on Horace (III, pp. 74–5 n.1).

Boswell also manages to present himself as a man with definite fixed ideas, but without prejudices (this from an eighteenth- rather than a twentieth-century point of view). He comments of the strengths, for example, of Churchill's poetry (I, pp. 419–20), although disagreeing with him in principle. He lays out categorically the evidence for and against Savage's authenticity (I, pp. 170–4), and is not afraid to reach no decision. He frankly owns his incompetence to judge of Johnson's Latin (I, p. 62), but considers himself fit to censure his taste with regard to the value of statuary (II, p. 439). And he even tries to maintain an impression of fairness concerning Sir John Hawkins:

> In Sir John Hawkins's compilation, there are, however, some passages concerning Johnson which have unquestionable merit. One of them I shall transcribe, in justice to a writer whom I have had too much occasion to censure, and to shew my fairness as the biographer of my illustrious friend. (IV, p. 371 n. 2)

Particularly important for Boswell's own image are the places where he demonstrates his independent judgement by disagreeing with Johnson. There are many instances of this, including some where Boswell's opinion is expressed only to the reader, as on 'the power of rhetorical action upon human nature' (II, p. 211), or on general warrants (II, p. 75), or slavery (III, p. 203); and some where he actually disputes an issue with Johnson himself, as on the happiness of one's boyhood (I, p. 451), the happiness of feudalism (II, p. 178), or on knowledge and the sense of personal superiority (II, p. 220). The balance Boswell is seeking to maintain is between sufficient agreement with Johnson to make him an understanding biographer, and sufficient evidence of independence to allow himself a mind and character of his own.

It is essential for the success of the *Life*, as Boswell realised, that we find him, on the whole, a sympathetic figure, for he provides in many places the emotional focus for our reactions to Johnson. From the beginning of the *Life*, Boswell emphasises that he is writing about a man who was, above all else, his friend: 'I had the honour and happiness of enjoying his friendship for upwards of twenty years' (I, p. 25). He loses few opportunities of stressing this fact. Of *Rasselas*, for example, he writes,

> I am not satisfied if a year passes without my having read it through; and at every perusal, my admiration of the mind which produced it is so highly raised, that I can scarcely believe that I had the honour of enjoying the intimacy of such a man. (I, p. 342)

By the time that Johnson actually appears in person, Boswell is already closely attached to him in the reader's mind, and while the entrance adds a new dimension to the portrait, Boswell can automatically assume the role of emotional intermediary.

Their introduction, in fact, demonstrates this well. We already share Boswell's impatience for a meeting with 'the extraordinary man whose works I highly valued, and whose conversation was reported to be so peculiarly excellent' (I, p. 391). When his 'aweful approach' is actually announced by Davies, we can sympathise with Boswell's agitation (I, p. 392). Johnson's two sharp rebuffs increase the atmosphere of nervousness:

> I now felt myself much mortified, and began to think that the hope which I had long indulged of attaining his acquaintance was blasted. And, in truth, had not my ardour been uncommonly strong, and my resolution uncommonly persevering, so rough a reception might have deterred me for ever from making any further attempts. (I, p. 393)

Boswell's 'reward' of 'hearing some of his conversation' successfully turns him and the reader into half-guilty eavesdroppers, but his later venturing 'to make an observation now and then, which he received very civilly' (I, p. 395), relieves the tension by giving us, as participants, more right to be there. Finally, we can share Boswell's glee when he subsequently finds a friendly reception at Johnson's own chambers:

> Before we parted, he was so good as to promise to favour me with his company one evening at my lodgings; and, as I took my leave, shook me cordially by the hand. It is almost needless to add, that I felt no little elation at having now so happily established an acquaintance of which I had been so long ambitious. (I, pp. 398–9)

And, in case his technique has not been fully successful, Boswell concludes the episode by reminding us that by the very act of having read the *Life* so far we are already committed to both his evaluation of his material and his way of presenting it:

> My readers will, I trust, excuse me for being thus minutely circumstantial, when it is considered that the acquaintance of Dr. Johnson was to me a most valuable acquisition, and laid the foundation of whatever instruction and entertainment they may receive from the collections concerning the great subject of the work which they are now perusing.
> (I, p. 399)

Throughout the *Life*, Boswell makes us feel with him in his relations with Johnson. When Johnson is irritated by an error of Boswell's, we 'bow to the storm' with him (I, p. 464). When Johnson unexpectedly announces, 'I look upon *myself* as a good humoured fellow' (II, p. 362), we share Boswell's amusement and wonder. Reconciliation after harshness can hardly fail to produce some effect:

> BOSWELL. 'I said today to Sir Joshua, when he observed that you *tossed* me sometimes – I don't care how often, or how high he tosses me, when only friends are present, for then I fall upon soft ground: but I do not like falling on stones, which is the case when enemies are present – I think this is a pretty good image, Sir.' JOHNSON. 'Sir, it is one of the happiest I have ever heard.' (III, p. 338)

Here the enjoyment is increased by some uncertainty in our reaction to Johnson's last remark: is there a note of sarcasm, and, if so, is Boswell aware of it? Then, as Johnson's death approaches, we can share Boswell's 'fearful apprehension' (IV, p. 226); we can enter into the warmth of friendship displayed in the emotional scene where Johnson learns about the proposed trip to Italy (IV, pp. 336–7); and, finally, we can react appropriately to Boswell's leave-taking as narrator shortly before the death: 'I now relieve the readers of this Work from any farther personal notice of its author, who if he should be thought to have obtruded himself too much upon their attention, requests them to consider the peculiar plan of his biographical undertaking' (IV, p. 380). Boswell's intermediary position has throughout been to the end of preventing the reader from feeling like an intruder into Johnson's private life: above all, he gives us the *right* to be there.

Clearly, though, this is also important for Boswell on a psychological level, for not only is he kept continuously in the reader's eye, but he has the satisfaction of being the essential medium through which Johnson affects our emotions. Confirmation of one inevitably involves confirmation of the other, even if that confirmation is in the form of a negative reaction of dislike. As R. D. Laing argues,

> The slightest sign of recognition from another at least confirms one's presence in *his* world.... A partially confirmatory response need not be in agreement, or gratifying, or satisfying. Rejection can be confirmatory if it is direct, not tangential, and recognizes the evoking action and grants it significance and validity.... An action 'rejected' is perceived and this perception shows that it is accepted as a fact. Direct 'rejection' is not tangential; it is not mocking or in other ways invalidating. It need neither depreciate nor exaggerate the original action. It is not synonymous with indifference or imperviousness.[25]

This is not to say that Boswell does not mind being disliked, but his most heartfelt resentment does seem to be against those 'shafts of ridicule' which seek to invalidate both his work and him personally. If, on the other hand, we are inclined to take Johnson warmly to our hearts, then Boswell has made sure that we will find it difficult to do so without taking his biographer as well – indeed, to despise Boswell must inevitably make us except from our admiration of Johnson his ability to judge of his friends. And Boswell's achievement here is to have translated a psychological need, which I have noted as an important factor in the writing of his journals, into artistic terms, and successfully catered for it through a literary genre.

Boswell does try to present himself as a likeable sort of man, though, and, in case his own self-portrait should be suspected of bias, he introduces other voices not only as testimonials of

Johnson, but also of himself. John Courtenay, for example, is quoted at length:

> Amid these names can BOSWELL be forgot,
> Scarce by North Britons now esteem'd a Scot?
> Who to the sage devoted from his youth,
> Imbib'd from him the sacred love of truth;
> The keen research, the exercise of mind,
> And that best art, the art to know mankind.
> (I, p. 223)

Boswell's admission that Courtenay is one of his friends reduces the value of his testimony, but adds to the atmosphere of comradeship which pervades the book.

Not surprisingly, in the light of my remarks elsewhere on Boswell's need for an impression of free and unrestrained communication, he is particularly assiduous in recording attestations of his ease and familiarity with Johnson. Sir William Forbes writes, 'I suppose there is not a man in the world to whom he discloses his sentiments so freely as to yourself' (III, p. 208), and Johnson himself 'was pleased to say to me', 'Boswell, I think, I am easier with you than with almost any body' (IV, p. 194). Boswell also mentions the point in a letter to Johnson: 'Please to consider, that to keep each other's kindness, we should every year have that free and intimate communication of mind which can be had only when we are together. We should have both our solemn and our pleasant talk' (III, p. 439). Sir John Hawkins, on the other hand, is 'a man, whom, during my long intimacy with Dr. Johnson, I never saw in his company, I think but once, and I am sure not above twice' (I, p. 27), and, 'from the rigid formality of his manners, it is evident that they could never have lived together with companionable ease and familiarity'.

Boswell, too, is seen in action in the conversations in which he is reported as a participant. Bertrand Bronson writes that Boswell's part in the conversation is important only in so far as it leads into Johnson's,[26] and Ralph Rader that he displayed Johnson's greatness 'to posterity shorn of accident and unblemished by any stain of his own private feeling or immense personal ego'.[27] This is not quite true, for Boswell not infrequently gives his own reported opinion more space than

Johnson's, and leaves the reader with the impression that he, and not Johnson, had the last word:

> This brought on a question whether one man is lessened by another's acquiring an equal degree of knowledge with him. Johnson asserted the affirmative. I maintained that the position might be true in those kinds of knowledge which produce wisdom, power, and force, so as to enable one man to have the government of others; but that a man is not in any degree lessened by others knowing as well as he what ends in mere pleasure:– eating fine fruits, drinking delicious wines, reading exquisite poetry. (II, p. 220)

> I argued warmly for the old feudal system. Sir Alexander opposed it, and talked of the pleasure of seeing all men free and independent. JOHNSON. ' I agree with Mr. Boswell that there must be a high satisfaction in being a feudal Lord; but we are to consider, that we ought not to wish to have a number of men unhappy for the satisfaction of one.' – I maintained that numbers, namely, the vassals or followers, were not unhappy; for that there was a reciprocal satisfaction between the Lord and them; he being kind in his authority over them; they being respectful and faithful to him. (II, p. 178)

Not that Boswell is deliberately falsifying the record: the journal record of the first example is missing (*Def.*, p. 191), and for the second Boswell's *Life* version is confirmed (*Def.*, p. 102). But he is certainly doing more than merely leading into Johnson's speech.

Sometimes Boswell introduces small alterations into his own speeches as we find them in the journal: an occasional 'indeed', for example, as in the discussion at Tom Davies's on immorality and gentility (*Life*, II, p. 340, and *OY*, p. 126). Such little touches, insignificant in themselves, make more convincing the evidence of Boswell's ease of communication with Johnson, as well as making him appear generally a more polished speaker. Later on the same occasion, Boswell assigns to himself the speech which draws to a close the discussion on judges and trading (II, p. 344), one which in the journal (*OY*, p. 128 and n. 7) appears to have been spoken by Johnson. This may be taken as an instance of Boswell's real memory being regarded as more accurate than the written one, or it may be a case of his giving himself the benefit of the doubt in an unclear passage.

Here again Boswell's problem is to maintain a balance, between on the one hand presenting his easy relationship with Johnson and giving some idea of his own aptitude for conversation, and on the other offering more evidence of vanity and foolishness. He wants to preserve his artistic integrity in portraying the true Johnson and the true Boswell, yet his immediate ease and reputation in the world demand that he should appear decently clad and bearing himself with dignity. Moreover, is his duty to fidelity and posterity more demanding than his duty to his friends and acquaintances and his desire to remain on good terms with them? As he writes to Temple, 'I may make many enemies, and even have quarrels' (*Corr.* II, p. lxxv).

In achieving this balance, Boswell depends upon the preservation in certain selected cases of anonymity rather than on the total suppression of information concerning himself or others. James Clifford describes Boswell's willingness 'to make changes to ease the resentment of persons who felt insulted by his revelations',[28] and Boswell himself writes in the Dedication to the *Life*,

> The world, my friend, I have found to be a great fool, as to that particular, on which it has become necessary to speak very plainly. I have, therefore, in this Work been more reserved; and though I tell nothing but the truth, I have still kept in my mind that the whole truth is not always to be exposed. (I, p. 4)

Yet it is not always easy to see upon what grounds Boswell chose whether the privilege of anonymity was to be granted. The 'demolition' of Moody, the Irish Jacobite (*OY*, p. 128), for example, is totally suppressed, and George Dempster, who gave Johnson 'such general displeasure' (I, p. 443), remains anonymous. 'Dodsley's brother', however, has his 'original low condition' (II, pp. 446–7) published, and the 'scene of too much heat between Dr. Johnson and Dr. Percy, which I should have suppressed, were it not that it gave occasion to display the truely tender and benevolent heart of Johnson' (III, p. 271), actually led to coldness between Boswell and Percy (cf. *Corr.* II, pp. 597–8). Boswell does permit himself one joke in this respect, and refers to an anonymous Sir Alexander Macdonald by his *Hebrides* title of 'a penurious gentleman of our acquaintance' (III, p. 40).

Understandably, though, it is for himself that Boswell most frequently claims anonymity. Instead of the talkative Boswell of the *Tour to the Hebrides*, there appears a glittering variety of 'gentlemen who were present': 'a young man who was uneasy from thinking that he was very deficient in learning and knowledge' (I, p. 454), one who told of 'the infidelity of his servant, who, he said, would not believe the scriptures, because he could not read them in the original tongues, and be sure that they were not invented' (II, p. 14), 'a gentleman who seemed fond of curious speculation' (II, p. 54), and one 'gentleman' who asks a foolish question when from the rest of the account Johnson and Boswell seem to be alone together (IV, p. 173). Boswell even introduces his own 'Ode to Mrs. Thrale, by Samuel Johnson, LL.D. on their supposed approaching Nuptials' without hinting as to the authorship (IV, p. 387 n. 1), and allows a reference to the first masquerade in Scotland to pass (II, p. 205 n. 2) without mentioning that he was himself present as a Dumb Conjuror, or quoting from any of the accounts he had written of it in the newspapers.[29]

This suppression of the self, finally, is particularly important for Boswell, for it represents the opening up of the private, egocentric world of his journals. The writing of the *Life* forced him to consider just what he should present to the public, and how much of himself he ought to make known. This exercise must have been at least as valuable as the writing of the journals in the real development of Boswell's self-awareness, and in his estimate of his relation to society. Like his use of the dramatic form at times in the journals, and his substitution of 'you' for 'I' in the memoranda, anonymity would help to increase the distance between Boswell and his experience, and hence to encourage objectivity in his naturally self-centred outlook. The necessity of judging how much the reader would be able to take of one man's voice, the whole balancing-act itself throughout the *Life*, could only be important and helpful influences for a melancholy man never completely sure of his own sanity and judgment, or of his position in the lives of others.

(iv)

Nevertheless, despite Boswell's minute attention, it is well known that the *Life of Johnson* produced a great deal of shock, and considerable derision of its author. Many readers, like Ralph Griffiths in the *Monthly Review*,[30] and the eminent persons Boswell mentions in the 'Advertisement to the Second Edition', declared themselves warm admirers of this type of biography. Others, including Percy,[31] were clearly unaware of just how much care Boswell had taken in his presentation of Johnson and his times. Even Wordsworth was later to pass a harsh censure on Boswell's work: 'The life of Johnson by Boswell had broken through many pre-existing delicacies, and afforded the British public an opportunity of acquiring experience, which before it had happily wanted.'[32] It is important to remember, though, that Boswell was prepared for such mixed reactions. He knew that he might make enemies, and that there would be 'cold-blooded and morose mortals who really dislike this Book' (*Life*, I, p. 12), which he did not know when he published the *Journal of a Tour to the Hebrides*. The risks were such as he had recognised and considered – though that did not make it any less painful when his fears were unfortunately realised:

> I am certain that there is not in reality a more benevolent man than myself in the World; and yet, from my having indulged myself without reserve in discriminative delineations of a variety of people, I know I am thought by many to be ill-natured; nay, from the specimens which I have given the World of my uncommon recollection of conversations, many foolish persons have been afraid to meet me, vainly apprehending that *their* conversation would be *recorded*. No study, however, is more improving than the study of Man. (7 Feb 1794, *BP*, XVIII, p. 319)

It would not, I suggest, be overstating the case to say that Boswell sacrificed what remained of his public image to the art of biography.

# 8 Conclusion: the Final Reckoning

By way of conclusion, I should like to discuss Boswell's writing of the *Life of Johnson* with regard to the actual work involved. What effect did this prolonged effort have upon his mental condition? How did it differ from the salutary effects of journalising? And, finally, what was the impetus that kept him to his task – what, in other words, did Johnson mean to him, that he should devote so much energy and attention to the writing of his biography?

Boswell's final journals do not make pleasant reading. The sense of dejection and failure which pervades them is given poignancy by our knowledge that they *were* the records of his final years. We seem to be witnessing the inevitable breakdown of a balance precariously maintained over thirty years; the gloom of melancholy infiltrates and blends with the few patterns of light which remain in a darkening mind:

> What sunk me very low was the sensation that I was precisely as when in wretched low spirits thirty years ago, without any addition to my character from having had the friendship of Dr. Johnson and many eminent men, made the tour of Europe, and Corsica in particular, and written two very successful Books. I was as a board on which fine figures had been painted, but which some corrosive application had reduced to its original nakedness.
>
> (*BP*, XVIII, pp. 70–1)

Only eighteen months earlier, in 1789, he could still write pathetically, but hopefully, to his dying wife, 'Fortune, I trust, will at last favour me, for I am sure that I deserve it' (*BP*, XVII, p. 143). Now he has lost not only any sense of deserving favour, but all certainty of his worth as a person. At times, only

## CONCLUSION: THE FINAL RECKONING

the unwillingness to surrender totally to the reality of failure kept Boswell in London at work on the *Life*:

> Felt myself shrink from London and all its Society. I believe I should have stolen away to Auchinleck had I not recollected the ambitious thoughts which I had all my life indulged, and which now seemed to be totally blasted.
> (*BP*, XVIII, p. 104)

Boswell is so frequently melancholy during this period of his life that he finds the fact scarcely worth recording: 'N.B. Understood *not well* till a change is marked' (*BP*, XVII, p. 47). And remarks which earlier in his life would have seemed the posturings of vanity, or excuses to a flexible conscience, are now readily accepted by the reader as sincere indications of Boswell's state of mind: 'I am conscious that I can expect only temporary alleviation of misery, and some gleams of enjoyment. But these it is my *right*, nay I think my *duty* to have' (*BP*, XVIII, p. 274).

But other factors contributed to Boswell's mental condition at this time and aggravated his sense of failure. One was undoubtedly his degrading and servile position in the association with Lord Lonsdale, which was not broken off until the summer of 1790. The demands of 'the great Earl' frequently hindered Boswell's work on the *Life*: 'It vexed me that I was dragged away from the printing of my *Life of Johnson*, and that perhaps Malone might be gone to Ireland, before I could get back to London' (*Corr.* II, p. lxix). The publication of Mrs Piozzi's *Letters to Dr. Johnson* in 1788 had also caused him distress, and impeded the progress of the *Life* in so far as it reduced, if only temporarily, his ardour for the task, and reminded him of the painful social effect of the *Journal of a Tour to the Hebrides*:

> I was disappointed a good deal, both in finding less able and brilliant writing than I expected, and in having a proof of his fawning on a woman whom he did not esteem, because he had luxurious living in her husband's home; and in order that this fawning might not be counteracted, treating me and other friends much more lightly than we had reason to expect. This publication *cooled* my warmth of enthusiasm

for 'my illustrious friend' a good deal. I felt myself degraded from the consequence of an ancient Baron to the state of an humble attendant on an Author; and what vexed me, thought that my collecting so much of his conversation had made the World shun me as a dangerous companion. (*BP*, XVII, pp. 74–5)

In these circumstances, the satisfaction of keeping a journal seems to be totally overwhelmed by the misery of the life which is recorded: 'What a wretched Register is this! "A Lazarhouse it seem'd." It is the Journal of a diseased mind. I had passed a very uneasy night' (*BP*, XVIII, p. 66).

This, then, was Boswell's general state of mind during the composition of the bulk of the *Life of Johnson*. Not that he does not sometimes record pleasant occasions or feelings of happiness, but the recurring theme in his account is dejection, and, in particular, Boswell has come to regard this as the norm. Nor does his biographical work itself seem to have afforded him a great deal of pleasure. As Geoffrey Scott writes,

> Boswell formed no exultant vision of his achieved task. He, who so often glowed with self-applause on small occasions, was scarcely roused from dejection, as he contemplated the masterpiece which, more than most great books, has added to the stock of happiness. The *Life* to him had not been a clear creative act; the zest and eager humanity which permeates it, he had experienced long ago; the communicable spark was still burning in the original records which, in a kind of discharge of destiny, he scrupulously and often diffidently wove together; but now it seldom lit his own darkened mind. (*BP*, VI, p. 290)

Boswell's own remarks during the writing scarcely suggest unstinted enjoyment: 'O! if this Book of mine were done. Job says, "O that mine ennemy *had written* a Book!" I shall rejoice when I can speak in the *past* tense. I *do* hope to be *Finis* in ten days' (*Corr*. II, p. lxv). His usual word for the task is 'laboured': 'Sat at home and laboured at *Life* all the evening' (p. lxxii). Even nearing the completion of the work seemed to give him little pleasure: 'I have now desired to have but one compositor. Indeed I go sluggishly and comfortlessly about my

## CONCLUSION: THE FINAL RECKONING

work.... I went to the Printinghouse a cold raw day; had no pleasure from my Book' (p. lxxii). In fact, one reason for Boswell's melancholy condition was his worries about money generally, and about the financial success of the *Life* itself: 'Kemble came to me in the morning, and made out a note of Dr. Johnson's conversation with Mrs. Siddons, for my Book. He encouraged me to hope that there would be a great sale, of which I was now despairing' (ibid.).

Despite the labour and worry involved, however, Boswell did seem to find his work on the *Life* something of a consolation. The Boswell *in* the *Life*, even with the traces of bitterness, is a very different person from the melancholy man of the final journals; it is almost as if he found in the world of the biography a therapeutic release from the present through the memory of the past. Whilst losing none of his artistic awareness or nicety of judgement, Boswell seems to have been able to return and 'as it were see each scene as it happened' (*Corr.* II, p. lxii) as he recounted the events of a happier part of his life. Drawn by the written memory in the raw material of the journals into the world of the past, it was nevertheless a world he was recreating and reshaping even as he entered it, for he took with him the knowledge and sense of responsibility acquired through the *Hebrides* experience. Without this dual capability, at the same time re-entering and standing apart from the world of memory, the portrait of Johnson would certainly have been less vivid and convincing, and without the element of pleasurable release Boswell might even have found his task too exacting for completion. Perhaps, then, we owe the accomplishment of the *Life of Johnson* to the misery of Boswell's final years.

Moreover, Boswell's literary labours seem to have provided a core to his life around which to group his fluctuating hopes for the future, though he hardly dares to formulate his feelings into anything so concrete as hope: 'Let me not *think* at present; far less *resolve*. The *Life of Johnson* still keeps me up. I *must* bring that forth' (*Letters*, II, p. 378). Only occasionally, though, is he prepared to allow it an overriding significance: by his enforced trip to Carlisle he has been obliged 'to interrupt my *Life of Dr. Johnson*, the most important, perhaps *now* the only, concern of any consequence that I ever shall have in this world' (*BP*, XVIII, p. 286). And, even when the *Life* has proved successful, he shows reluctance to accept himself only as the great biographer:

> As my friend and I rode calmly between his Churches, I observed that he held a creditable actual station in Society, whereas I held none. Yet we both agreed that I was better as the distinguished Biographer than as a Lord of Session.
> (*BP*, XVIII, p. 153)

> My constant cause of repining is having indulged hopes of attaining both to consequence and wealth, so as to raise my family to higher consideration; and finding no prospect of attaining my ambitious objects, I tried to soothe myself with the consideration of my fame as a Writer, and that by the good management of my Estate, and saving, I might in time pay my debts. (*BP*, XVIII, p. 262)

Boswell throughout his life often speaks of the importance of activity in combating melancholy – even before the personal influence of Johnson he had discovered this fact. One reason for keeping a journal is that it will 'save me from indolence and help to keep off the spleen' (*LJ*, p. 67).[1] In Edinburgh in 1780 he saw his brother David as an example of a man whose way of life allowed no room for melancholy: 'David had appeared to me yesterday very intelligent and firm. I saw that much of my unhappiness was *mouldy imagination*. I ought therefore to keep my mind clear by *realities* and activity' (*BP*, XIV, p. 101). In the elections of the following spring, Boswell himself experienced how salutary an effect a full commitment to business could produce: 'I was now kept quite in a fever with it, I was so keen. The agitation kept off all melancholy' (*BP*, XIV, p. 159); 'It is amazing how the warmth of my anxiety for Major Montgomery's Election cleared my mind of all gloomy vapours' (XIV, p. 160); 'In short, I was active and animated and full of hope. How very different from the dreary metaphysical Wretch that I had been!' (XIV, p. 164). Boswell almost sounds as though he had never been *really* aware of the therapeutic effects of activity (although we should not assume that he was unaware of the benefit he derived from the activity of ordering his experience in his journal), or that he had been melancholy for so long that he had quite forgotten the fact.

## CONCLUSION: THE FINAL RECKONING

With this recent experience in mind, it seems probable that one of the effects of the writing of the *Life* was to prevent Boswell from sinking into so deep a melancholy as he might otherwise have experienced. Certainly, it involved him in a great deal of real activity, and this, despite his complaints, served to keep his mind on something real and tangible:

> You cannot imagine what labour, what perplexity, what vexation I have endured in arranging a prodigious multiplicity of materials, in supplying omissions, in searching for papers buried in different masses – and all this besides the exertion of composing and polishing. Many a time have I thought of giving it up. (*Corr.* II, pp. lxv–lxvi)

> I was as far as Mr. Sewel's in Cornhill to get some little information for Johnson's *Life*. Hundreds of such pieces of trouble have I been obliged to take, in the course of the printing. (Ibid., p. lxix)

With the *Life* continuing Boswell had less cause to feel guilty about being able to do little else:

> My life at present, though for some time my health and spirits have been wonderfully good, is surely as idly spent, as can almost be imagined. I merely attend to the progress of my *Life of Johnson*, and that by no means with great assiduity such as that which Malone employs on Shakspeare.
> (Ibid., p. lxxi)

Work on the *Life*, too, provided an incentive to his friendship with Malone, perhaps one of the most trouble-free of his whole life. All this could not be anything but beneficial to Boswell, who, with his failure at the English bar, had nothing else to do. And after the publication of the *Life* he is again without employment:

> I often called on Malone, and found him fully occupied in historical and biographical researchers, on which he was intent, while I had absolutely no pursuit whatever. The delusive hope of *perhaps* getting into some practice at the bar, was *now* dead, or at least torpid. The printing of my

second edition of Dr. Johnson's *Life* was the only thing I had to do. That was little, and was now nearly ended.

(*Corr*. II, p. lxxvi)

The very business of writing, then, was probably important in maintaining Boswell in a less unbearable condition during this final period of his life. Also of value, though, must have been the fact that he was being forced to concentrate his mind upon the reality of Johnson and on what he had meant for him personally and for the public as a whole. This, like the biographical problem of selection of material and of the need for occasional anonymity, made it necessary for Boswell to step out of himself and see Johnson from a different point of view. His method of drawing Johnson for his own benefit in the journals had always been that of the realist, the 'Flemish painter' (*OY*, p. 103). He now had to present for public approval Johnson as a real and living man, and yet also as surpassing the limits imposed by mere flesh and blood and achieving the status of a symbol fit to be reverenced as Boswell reverenced him. In Marshall Waingrow's words,

> If Johnson alive was that something steady, and steadying, of which Boswell stood in awesome contemplation, the writing of the *Life* was more than memorial therapy, the patient ministering to himself; the hypochondriac turned artist steadied his own doctor and consoled *us* with the contemplation of something at least comparatively great. (*Corr*. II, p. 1)

In this way, contemplation of Johnson's image may be seen as an antidote to the nothingness of the increasingly melancholy world of Boswell's imagination – or at least, looking back to Sartre, its nothingness in relation to the 'real' world.[2] Johnson's inviolable reality is proof against the images which 'pertain to the void', which remove all that they can embrace to a world which is 'other' than the real one. As the *Spectator* says, 'Our Imagination loves to be filled with an Object, or to grasp at any thing that is too big for its Capacity.'[3] Concentration upon the reality of Johnson restricts the influence of that abyss of vacuity in the mind in which melancholy can function freely. As Boswell slowly pieced together the *Life*, he rendered concrete and permanent the image of the man who, for him, had been the representative of common-sense and reality:

> After we came out of the church, we stood talking for some time together of Bishop Berkeley's ingenious sophistry to prove the non-existence of matter, and that every thing in the universe is merely ideal. I observed, that though we are satisfied his doctrine is not true, it is impossible to refute it. I never shall forget the alacrity with which Johnson answered, striking his foot with mighty force against a large stone, till he rebounded from it, 'I refute it *thus*.'
> (*Life*, I, p. 471)

Boswell's worship of Johnson is significant in this respect, for the God of Boswell's religious leanings may also belong to the unreal world of his own imagination. Boswell, who was always attracted to the external splendours of any manner of worship (cf. *LJ*, p. 80), seems to have found it difficult to maintain any fixed idea of what he meant by God, and what other people meant when they spoke of the deity. Religious devotion he could appreciate, particularly when in a state of physical well-being,[4] but devotion for what? As Edmund Burke guardedly writes,

> whilst we consider the Godhead merely as he is an object of the understanding, which forms a complex idea of power, wisdom, justice, goodness, all stretched to a degree far exceeding the bounds of our comprehension, whilst we consider the divinity in this refined and abstracted light, the imagination and passions are little or nothing affected. But because we are bound by the condition of our nature to ascend to these pure and intellectual ideas, through the medium of sensible images, and to judge of these divine qualities by their evident acts and exertions, it becomes extremely hard to disentangle our idea of the cause from the effect by which we are led to know it.[5]

In Johnson, however, Boswell found a man of exemplary piety and goodness, one in whose life and deeds could be observed real proof of the existence of an active and benevolent divinity. The image of God could be apprehended through the example of a man who overcame his very human limitations and attained to a state of grace rarely achieved in a postlapsarian world, and who at the same time avoided the sin of pride through strongly felt doubts of his own worth. For Boswell, man was, in Johnson, made in God's own image.

Boswell's final character-sketch of Johnson in the *Life* attempts to sum up all that Johnson stood for. The quality that is insisted upon as most characteristic is that all of Johnson's wisdom and piety was directed towards practical ends – the conduct of life in the world. The divine and the unquestionably human are combined in the example of his life and writings:

> But his superiority over other learned men consisted chiefly in what may be called the art of thinking, the art of using his mind; a certain continual power of seizing the useful substance of all that he knew, and exhibiting it in a clear and forcible manner; so that knowledge, which we often see to be no better than lumber in men of dull understanding, was, in him, true, evident, and actual wisdom. His moral precepts are practical; for they are drawn from an intimate acquaintance with human nature. His maxims carry conviction; for they are founded on the basis of common sense, and a very attentive and minute survey of real life.... he was too conscientious to make errour permanent by deliberately writing it; and, in all his numerous works, he earnestly inculcated what appeared to him to be the truth; his piety being constant, and the ruling principle of all his conduct. (*Life*, IV, pp. 427-9)

Johnson, then, in the image Boswell has conveyed to us, makes truth and reality permanent for all time and all people. And, by means of the *Life*, Boswell has saved from time's destruction both Johnson and himself. The authenticity of Johnson's image is guaranteed because Boswell is actually in the *Life* as an assurance that Johnson really was such a man, and really did represent these qualities. Francis Hart writes,

> The emergence of Romantic historicism implies the approving recognition of historical relativism, and in biography this meant the recognition that a memoir would

## CONCLUSION: THE FINAL RECKONING 193

inevitably be dominated by the personality and experience of the memoirist. Indeed, personal consistency was the guarantee of authenticity; authenticity was a function of the memoirist's access to and relationship with his subject. Authenticity had come to mean something akin to originality, to delineate an immediate, unadulterated connection between a testimony and the origin of that testimony in the personality and experience of the witness.[6]

Boswell, as we have seen, took immense pains to present a consistent portrait not only of Johnson, but also of himself, for he realised that his own crucial role in the biography depended above all upon the presentation of his attitude towards his subject, and of his own personality as it was illustrated and defined by that attitude. In the final analysis, it was Boswell's conscious artistry and integrity, his willingness to accept in all its implications his role as an author, that made it possible for him to carry to the *Life* the subjective truth of his journals, and yet able to prune that truth of the self-obsession which unbalanced the whole of his life.

# Notes

NOTES TO CHAPTER ONE: INTRODUCTION

1. John Locke, *Essay Concerning Human Understanding* (1690) II, i, p. 25.
2. Paul Fussell, *The Rhetorical World of Augustan Humanism* (1965) p. viii.
3. John Berger, *Ways of Seeing* (1972) p. 46.
4. Cited by M. H. Abrams, *The Mirror and the Lamp* (1953) p. 77.
5. Ibid., p. 140.
6. Mme de Stael, *De l'Allemagne* (1852), cited ibid., p. 91.

NOTES TO CHAPTER TWO: MELANCHOLY AND THE IMAGINATION

1. Bridget Gellert Lyons, *Voices of Melancholy: Studies in Literary Treatments of Melancholy in Renaissance England* (1971).
2. Ibid., p. 3.
3. Robert Burton, *Anatomy of Melancholy*, 3 vols (1932 edn) I, p. 201.
4. Ibid., I, p. 175.
5. Ibid., I, p. 220.
6. Ibid., II, p. 242.
7. Ibid., I, p. 11.
8. Ibid., I, p. 406.
9. Ibid., I, pp. 406–7.
10. Ibid., I, p. 12.
11. Ibid., I, p. 171.
12. Ibid., I, p. 252.
13. Ibid., I, p. 424.
14. Ibid., II, p. 109.
15. Ibid., III, p. 417.
16. Cited by Michel Foucault, *Madness and Civilization*, trs. Richard Howard (1967) p. 131.
17. Cited by Richard Hunter and Ida Macalpine, *Three Hundred Years of Psychiatry: 1535–1860* (1963) p. 840.
18. Timothy Bright, *A Treatise of Melancholie*, cited by Hunter and Macalpine, *Three Hundred Years*, p. 39.
19. Cited ibid., p. 321. Swift, of course, draws upon such ideas for satiric use in *Tale of a Tub*, particularly in section IX, the digression on madness. On this topic, see also Michael V. DePorte, *Nightmares and Hobbyhorses* (1974) esp. chs 1 and 2.
20. Thomas Willis, *Pathologiae cerebri, et nervosi generis specimen* (1667, trs.

1681), cited by Hunter and Macalpine, *Three Hundred Years,* p. 191.
21. Foucault, *Madness and Civilization*, pp. 131–2.
22. Cited by Hunter and Macalpine, *Three Hundred Years*, p. 322.
23. Richard Baxter, *Reliquiae Baxteriaenae* (1696), cited ibid., p. 240.
24. Thomas Hobbes, *Leviathan*, I, p. 8.
25. *The Signs and Causes of Melancholy... Collected... by Samuel Clifford* (1716), cited by Hunter and Macalpine, *Three Hundred Years*, p. 241.
26. John Moore, *Of Religious Melancholy, a Sermon* (1692), cited ibid., p. 252.
27. Jeremy Taylor, *Ductor dubitantium, or the Rule of Conscience* (1660), cited ibid., p. 165.
28. Cited ibid., p. 37.
29. J. G. Zimmerman, *Solitude: or the Influence of Retirement on the Mind and the Heart* (1824 edn) p. 242.
30. Ibid., p. 356.
31. Ibid., p. 303.
32. Ibid., p. 339.
33. Ibid., p. 347.
34. *The Rambler*, 150 (*Works,* V, p. 36). (References to Johnson's *Works* are to the Yale edn. See Bibliography for details.)
35. *The Rambler*, 89 (*Works,* IV, p. 107).
36. *The Rambler*, 85 (*Works,* IV, pp. 86–7).
37. Roger Lonsdale in a note on the Epitaph to Gray's *Elegy – Poems of Gray, Collins, and Goldsmith* (1969) p. 139 – points out a 'favourable sense of "melancholy", implying a valuable kind of sensibility' expressing itself 'in benevolence and other social virtues, rather than merely in solitary wandering'.
38. Oliver Goldsmith, *The Citizen of the World* (1762) letter xc.
39. John 8: 12.
40. *Westminster Confession of Faith* (1643) XI, 3.
41. Ibid., XI, 4.
42. With this in mind, it is distressing to find Boswell frightening his own children with devils and hell, 'a dark place, (for I had not yet said any thing of *fire* to them, and perhaps never will).... Yet without mixing early some *fear* in the mind, I apprehend Religion will not be lasting' (*BP*, XIV, p. 20).
43. Mark 9: 43–4.
44. In 1772, for example, Boswell and Johnson discuss whether fornication is a sin 'of a heinous nature', but it is with reference not to Boswell himself but to 'a cause in which I had appeared as counsel at the bar of the General Assembly of the Church of Scotland' (*Life*, II, pp. 171–2; also *Def.*, pp. 97–8).
45. Foucault, *Madness and Civilization*, p. 217.
46. On this topic cf. J. T. Boulton in Howard Anderson *et al.* (eds), *The Familiar Letter in the Eighteenth Century*, (1966) p. 208. For the enormous topic of 'man as machine' see most relevantly Nicolas Malebranche, *De la Recherche de la Vérité* (1674), and J. O. de La Mettrie, *L'Homme Machine* (1747; trs. Gertrude Carmen Bussey as *Man a Machine*, 1912).
47. Fussell, *The Rhetorical World of Augustan Humanism*, p. 169.
48. Ibid., p. 142.

49. Ibid., p. 141.
50. Ibid., p. 149.

NOTES TO CHAPTER THREE: MADNESS AND THE ROLE OF THE IMAGE

1. Cited by Hunter and Macalpine, *Three Hundred Years*, p. 561.
2. Locke, *Essay Concerning Human Understanding*, I, i, p. 1.
3. Alexander Smith, 'Philosophy of Poetry' (1835) cited by Abrams, *The Mirror and the Lamp*, p. 153.
4. Ibid., p. 158.
5. Jean-Paul Sartre, *The Psychology of Imagination*, Eng. trans. (1972) p. 96.
6. Ibid., pp. 109–10.
7. Ibid., pp. 126–8.
8. Ibid., p. 133.
9. Ibid., pp. 136–7.
10. Ibid., pp. 158–60.
11. Samuel Johnson, *Rasselas*, ch. 44, ed. J. P. Hardy (1968) p. 105.
12. Foucault, *Madness and Civilization*, pp. 93–4.
13. *Rasselas*, pp. 104–5.
14. Foucault, *Madness and Civilization*, p. 105, quoting *Encyclopédie* article on mania.
15. Ibid., p. 104.
16. Cf. Bernard L. Einbond, *Samuel Johnson's Allegory* (1971) p. 34ff.
17. Cited by Abrams, *The Mirror and the Lamp*, p. 286.
18. Sartre, *The Psychology of Imagination*, pp. 132–3.
19. *Rasselas*, p. 104.
20. A similar idea occurs in a letter to Johnston: 'If the gloomy fiend shows his black visage on the frontiers of my Mind a detachment of brisk animal spirits like a Corps of light troops give him a reception so smart that he is glad to retreat with grumbling precipitation' (*Corr.* I, p. 136). Here, though, the disturbance is not a civil one but an invasion from outside. Internal warfare is more serious.
21. *Rasselas*, p. 105.
22. *The Idler*, 32 (Johnson, *Works*, II, p. 101).
23. Sartre, *The Psychology of Imagination*, p. 155.
24. Ibid., p. 140.
25. Ibid., p. 141.
26. Ibid., p. 156.
27. Foucault, *Madness and Civilization*, pp. 106–7.
28. Sartre, *The Psychology of Imagination*, p. 217.

NOTES TO CHAPTER FOUR: THE PRESSURES OF SOCIETY

1. Lord Chesterfield, *Letters to his Son and Others*, intro. R. K. Root (1929) p. 1.
2. George Cheyne, *Essay on Regimen*, pp. x–xi; cited by A. A. Wheater, 'Studies in Melancholy and Sentiment' (unpublished Ph D thesis, University of Nottingham, 1958) p. 145.

3. Sigmund Freud, *Totem and Taboo*, trs. James Strachey (1960 edn) pp. 33, 72.
4. Bartholomaeus Anglicus, *De proprietatibus rerum* (1535), cited by Hunter and Macalpine, *Three Hundred Years*, p. 2.
5. John Hill, *Hypochondriasis* (1766) ed. G. S. Rousseau, Augustan Reprint Society no. 135 (1966) p. 14.
6. John Moore, *Medical Sketches* (1786), cited by Hunter and Macalpine, *Three Hundred Years*, p. 497.
7. Reference is made to 'the contagious quality of mental depression' by John Reid, *Essays on Insanity* (1816), cited by Hunter and Macalpine, *Three Hundred Years*, p. 724.
8. Thomas Fitzgerald, *Poems on Several Occasions* (1733), cited by Hunter and Macalpine, *Three Hundred Years*, pp. 356–7.
9. Foucault, *Madness and Civilization*, pp. 211–12.
10. R. D. Laing, *Knots* (1970) p. 1.
11. Hunter and Macalpine, *Three Hundred Years*, p. 821.
12. Foucault, *Madness and Civilization*, p. 157.
13. Burton, *Anatomy of Melancholy*, I, p. 330ff., argues that, among other factors, a lax or excessively severe education can aggravate the tendency to melancholy.
14. John Locke, *Some Thoughts Concerning Education* (1693) p. 2.
15. F. A. Pottle, *James Boswell: the Earlier Years 1740–1769* (1966), relates what little is known of Boswell's early education.
16. Chesterfield, *Letters*, p. 1.
17. Boswell does add, though, 'It seemed to me, however, that his oratory rather tended to distinguish himself than to assist his cause. There was amusement instead of persuasion' (*Def.*, p. 169). Burke apparently was not completely attuning himself to the circumstances.
18. A. J. Tillinghast, 'A Critical Study of the Writings of James Boswell' (unpublished Ph D thesis, University of Nottingham, 1962) p. 152.
19. Foucault, *Madness and Civilization*, pp. 253–4.
20. Freud, *Totem and Taboo*, p. 60; cf. Foucault, *Madness and Civilization*, pp. 209–10, where Foucault speaks of 'the strange contradiction of human appetites'.
21. Foucault, *Madness and Civilization*, pp. 264–5.
22. A similar piece of sophistry is described by Johnson in *The Rambler* 28: 'The tribe is likewise very numerous of those who regulate their lives, not by the standard of religion, but the measure of other men's virtue; who lull their own remorse with the remembrance of crimes more atrocious than their own, and seem to believe that they are not bad while another can be found worse' (*Works*, III, p. 154).
23. Cited by Hunter and Macalpine, *Three Hundred Years*, p. 4.
24. Philip Barrough, *The Methods of Phisicke* (1583), cited by Hunter and Macalpine, *Three Hundred Years*, p. 28.
25. Alexander Chalmers (ed.), *British Essayists* (1808) XXIX, p. 258.

NOTES TO CHAPTER FIVE: FREEDOM AND THE PEN

1. Cited by Frank Brady, *Boswell's Political Career* (1965) p. 137.

2. Alexander Pope, *Moral Essays* (1735) II, pp. 199–200.
3. Ibid., II, p. 156.
4. Foucault, *Madness and Civilization*, p. 250.
5. Cf. *Ex.*, p. 84 and *BP*, XV, p. 49, where Boswell discusses casting off all life's accessories and moving one's residence frequently in order to perceive better the true self.
6. W. B. Yeats, 'A Dialogue of Self and Soul' (1933) ll. 50–4.
7. Chalmers, *British Essayists*, XXVIII, p. 115.
8. David L. Passler, *Time, Form, and Style in Boswell's 'Life of Johnson'* (1971) p. 94.
9. It would be interesting to examine Boswell's attitude to confessional literature. He finds, for example, Cleland's *Fanny Hill* a 'most licentious and inflaming book' (*Def.*, p. 84) – not an unexpected reaction. Perhaps, too, one of the elements of the Catholic faith which attracted him was the opportunity for self-exposure within the security of the confessional.
10. Freud, *Totem and Taboo*, p. 159.
11. Foucault, *Madness and Civilization*, p. 194.
12. *William Cowper's Letters: a Selection*, ed. E. V. Lucas (1908) p. 92.
13. Cf. *LJ*, p. 188: 'I could scarce keep my dreary humour from persuading me that she despised me, a sure sign of the spleen, which makes us always imagine that we are despised.'
14. Cited by G. S. Rousseau, in Hill, *Hypochondriasis*, p. v. Cf. Freud on the nature of the relationship between the psychoanalyst and the patient: 'One would have thought that the patient's relation to the analyst called for no more than a certain amount of respect, trust, gratitude, and human sympathy. Instead, there is this falling in love, which itself gives the impression of being a pathological phenomenon' (*Two Short Accounts of Psycho-Analysis*, trs. James Strachey, 1962 edn, p. 140).
15. *The Rambler* 59 (*Works*, III, p. 318).
16. *Some Thoughts Concerning Education*, in Locke, *Works*, 3rd edn (1727) III, p. 86. We must at the same time, however, remember Johnson's view: 'There is, indeed, no transaction which offers stronger temptations to fallacy and sophistication than epistolary intercourse' – 'Life of Pope', *Lives of the Poets*, ed. G. B. Hill, III, p. 207.
17. Naturally there was resentment when Boswell, by no means a Curll, actually did publish a man's private correspondence; see C. N. Fifer, 'Boswell and the Decorous Bishop', *JEGP*, LXI (1962) 48–56.
18. Cowper, *Letters*, p. 46.
19. *Works*, III, p. 74.
20. As R. D. Laing suggests, there are many ways in which a man may choose to display the 'real' self which is concealed in his everyday relations: 'The man who does not reveal himself or is not "seen" by the others when he does, may turn, in partial despair, to other modes of self-disclosure. The exhibitionist shows off his body, or some highly prized function or skill trying to overcome that haunting isolation and loneliness of one who feels his "real" or "true" self has never been disclosed to and confirmed by others' – *Self and Others*, 2nd edn (1969) pp. 130–1.

NOTES 199

21. Hill, *Hypochondriasis*, pp. 40–1.
22. Chalmers, *British Essayists*, I, p. xxiv.
23. Ibid., XVI, pp. x, xlvi.
24. *The Rambler* 208 (*Works*, V, p. 320).
25. *Gentleman's Magazine* (1786) LVI, p. 123.
26. Fussell, *The Rhetorical World of Augustan Humanism*, pp. 66–7.
27. Ibid., p. 67.
28. 'Peter Pindar' (John Wolcot), *Epistle to James Boswell* (1786), in *English Satiric Poetry*, ed. James Kinsley and J. T. Boulton (1966) pp. 134–5.
29. Tillinghast, 'A Critical Study of the Writings of Boswell', p. 270.
30. Introduction to the original journal of the tour, ed. F. A. Pottle and Charles H. Bennett (1936), pp. ix–x, 9 n. 11. Cf. L. F. Powell, 'Boswell's Original Journal of his Tour to the Hebrides and the Printed Version', *Essays and Studies*, XXIII (1937) 58–69, for a fuller discussion than Pottle's, but also for a different conclusion.
31. But see *BP*, XVI, pp. 110, 118, for Boswell's occasional twinges of conscience for what Macdonald might understand. I feel, though, that these are more attributable to Boswell's good nature than to any doubts over the validity of the criticisms.

**NOTES TO CHAPTER SIX: 'SCRIBO ERGO SUM'**

1. 'Boswell's Boswell', *Johnson Agonistes and Other Essays* (1946) p. 78.
2. This may seem rather odd in the light of what we know about Boswell's remarkable powers of memory – see F. A. Pottle, 'The Power of Memory in Boswell and Scott', *Essays on the Eighteenth Century Presented to David Nichol Smith* (1945) pp. 168–89. But Pottle also points out – 'The *Life of Johnson*: Art and Authenticity', in James L. Clifford (ed.), *Twentieth Century Interpretations of Boswell's 'Life of Johnson'* (1970) p. 68 – that Boswell's memory needed a clue to trigger it off, and that his notes were intended as these clues: 'Without such a note, his memory was no better than anyone else's.' A second memory in some form is essential to Boswell's recollection and recreation of the past.
3. A phrase used by Passler, *Time, Form, and Style*, ch. 1, with reference to the *Life*.
4. By Ralph H. Isham, in Clifford, *Twentieth Century Interpretations*, p. 90.
5. *The Rambler* 23 (*Works*, III, p. 125).
6. Clifford, *Twentieth Century Interpretations*, p. 12.
7. Cf. Freud's account of repression and distortion in *Two Short Accounts of Psycho-Analysis*, pp. 52–3, 56.
8. Sartre, *Psychology of Imagination*, p. 158.
9. See *Letters*, II Appendix, where Tinker reprints a large number of Boswell's detailed letters of instruction to the overseer of the Auchinleck estate.
10. Hill, *Hypochondriasis*, p. 26.
11. Ibid., pp. 27–9.
12. Ibid., pp. 27–8.
13. Matthew 21; 18–20.

14. W. K. Wimsatt, 'The Fact Imagined: James Boswell', *Hateful Contraries* (1965) pp. 182–3.

NOTES TO CHAPTER SEVEN: BALANCING THE ACCOUNTS

1. William R. Siebenschuh, *Form and Purpose in Boswell's Biographical Works* (1972) pp. 74–5.
2. Ralph W. Rader, 'Literary Form in Factual Narrative: the Example of Boswell's *Johnson*', in Philip B. Daghlian (ed.), *Essays in Eighteenth Century Biography* (1968) pp. 8–9.
3. *The Rambler* 56 (*Works*, III, p. 300).
4. Charles Churchill, *The Ghost* (1762), cited by James T. Boulton, *Johnson: the Critical Heritage* (1971) pp. 357–8.
5. Cited by Sir John Hawkins, *The Life of Samuel Johnson, LL.D.*, 2nd edn (1787) p. 170.
6. See 'Conjugal Fidelity: a Suppressed Dialogue between Boswell and Johnson', *Life and Letters*, IV (1930) 164–6.
7. Rader, in Daghlian (ed.), *Essays*, p. 36.
8. See Boulton, *Johnson: the Critical Heritage*, pp. 32–3, for further information on this subject.
9. Hawkins, *Life of Johnson*, pp. 73–6.
10. Siebenschuh, *Form and Purpose*, pp. 33–5.
11. *OY*, p. 116; the relevant portion of the original Hebrides manuscript is missing.
12. Siebenschuh, *Form and Purpose*, ch. 4.
13. See, too, Felicity A. Nussbaum, 'Boswell's Treatment of Johnson's Temper: "A Warm West-Indian Climate"', *SEL*, 14 (1974) 421–34.
14. James L. Clifford, 'How Much Should a Biographer Tell? Some Eighteenth-Century Views', in Daghlian (ed.), *Essays*, p. 86.
15. 'Pindar', *Epistle to James Boswell*, ll. 14, 3, 65–6, in *English Satiric Poetry*, ed. Kinsley and Boulton, pp. 133, 135.
16. Cited by Boulton, *Johnson: the Critical Heritage*, p. 358.
17. Robert Potter, *The Art of Criticism as Exemplified in Dr Johnson's 'Lives of the Most Eminent English Poets'* (1789), cited by Boulton, *Johnson: the Critical Heritage*, p. 306.
18. Ibid., p. 307.
19. Ibid., pp. 308–10.
20. Ibid., p. 309.
21. Rader, in Daghlian (ed.), *Essays*, p. 31.
22. Joseph Towers, *An Essay on the Life, Character, and Writings of Dr. Samuel Johnson* (1786), cited by Boulton, *Johnson: the Critical Heritage*, p. 381.
23. See Clifford, in Daghlian (ed.), *Essays*, pp. 86–9; and Lucyle Werkmeister, 'Jemmie Boswell and the London Daily Press, 1785–95', *Bulletin of the New York Public Library*, LXVII (1963) 82–114, 169–85 (repr. New York, 1963).
24. Paul K. Alkon, 'Boswell's Control of Aesthetic Distance', in Clifford, *Twentieth-Century Interpretations*, p. 60.
25. Laing, *Self and Others*, pp. 98–9.

26. Bronson, in *Johnson Agonistes and Other Essays*, p. 77.
27. Rader, in Daghlian (ed.), *Essays*, p. 37.
28. Clifford, ibid., pp. 85–6.
29. F. A. Pottle, *The Literary Career of James Boswell, Esq.* (1929) pp. 223–4, 252–3, finds accounts attributable to Boswell in the *London Magazine*, XLIII (1774) 26, and the *Edinburgh Advertiser*, XXX (Jan–June 1773) 44.
30. Cited by Clifford, in Daghlian (ed.), *Essays*, pp. 92–3.
31. See Fifer, in *JEGP*, LXI, 49, 55.
32. William Wordsworth, 'A Letter to a Friend of Robert Burns', *Prose Works*, ed. A. B. Grosart (1873), II, p. 9.

**NOTES TO CHAPTER EIGHT: CONCLUSION: THE FINAL RECKONING**

1. See Arieh Sachs, *Passionate Intelligence* (1967) p. 15ff., for an account of Johnson's ideas on activity and salvation.
2. See above, p. 61.
3. *Spectator* 412; in Chalmers, *British Essayists*, XII, p. 135.
4. Cf. *BP*, XVII, p. 25: 'I was quite convinced that our spirits depend chiefly upon what we throw into the stomack.'
5. Edmund Burke, *A Philosophical Enquiry into the Origin of our Ideas of the Sublime and Beautiful* (2nd edn, 1759), ed. James T. Boulton (1958) p. 68.
6. Francis R. Hart, 'Boswell and the Romantics', *ELH*, XXVII (1960) 59–60.

# Bibliography

BOSWELL

I. *Works*

*Private Papers of James Boswell from Malahide Castle*, ed. Geoffrey Scott and Frederick A. Pottle (New York, 1928–34) 18 vols.
*Boswell's London Journal, 1762–1763*, ed. F. A. Pottle (London, 1951).
*Boswell's London Journal, 1762–1763, and Journal of my Jaunt, Harvest 1762*, ed. F. A. Pottle (London, 1951, de-luxe edn).
*Boswell in Holland, 1763–1764*, ed. F. A. Pottle (London, 1952).
*Boswell on the Grand Tour: Germany and Switzerland, 1764*, ed. F. A. Pottle (London, 1953).
*Boswell on the Grand Tour: Italy, Corsica and France, 1765–1766*, ed. Frank Brady and F. A. Pottle (London, 1955).
*Boswell in Search of a Wife, 1766–1769*, ed. Frank Brady and F. A. Pottle (London, 1957).
*Boswell for the Defence, 1769–1774*, ed. W. K. Wimsatt and F. A. Pottle (London, 1960).
*Boswell's Journal of a Tour to the Hebrides with Samuel Johnson, LL.D.*, ed. F. A. Pottle and Charles H. Bennett (London, 1936).
*Boswell: the Ominous Years, 1774–1776*, ed. Charles Ryskamp and F. A. Pottle (New York, 1963).
*Boswell in Extremes, 1776–1778*, ed. Charles McC. Weis and F. A. Pottle (London, 1971).
*Boswell's Notebook, 1776–1777*, ed. R. W. Chapman (Oxford, 1925).
*Boswell: Laird of Auchinleck, 1778–1782*, ed. Joseph W. Reed and F. A. Pottle (London, 1977).

*Boswelliana: the Commonplace Book of James Boswell*, ed. Rev. C. Rogers (London, 1874).
*Observations on the Minor, by a Genius* (Edinburgh, 1760).
*Elegy on the Death of an Amiable Young Lady* (Edinburgh, 1761).
*Ode to Tragedy* (Edinburgh, 1761 [dated 1661]).
*The Cub at Newmarket* (London, 1762).
*Critical Strictures on Elvira* (London, 1763).
*Critical Strictures on the New Tragedy of Elvira written by Mr David Malloch, 1763. By James Boswell, Andrew Erskine, and George Dempster*, introduction by F. A. Pottle, Augustan Reprint Society no. 35 (Los Angeles, 1952).
*Letters between the Honourable Andrew Erskine and James Boswell, Esq.* (London, 1763).
*Boswell's Correspondence with the Hon. Andrew Erskine and his Journal of a Tour to Corsica*, ed. George Birkbeck Hill (London, 1879).
*Thesis in Civil Law* (Edinburgh, 1766).
*The Douglas Cause* (1767).
*Dorando, A Spanish Tale* (London, 1767).
*Dorando, A Spanish Tale, by James Boswell* (London, 1930).
*The Essence of the Douglas Cause* (London, 1767).
*Letters of Lady Jane Douglas*, ed. James Boswell (London, 1767).
*An Account of Corsica* (Glasgow, 1768).
*British Essays in Favour of the Brave Corsicans*, ed. James Boswell (London, 1769).
*'On the Profession of a Player': Three Essays Reprinted from the London Magazine for August, September, and October, 1770* (London, 1929).
*Reflections on the Late Alarming Bankruptcies in Scotland* (Edinburgh, 1772).
*Decision of the Court of Session upon the Question of Literary Property* (Edinburgh, 1774).
*A Letter to Lord Braxfield* (Edinburgh, 1780).
*The Hypochondriack: Essays Appearing in the London Magazine from November, 1777, to August, 1783*, ed. Margery Bailey (Palo Alto, Calif., 1928) 2 vols.
*Boswell's Column (The Hypochondriack)*, ed. Margery Bailey (London, 1951).
*Letter to the People of Scotland, on the Present State of the Nation* (Edinburgh, 1783).

*Letter to the People of Scotland . . . on Diminishing the Number of the Lords of Session* (London, 1785).
*Journal of a Tour to the Hebrides, with Samuel Johnson, LL.D.* (London, 1785).
*Ode by Dr. Samuel Johnson to Mrs. Thrale* (London, 1788 [dated 1784]).
*The Celebrated Letter from Samuel Johnson to the Earl of Chesterfield* (London, 1791 [dated 1790]).
*A Conversation between George III and Samuel Johnson* (London, 1790).
*No Abolition of Slavery: or the Universal Empire of Love* (London, 1791).
*The Life of Samuel Johnson, LL.D.* (London, 1791) 2 vols; 2nd edn (London, 1793), 3 vols.
*Principal Corrections and Additions to the First Edition of Mr. Boswell's Life of Dr. Johnson* (London, 1793).
*The Life of Samuel Johnson, LL.D., together with Boswell's Journal of a Tour to the Hebrides and Johnson's Diary of a Journey into North Wales*, ed. George Birkbeck Hill, rev. L. F. Powell (Oxford) 6 vols (I-IV, 1934; V-VI, 1950; rev. 1964).
'Memoirs of James Boswell, Esq.', repr. from the *European Magazine* (May, June 1791), in F. A. Pottle, *The Literary Career of James Boswell, Esq.* (Oxford, 1929).
*Letters of James Boswell, Addressed to the Rev. W. J. Temple*, ed. Sir Phillip Francis (London, 1857; republished with Introduction by Thomas Seccombe, London, 1908).
*Letters of James Boswell*, ed. C. B. Tinker (Oxford, 1924) 2 vols.
*Correspondence of James Boswell and John Johnston of Grange*, ed. Ralph S. Walker (London, 1966).
*Correspondence and Other Papers of James Boswell Relating to the Making of the 'Life of Johnson'*, ed. Marshall Waingrow (London, 1969).


II. *Reference and Bibliography*

Abbott, C. Colleer, *A Catalogue of Papers Relating to Boswell, Johnson and Sir William Forbes, Found at Fettercairn House* (Oxford, 1936).
Adam, R. B., *Catalogue of the Johnsonian Collection* (Buffalo, New York, 1921).

Brown, Anthony E., 'Boswellian Studies: a Bibliography', *Cairo Studies in English* (1963–6) 1–75.
——, *Boswellian Studies: a Bibliography* (Hamden, Conn., 1972).
Clifford, James L. and Greene, Donald J., 'A Bibliography of Johnsonian Studies, 1950–1960', in Magdi Wahba (ed.), *Johnsonian Studies* (Cairo, 1962).
Clifford, James L., *Samuel Johnson: a Survey and Bibliography of Critical Studies* (Minneapolis, 1970).
Pottle, F. A. and Pottle, Marion S., *The Private Papers of James Boswell from Malahide Castle in the Collection of Lt.-Colonel Ralph Heyward Isham: a Catalogue* (Oxford, 1931).
Pottle, F. A. *et al.*, *Index to the Private Papers of James Boswell from Malahide Castle* (Oxford, 1937).
Pottle, F. A., *The Literary Career of James Boswell, Esq.* (Oxford, 1929).

III. *Criticism and Biography*

(a) Books

Brady, Frank, *Boswell's Political Career* (New Haven, Conn., 1965).
Clifford, James L. (ed.), *Twentieth-Century Interpretations of Boswell's 'Life of Johnson'* (Englewood Cliffs, N. J., 1970).
Collins, P. A. W., *James Boswell* (London, 1956).
Fitzgerald, Percy, *Boswell's Autobiography* (London, 1912).
Passler, David L., *Time, Form, and Style in Boswell's 'Life of Johnson'* (New Haven, Conn., and London, 1971).
'Pindar, Peter' (John Wolcot), *A Poetical and Congratulatory Epistle to James Boswell, Esq., on his Journal of a Tour to the Hebrides* (London, 1786); in *English Satiric Poetry*, ed. James Kinsley and James T. Boulton (London, 1966) pp. 132–43.
Pottle, F. A., *Boswell and the Girl from Botany Bay* (New York, 1937).
——, *James Boswell: the Earlier Years, 1740–1769* (New York, 1966).
Scott, Geoffrey, *The Making of the 'Life of Johnson'* (New York, 1929); vol. VI of the *Private Papers*.
Siebenschuh, William R., *Form and Purpose in Boswell's Biographical Works* (London, 1972).
Spacks, Patricia, *Imagining a Self: Autobiography and Novel in*

*Eighteenth-Century England* (Cambridge, Mass., 1977).
Tinker, Chauncey Brewster, *Young Boswell* (London, 1922).

(b) Articles and Essays

Alkon, Paul K., 'Boswell's Control of Aesthetic Distance', *University of Toronto Quarterly*, XXXVIII (Jan 1969) 174–91; abridged and repr. in Clifford, *Twentieth-Century Interpretations of Boswell's 'Life of Johnson'*, pp. 51–65.

Bronson, Bertrand H., 'Boswell's Boswell', *Johnson Agonistes and Other Essays* (Cambridge, 1946) pp. 53-99.

Carlyle, Thomas, 'Boswell's Life of Johnson', *Fraser's Magazine*, V (May 1832) 379–413; repr. in *Critical and Miscellaneous Essays* (London, 1888) vol. III, pp. 49–104.

Clifford, James L., 'How Much Should a Biographer Tell? Some Eighteenth-Century Views', in Philip B. Daghlian (ed.), *Essays in Eighteenth-Century Biography* (Bloomington, Ind., and London, 1968) pp. 67–95.

'Conjugal Fidelity: a Suppressed Dialogue between Boswell and Johnson', *Life and Letters*, IV (1930) 164–6.

Copeland, Thomas W., 'Boswell's Portrait of Burke', in *The Age of Johnson: Essays Presented to C. B. Tinker* (New Haven, Conn., 1949) pp. 27–39.

Fifer, C. N., 'Boswell and the Decorous Bishop', *JEGP*, LXI (Jan 1962) 48–56.

Gulick, Sidney L., Jr, 'Johnson, Chesterfield, and Boswell', in *The Age of Johnson: Essays Presented to C. B. Tinker* (New Haven, Conn., 1949) pp. 329–40.

Hart, Francis R., 'Boswell and the Romantics: a Chapter in the History of Biographical Theory', *ELH*, XXVII (1960) 44–65.

Hitschman, Edward, 'Boswell: the Biographer's Character', *Psychoanalytic Quarterly*, XVII (1948) 212–25; repr. in *Great Men: Psychoanalytic Studies* (New York, 1956) pp. 186–98.

Isham, Ralph H., Krutch, Joseph Wood, and Van Doren, Mark, 'Boswell: the *Life of Johnson*', in Mark Van Doren (ed.), *New Invitations to Learning* (New York, 1942) pp. 285–96; repr. in Clifford, *Twentieth-Century Interpretations of Boswell's 'Life of Johnson'* (Englewood Cliffs, N. J., 1970) pp. 90–6.

Jack, Ian, 'Two Biographers: Lockhart and Boswell', in *Johnson, Boswell, and their Circle: Essays Presented to L. F. Powell* (Oxford, 1965) pp. 268–85.

Macaulay, Thomas B., Review of Croker's edition of the *Life*, *Edinburgh Review*, LIV (Aug–Sep 1831) 1–38.

Nussbaum, Felicity A., 'Boswell's Treatment of Johnson's Temper: "A Warm West-Indian Climate" ', *SEL*, 14 (1974) 421–34.

Pottle, F. A., 'Boswell's University Education', in *Johnson, Boswell and their Circle: Essays Presented to L. F. Powell* (Oxford, 1965) pp. 230–53.

——, 'Dark Hints of Sir John Hawkins and Boswell', *MLN*, LVI (1941) 325–9; repr. and enlarged in F. W. Hilles (ed.), *New Light on Dr. Johnson* (New Haven, Conn., 1959) pp. 153–62.

——, 'James Boswell, Journalist', in *The Age of Johnson: Essays Presented to C. B. Tinker* (New Haven, Conn., 1949) pp. 15–25.

——, 'The Life of Johnson: Art and Authenticity', in Clifford, *Twentieth-Century Interpretations of Boswell's 'Life of Johnson'* (Englewood Cliff, N. J., 1970) pp. 66–73.

——, 'The Power of Memory in Boswell and Scott', in *Essays on the Eighteenth Century Presented to David Nichol Smith* (Oxford, 1945) pp. 168–89.

Powell, L. F., 'Boswell's Original Journal of his Tour to the Hebrides and the Printed Version', *Essays and Studies*, XXIII (1938) 58–69.

Rader, Ralph W., 'Literary Form in Factual Narrative: the Example of Boswell's *Johnson*', in Philip B. Daghlian, *Essays in Eighteenth-Century Biography* (Bloomington, Ind., and London, 1968) pp. 3–42.

Rae, Thomas I. and Beattie, William, 'Boswell and the Advocates' Library', in *Johnson, Boswell, and their Circle: Essays Presented to L. F. Powell* (Oxford, 1965) pp. 254–67.

Reiberg, Rufus, 'James Boswell's Personal Correspondence: the Dramatized Quest for Identity', in H. Anderson, P. B. Daghlian and I. Ehrenpreis (eds), *The Familiar Letter in the Eighteenth Century* (Lawrence, Kansas, 1966) pp. 244–68.

Stewart, Mary M., 'Boswell's Denominational Dilemma', *PMLA*, LXXVI (Dec 1961) 503–11.

Tillinghast, Anthony J., 'Boswell Playing a Part', *Renaissance and Modern Studies*, IX (1965) 86–97.

——, 'The Moral and Philosophical Basis of Johnson's and Boswell's Idea of Biography', Magdi Wahba (ed.), *Johnsonian Studies* (Cairo, 1962) pp. 115–31.

Werkmeister, Lucyle, 'Jemmie Boswell and the London Daily Press, 1785-95', *Bulletin of the New York Public Library*, LXVII (1963) 82-114, 169-85 (repr. New York, 1963).

Wimsatt, W. K., 'The Fact Imagined: James Boswell', *Hateful Contraries* (Lexington, Kentucky, 1966) pp. 165-83.

——, 'James Boswell: the Man and the Journal', *Yale Review*, XLIX (Sep 1959) 80-92.

(c) Theses

Brooks, Alfred R., 'The Literary and Intellectual Foundations of James Boswell' (University of Wisconsin, 1957).

Tillinghast, Anthony J., 'A Critical Study of the Writings of James Boswell' (University of Nottingham, 1962).

OTHER WRITERS

(a) Books

Abrams, M. H., *The Mirror and the Lamp* (Oxford, 1953).

Anderson, Howard, Daghlian, Philip B. and Ehrenpreis, Irvin (eds), *The Familiar Letter in the Eighteenth Century* (Lawrence, Kansas, 1966).

Berger, John, *Ways of Seeing* (London, 1972).

Boulton, James T., *Johnson: the Critical Heritage* (London, 1971).

Burke, Edmund, *A Philosophical Enquiry into the Origin of our Ideas of the Sublime and Beautiful*, ed. James T. Boulton (London, 1958).

Burton, Robert, *Anatomy of Melancholy* (London, 1932 edn) 3 vols.

Chalmers, Alexander (ed.), *British Essayists* (London, 1808) 45 vols.

Chesterfield, Philip Dormer Stanhope, Earl of, *Letters to his Son and Others*, intro. R. K. Root (London, 1929).

Cowper, William, *William Cowper's Letters: a Selection*, ed. E. V. Lucas (London, 1908).

Einbond, Bernard L., *Samuel Johnson's Allegory* (The Hague, 1971).

Foucault, Michel, *Madness and Civilization*, trs. Richard Howard (London, 1967).

Freud, Sigmund, *Totem and Taboo*, trs. James Strachey (London, 1960 edn).

——, *Two Short Accounts of Psycho-Analysis*, trs. and ed. James Strachey (Harmondsworth, 1962 edn).
Fussell, Paul, *The Rhetorical World of Augustan Humanism* (Oxford, 1965).
Hawkins, Sir John, *The Life of Samuel Johnson, LL.D.* (Dublin edn, 1787).
Hill, John, *Hypochondriasis: a Practical Treatise*, ed. G. S. Rousseau, Augustan Reprint Society no. 135 (Los Angeles, 1966).
Hunter, Richard and Macalpine, Ida, *Three Hundred Years of Psychiatry: 1535–1860* (London, 1963).
Johnson, Samuel, *A Dictionary of the English Language*, 8th edn (London, 1799) 2 vols.
——, *Diaries, Prayers and Annals*, ed. E. L. MacAdam, Jr, with Donald and Mary Hyde (New Haven, Conn., and London, 1958); vol. I of Yale edn of the *Works*.
——, *The Idler and the Adventurer*, ed. W. J. Bate, J. M. Bullit and L. F. Powell (New Haven, Conn., and London, 1963); vol. II of Yale edn of the *Works*.
——, *The Rambler*, ed. W. J. Bate and Albrecht B. Strauss (New Haven, Conn., and London, 1969); vols III–V of Yale edn of the *Works*.
——, *Poems*, ed. E. L. MacAdam, Jr, with George Milne (New Haven, Conn., and London, 1964); vol. VI of Yale edn of the *Works*.
——, *A Journey to the Western Islands of Scotland*, ed. Mary Lascelles (New Haven, Conn., and London, 1971); vol. IX of Yale edn of the *Works*.
——, *Lives of the Poets*, ed. G. B. Hill (Oxford, 1905) 3 vols.
——, *Letters of Samuel Johnson*, ed. R. W Chapman (Oxford, 1952) 3 vols.
——, *Rasselas*, ed. J. P. Hardy (Oxford, 1968).
Laing, R. D., *Knots* (London, 1970).
——, *Self and Others*, 2nd edn (London, 1969).
Locke, John, *Some Thoughts Concerning Education* (1693; repr. Menston, Yorks., 1970); and in *Works*, 3rd edn (London, 1727) vol. III.
Lyons, Bridget Gellert, *Voices of Melancholy: Studies in Literary Treatments of Melancholy in Renaissance England* (London, 1971).

Sachs, Arieh, *Passionate Intelligence: Imagination and Reason in the Work of Samuel Johnson* (Baltimore, 1967).
Sartre, Jean-Paul, *The Psychology of Imagination*, Eng. trans. (London, 1972).
Torrance, Thomas F., *The School of Faith: the Catechisms of the Reformed Church* (London, 1959).
Wordsworth, William, *Prose Works*, ed. A. B. Grosart (London, 1873) 3 vols.
Zimmerman, Johann Georg, *Solitude; or the Influence of Retirement on the Mind and the Heart* (London, 1824 edn).

(b) Thesis

Wheater, A. A., 'Studies in Melancholy and Sentiment' (University of Nottingham, 1958).

# Index

Abrams, M. H., 5, 8, 49
acting, 6, 8, 43, 72, 79–80, 92–3, 96, 108, 114, 118, 132
Adams, Dr William, 173
Addison, Joseph, 61, 154
  *Spectator*, 75, 111, 116, 190
Aeneas, 122–3, 143
Alkon, Paul, 173
America, 7
Aristotle, 11, 12
Ashbourne, 54, 130
Atterbury, Francis, Bishop of Rochester, 2
Auchinleck (Alexander Boswell), Lord, father of Boswell, 7, 19, 78, 82–4, 87, 113, 135, 141
Auchinleck, 9, 42, 44, 83, 123, 142, 174, 185, 199n.9
authorship
  and anonymity, 111–13, 181–2, 190
  and deception, 108, 109, 110
  and readers, 3, 5, 23, 25, 49–50, 106–8, 109–10, 111, 114, 126, 130, 135, 138–43, 151–2, 153, 154, 171–4, 176–8, 183, 190, 192–3
  and society, 112–13, 115–16, 153, 161, 178, 188, 192–3
  *see also* communication, periodical essays, publication, society

Bacon, Sir Francis, 25
Baden-Durlach, 33
Barrough, Philip
  *Methods of Phisicke*, 90
Bartholomaeus Anglicus
  *De proprietatibus rerum*, 70, 90
Baxter, Richard
  *Reliquiae Baxterianae*, 15

Beauclerk, Topham, 101
Berger, John, 3
Berkeley, George, Bishop of Cloyne, 191
Bewdoc, 144
Bible, 27–8, 29, 36–7, 150, 186
Bickerstaffe, Isaac
  *Love in a Village*, 4
biography, 112, 114–15, 117, 153–4, 158, 160, 167, 169, 173, 175, 177–8, 183, 184–90 *passim*, 192–3
Birmingham, 165
Blackmore, Sir Richard, 24
  *Treatise of the Spleen and Vapours*, 15
Blair, Catherine, 8
Blair, Dr Hugh, 29
Blenheim, 101
Bolton, Matthew, 165
Boswell, Alexander, son of JB, 116
Boswell, Charles, cousin of JB, 123
Boswell, Charles (Doig), natural son of JB, 41
Boswell, David (later Thomas David), brother of JB, 61, 81–2, 87, 174, 188
Boswell, James
  *Account of Corsica*, 109, 115, 118, 154, 174
  'Boswelliana', 93, 145, 148
  *Correspondence of James Boswell and John Johnston of Grange*, 10, 56, 66, 82–3, 106, 113, 135, 148, 196n.20
  *Correspondence... Relating to the Making of the 'Life of Johnson'*, ix, 158, 181, 182, 185, 186–7, 189–90
  *Cub at Newmarket*, 113

## 212 INDEX

Boswell, James (*Contd.*)
  *Boswell for the Defence*, 8, 34, 37, 45, 55, 81, 88, 125, 138, 147, 180, 195n.44, 198n.9
  *Dorando*, 8
  *Douglas Cause*, 174
  *Boswell in Extremes*, 7, 22, 29, 36–7, 54, 78, 81, 83, 84, 87, 89, 97–8, 119–20, 122, 128, 130–1, 132, 137, 168–9, 198n.5
  *Boswell on the Grand Tour: Germany and Switzerland*, 5, 7, 17, 27, 30, 33, 38, 41, 42, 44, 46, 55–6, 59, 100, 102, 103, 121, 123, 125, 126, 142, 149
  *Boswell on the Grand Tour: Italy, Corsica and France*, 29, 30–1, 54, 69, 77, 80, 103, 129
  *Boswell in Holland*, 6, 19, 27, 34, 38, 40–2, 59, 69, 88, 106, 121, 134, 136–7, 150
  *The Hypochondriack*, viii, 17, 18, 22–4, 25, 27, 33, 34, 66–7, 68, 71, 79, 93–4, 97, 98, 99–101, 102, 105, 107–8, 109–10, 112, 118, 119, 121, 124, 125, 130, 135, 137, 139, 140, 144, 145–6, 147, 148, 150, 151, 173
  *Journal of a Tour to the Hebrides*, viii, 81, 112–17, 137, 147, 153–4, 158, 160, 161–6, 171–4, 182, 183, 185, 187, 199n.30
  *Journal of a Tour to the Hebrides* (manuscript journal), 4, 28, 72–3, 78, 101, 115, 119, 127, 147, 199n.30, 200n.11
  *Boswell, Laird of Auchinleck*, 18, 22, 23
  *Letters between the Honourable Andrew Erskine and James Boswell, Esq.*, 113
  *Letters of James Boswell*, 67, 68, 72, 102, 108, 120, 126–7, 142, 187, 199n.9
  *Letter to the People of Scotland ... on Diminishing the Number of the Lords of Session*, 92, 174
  *Life of Johnson*, viii, ix, 2, 3, 26, 33, 80, 81, 95, 107, 117, 141, 143, 151, 152, 153–93, 195n.44
  *Boswell's London Journal*, 4, 9, 20–1, 29, 33, 46, 54, 60, 61, 67, 68, 69, 73, 79, 80, 105, 106, 113, 119, 120, 121–2, 124, 129, 130, 135, 136, 138, 140, 142, 147, 188, 191, 198n.13
  newspaper publications, 113, 182, 201n.29
  *Ode by Dr. Samuel Johnson to Mrs. Thrale*, 182
  *Boswell: the Ominous Years*, 7, 17, 29–30, 31–2, 35–6, 37, 38, 46–8, 54, 59, 61, 73, 82, 83, 84, 90, 92, 94, 101, 105, 107, 108, 120, 121, 125, 129, 131–2, 133, 138, 147, 148, 180, 190, 200n.11
  *Boswell Papers*, 3, 4, 8, 9, 10, 17, 18, 38, 56, 60, 61, 66, 68, 69–70, 72, 73–5, 78, 80, 81–2, 85–7, 88–9, 92, 94, 96, 98–9, 101, 104, 115–16, 119, 120, 127–8, 139, 141–2, 144, 149, 183, 184–8, 195n.42, 198n.5, 198n.31, 201n.4
  'On the Profession of a Player', 92–3, 96, 118
  *Boswell in Search of a Wife*, 7–8, 9, 16, 33–4, 53, 56, 70, 72, 109, 123, 125, 134, 137, 139, 140
Boswell, John, brother of JB, 83–4
Boswell, Margaret, wife of JB, 7, 32, 53–4, 55, 84–6, 97–8, 135, 139, 141, 184
Boyd, Marianne, 53
Bright, Timothy
  *Treatise of Melancholie*, 15, 16
Bronson, Bertrand, 119, 179
Bunyan, John, 39
Burke, Edmund, 3, 4, 39, 80–1, 197n.17
  *Enquiry*, 191
Burton, Robert, 24, 146
  *Anatomy of Melancholy*, 12–14, 197n.13
Bute, John Stuart, 3rd Earl of, 127–8

# INDEX 213

Campbell, Dr Thomas, 133–4
Carlisle, 66, 187
Castiglione, 112
castle-building, 9, 13, 60
Catholicism, 29
Cervantes Saavedra, Miguel de
  *Don Quixote*, 60
Chalmers, Alexander
  *British Essayists*, 111
Chesterfield, Philip Dormer Stanhope, 4th Earl of, 155
  *Letters to his Son*, 65, 66, 78, 82, 95, 116
Cheyne, George
  *Essay on Regimen*, 65–6, 75
Churchill, Charles, 175
  *The Ghost*, 155, 166
Clarke, Rev. Dr Samuel, 171
Cleland, John
  *Fanny Hill*, 198n.9
Clifford, James, 133–4, 166, 181
Coleridge, Samuel Taylor, 170
Coll, 164
communication, 2, 3, 26, 102–3, 120, 129–30, 138–40, 179, 180
  and letters, 103, 105, 106, 108, 109, 130, 198n.16, 198n.17
  and melancholy, 103–5, 109–11, 139, 186
  and publication, 106–8, 109–11, 114, 115, 171
  *see also* authorship, friendship, periodical essays, publication
conversation, 2, 3–4, 61, 81, 88, 98, 106, 108, 109, 124, 130–4, 180–1, 183
  Johnson's, 3, 80, 116, 132, 133–4, 147, 155–7, 163, 165, 168–9, 174, 175, 176, 179–80, 186, 195n.44
  *see also* Johnson
Cornwall, 72, 144
Corsica, 42, 80, 103, 132, 184
countryside, 70, 72, 74, 79, 143–50
Courtenay, John, 72, 116, 179
Covington (Alexander Lockhart), Lord, 99
Cowper, William, 103, 106
Crichton, Sir Alexander

*Inquiry into... Mental Derangement*, 45

Davies, Thomas, 176, 180
Dawkins, James ('Jamaica'), 9
Dempster, George, 56, 129, 136, 181
Derby, 130
Derrick, Samuel, 174
Desmaiseaux, Pierre, 173
Dick, Sir Alexander, 72
Digges, West, 61, 80
Dilly, Edward, 163, 168
Dodds, Mrs, 123
Dodsley, James, 181
Dodsley, Robert, 159, 181
Douglas Cause, The, 174
Dryden, John, 58
Dunbar, Dr James, 22
Dundas, Henry, Lord Advocate, 3, 92
Dundas, Robert, Lord President of the Court of Session, 82

Eardley, Sampson (formerly Sampson Gideon), Lord, 142
Edinburgh, 20, 21, 29, 46, 74, 82, 113, 122, 123, 170, 188
education, 12, 29, 66, 78, 82, 99, 174, 197n.13, 197n.15
Edward Augustus, Duke of York, 113
Eglinton, Alexander Montgomerie, 10th Earl of, 21, 87, 113, 174
Erskine, Hon. Andrew, 4, 88–9, 104, 113, 129, 136
Essex Sessions, 75

Falmouth, 144
fancy, 2, 18, 37, 38, 41, 46, 50, 55, 56, 57, 60, 73, 87, 106, 127, 129, 140, 163, 172
  *see also* imagery, imagination, melancholy
Fielding, Henry, 85
Fitzgerald, Thomas
  'Bedlam', 75, 76
Forbes, Sir William, 179

# 214  INDEX

Foucault, Michel
  *Madness and Civilization*, 15, 17, 32, 57–8, 62, 75–7, 83, 87–8, 95, 103, 197n.20
Freud, Sigmund
  *Totem and Taboo*, 67–8, 75, 84, 102
  *Two Short Accounts of Psycho-Analysis*, 198n.14, 199n.7
friendship, 6, 23, 26, 27, 31, 89, 92, 97, 101, 106, 109–11, 128, 129, 154, 157, 171–2, 175–6, 177, 178, 179, 181, 184, 189
  *see also* authorship, communication, Johnson, periodical essays
Fussell, Paul, 2, 39, 112, 113

Galloway, Alexander Stewart, 6th Earl of, 87
Garrick, David, 139
Gay, John
  *Beggar's Opera*, 8, 46
Geneva, 41, 75
Germany, 42
Gibbon, Edward
  *Decline and Fall of the Roman Empire*, 107
Glasgow, 20
Goldie, George, 88
Goldsmith, Oliver, 88, 157, 167
  *Citizen of the World*, 26–7
Grant, Peggy, 97
Gray, Thomas, 166, 167
  'Elegy', 195n.37
Griffiths, Ralph, 183

Hague, The, 41
Hamilton, John, of Sundrum, 22
Hammond, James, 167
Hampden, John, 170
Harris, James ('Hermes'), 89
Hart, Francis R., 192–3
Hartley, David, 36
Harwood, Dr E., 35
Hawkins, Sir John, 159–60, 172, 179
  *Life of Samuel Johnson*, 159–60, 175
Hay, Charles, 8
Hazlitt, William, 170

Heraclitus, 70
Hill, Dr John
  *Hypochondriasis*, 70–1, 110–11, 149–50
Hippocrates, 12
Hobbes, Thomas
  *Leviathan*, 16
Holland, 6, 18–19, 34, 40–1, 134
Home, John, 174
Hoole, John, 108
Horace, 174
Hume, David, 36–8, 43
Hunter, Richard and Ida Macalpine, 76
Hunter, Dr William, 35
hypochondria, *see* melancholy

imagery, 81, 82, 108, 125, 127, 141, 147–8, 177, 191–2
  and behaviour, 30–1, 38–42, 53–7, 61–2, 63, 89–90
  definitions, 1–3, 49–50
  and feeling, 47–9, 52–4, 165
  of Johnson, 154–70, 171, 190–3
  and judgement, 51, 57, 62, 88
  and knowledge, 50–1, 53
  and language, 50, 138–9
  and madness, 2, 57–64, 88
  of melancholy, 15–18, 25, 43, 59–60
  of the self, 3–9, 32–6, 38–43, 72, 95, 96, 136–7, 150, 170–83
  and self-analysis, 8–10, 34, 46–50, 63, 79, 81
  and thought, ix, 45–64
  and unreality, 53, 56, 60–4, 95, 128, 136, 190–1
  *see also* conversation, fancy, imagination, journals, madness, melancholy, society
imagination, 3, 8, 9, 30, 36–8, 79, 85, 102, 103, 106, 108, 124, 128, 191
  and melancholy, 10, 13, 15, 18, 24–6, 44, 61, 63, 70, 190, 191
  psychology of, 50–64
  and time, 25–6, 88–9, 128, 136
  *see also* imagery, madness, mania, melancholy, reason

inactivity, 11, 12, 13, 15, 19, 22–3, 24–6, 32, 33–5, 41, 88–9, 119, 120–1, 126, 132–3, 144–6, 150, 188–90
  *see also* melancholy
Ireland, 185
Italy, 30–1, 42, 54, 122, 160, 177

'Jachone', 129–30
James, Robert
  *Medicinal Dictionary*, 104
Jerusalem, 55
Johnson, Samuel, 1, 26, 27, 29, 31, 37, 39, 54, 55, 72, 80, 81, 88, 95, 96, 99, 101, 107, 108, 114, 116, 125, 127, 130–1, 132, 134, 135, 139, 143, 147, 151, 152–93, 195n.44, 201n.1
  'character', 108, 161–3, 192
  and friendship, 101, 154, 157, 171–2, 175–6, 177–8, 184, 185, 192–3
  and melancholy, 25–6, 31, 33, 37, 39, 59, 69, 104, 146, 155–6, 157–8
  and society, 80, 92, 155–6, 170, 190
  and virtue, 154, 156–7, 162, 172, 191–2, 197n.22
  works concerning, 114, 155, 158–9, 160–1, 166–7, 170
  *Dictionary*, 2, 11, 12, 15, 16, 25, 133
  *Idler*, 60
  *Lives of the Poets*, 166–7, 172, 198n.16
  *Prayers and Meditations*, 157
  *Rambler*, 25–6, 104, 108, 111–12, 114, 130, 161, 166, 197n.22
  *Rasselas*, 9, 57–8, 59, 60, 63, 175–6
  *see also* biography, conversation, imagery, periodical essays, religion, society
Johnston, John, of Grange, 7, 10, 22, 30, 41–2, 56, 66, 71, 74, 82–3, 106, 113, 129, 130, 147, 149, 196n.20
journals, viii, ix, 3–4, 35, 36, 51, 68, 69, 78, 86, 89, 109, 117, 139, 152, 163, 164, 168, 178, 193
  and experience, 1, 119–21, 123, 125, 132, 148–9
  and melancholy, 18, 24, 121, 125–6, 143, 150–1, 184–6, 187, 188
  and privacy, 92, 97–8, 130–2, 135–6
  and reality, 128–9, 132, 133–5, 136–43
  and satisfaction, 120–1, 147–51, 184, 186, 188
  and the self, 34, 45, 50, 81, 92, 121–37, 143, 151, 171, 182, 193, 198n.5
  and time, 119–21, 123, 126–7, 133, 141
  *see also* imagery, madness, melancholy, memory, society, style, time

Kemble, John Philip, 187
Knowles, Mrs Mary, 168

Laing, R. D., 5, 76, 178, 198n.20
Langton, Bennet, 104, 173
law, 19, 23, 54, 71, 74–5, 82, 94, 113, 122, 123, 137, 147, 188, 189, 195n.44
Lee, John, 92, 113
Leith, 160
Lewis, Mrs ('Louisa'), 54, 142
Leyden, 19
Lichfield, 30
Locke, John
  *Essay Concerning Human Understanding*, 1, 45–6, 124
  *Some Thoughts Concerning Education*, 78, 105
London, 19–20, 21, 31, 40, 43, 54–5, 61, 69, 72, 74, 75, 85, 89, 104, 122, 129, 131, 141–2, 143, 147, 161, 185
*London Chronicle*, 113, 159
Lonsdale, James Lowther, 1st Earl of, 185
Lonsdale, Roger, 195n.37
'Louisa', *see* Mrs Lewis

# INDEX

Lowth, Robert, Bishop of London *Lectures on the Sacred Poetry of the Hebrews*, 5
Lyons, Bridget Gellert, 11

Macdonald, Sir Alexander, 115, 180, 182, 199n.31
Macdonald, Sir James, 20
Macfarlane, Walter, of Macfarlane, 4
machines, 32–6, 38, 41, 43, 56, 59, 137, 165, 195n.46
*see also* imagery
Maclaurin, John (later Lord Dreghorn), 21, 94
Macleod, John, of Rasay, 164
McQuhae, Rev. William, 129, 130
madness, 2, 11, 12, 14, 15, 19, 43, 57–64, 69, 75–7, 83–4, 87–8, 95, 103, 130, 135, 137, 151, 194n.19
*see also* imagery, imagination, mania, melancholy, society
Malone, Edmond, 115, 185, 189
mania, 11, 14–16, 27, 30, 67–8, 87, 196n.14
Marchmont, Hugh Hume Campbell, 3rd Earl of, 92
Marischal, George Keith, 10th Earl, 149
Marlborough, George Spencer, 4th Duke of, 101
marriage, 3, 7, 33, 46–7, 106, 156
melancholy, ix, 85, 96–7, 112, 138, 139, 149–51, 197n.13
  background, 11–16, 24–5
  depression, 7, 10, 16, 18–24, 37–8, 40–2, 46, 69, 73–5, 99, 106, 126, 141–3, 144, 146, 184–90
  distraction from, 12, 109, 120–1, 188–9
  and the family, 78, 81–7
  imaginings, 2, 12–19, 23–4, 25, 39, 41–2, 43, 47, 61, 63, 74, 87, 104, 125, 126, 196n.20, 198n.13
  melancholy-mania, 14, 15, 16, 17, 64, 69
  and nothingness, 2, 18–19, 22–4, 42, 44, 63, 69–70, 73, 77, 88–9, 120–1, 190
  and religion, 12, 24–32, 37
  and sex, 29–32
  and society, 65–91, 104–5, 109–12, 115, 138, 155–6, 182–3
  status of, 10, 18, 24, 121, 123–4, 157–8
  temperamental, ix, 1, 12, 16, 21, 163
  types, 12–13, 195n.37
  *see also* education, imagery, imagination, journals, madness, mania, religion, sexual indulgence, society
memory, 13, 22, 25, 86, 124, 127–9, 133, 136
  and writing, 114, 118–28, 135, 137, 141, 154, 173, 181, 187, 190, 192–3, 199n.2
  *see also* journals, time
Milton, John, 39
  *Paradise Lost*, 16
*Mirror, The*, 90–1, 96
Mitchell, Sir Andrew, 106
Monboddo (James Burnett), Lord, 115, 121
Montgomerie, Major Hugh, 21–2, 188
*Monthly Review*, 183
Moody, John, 181
Murray, Alexander, Solicitor-General (later Lord Henderland), 89
music, 33, 89–90, 102, 103, 106, 150, 164
Musselburgh, 84

Nairne, William (later Lord Dunsinnan), 89
Nash, Richard, 171
Newton, Sir Isaac, 27
Northumberland, Elizabeth Seymour, Duchess of, 198n.13

Osborne, Francis, 107
Oxford, 20–1

Paoli, Pasquale de, 80, 130, 132, 165

Parnell, Thomas, 154
Passler, David, 99
Paul, Saint, 39
Pepys, William Weller, 20
Percy, Dr Thomas, Bishop of Dromore, 181-2, 183, 198n.17
periodical essays, 18, 22-4, 107-8, 109-12, 116, 120-1
  see also authorship, communication, friendship, publication, society
philosophy, 72-3, 85, 162
Piozzi, Hester Lynch (formerly Mrs Thrale), 36, 159, 160
  *Anecdotes of the Late Samuel Johnson, LL.D.*, 160
  *Letters To and From the Late Samuel Johnson*, 116, 185
Pope, Alexander, 198n.16
  *Essay on Man*, 93
  *Moral Essays*, 93
Potter, Robert
  *The Art of Criticism*, 166-7
Pottle, Frederick A., 115, 119, 197n.15, 199n.30, 199n.2, 201n.29
Powell, L. F., 199n.30
Presbyterianism, 28-9, 170
Prichard, James Cowles
  *Treatise on Insanity*, 14
Priestley, Dr Joseph, 35, 36, 37, 131
Pringle, Sir John, 22, 31, 33, 34-5, 131
Prussia, 55
Publication, ix, 1, 4, 21, 24, 81, 91, 105, 109-17, 118, 158-9, 174, 183, 189, 198n.17
  see also authorship, communication, periodical essays, society, style

Rader, Ralph, 154, 157, 169, 179
reason, 13, 19, 24, 30, 31, 36-8, 56, 57, 59, 60, 70, 75, 83, 93, 94, 125
Reid, Rev. George, 135
Reid, John, 8
Reid, John
  *Essays on Insanity*, 197n.7

religion, 8, 14, 15-16, 18, 24-32, 35-8, 41, 54, 61, 66, 72, 78, 81, 82, 85, 94, 99, 129, 131-2, 154, 156, 157, 163, 164, 170, 182, 191-2, 195n.42, 197n.22, 198n.9, 201n.1
  see also education, imagination, Johnson, melancholy
Reynolds, Sir Joshua, 163, 177
Robertson, Dr William, 170
Rome, 28-9, 53
Rotterdam, 18
Rousseau, Jean-Jacques, 27, 42, 54, 75, 100, 106, 108, 149
Rudd, Mrs Margaret Caroline, 90
Rutty, Dr John, 151

St Andrews, 163
Sachs, Arieh, 201n.1
Sartre, Jean-Paul
  *Psychology of Imagination*, 50-3, 58-62, 63, 136, 137, 190
Savage, Richard, 156, 175
Scotland, 4, 129, 149, 162, 164, 174, 182
Scott, Geoffrey, 96, 186
Seward, Anna, 129
Seward, William, 104
Sewel, Mr, 189
sexual indulgence, 29-32, 41, 46-7, 53, 54, 84, 86, 97-8, 99, 129, 131-2
  see also imagination, journals, mania, melancholy, religion, society
Shakespeare, William, 39, 189
  *Hamlet*, 8, 90-1, 151
  *King Lear*, 8
  *Macbeth*, 79
Shenstone, William, 166, 167
Shepherd, Richard, 21
Sheridan, Charles
  *History of the Late Revolution in Sweden*, 168
Siddons, Mrs Sarah, 187
Siebenschuh, William, 153, 161, 164
Siena, 77
Smith, Sir Alexander
  'Philosophy of Poetry', 47-8

# INDEX

society, 3, 26, 39, 47, 63–4, 109, 135–6, 138, 144, 157, 170, 174, 190, 192, 198n.20
  and appearances, 70–2, 74, 79, 86, 90–1, 92–102, 105, 106, 109, 130
  and enjoyment, 74, 77–8, 85–6, 92, 94, 103, 145, 150
  and the family, 78, 81–6, 97–8
  and mania, 67, 68, 69, 75
  and melancholy, 68, 70–1, 73–8, 79, 80, 90, 104, 115, 143, 195n.37
  and propriety, 65–9, 77–81, 84, 86–90, 95, 98, 101–2, 103, 104–5, 111, 112–15, 116, 129, 137, 153–4, 155, 160, 161–2, 181–3
  and punishment, 67–8, 71, 75–7, 102, 109, 112, 116, 130, 145, 171, 185–6
  *see also* Johnson, journals, mania, melancholy, publication
soldiers, 21, 38–43, 55–6, 59, 72, 73, 80, 99, 103, 196n.20
Spenser, Edmund
  *Colin Clout*, 144
Stael, Mme de
  *De l'Allemagne*, 10
Steele, Richard, 61
  *Guardian*, 116
  *Tatler*, 116
Stewart, Francis, 134
Stewart, Houston (later Stewart-Nicholson), 88
Stockdale, Rev. Percival, 99
Strahan, Rev. George, 157
Strange, Mrs Isabella, 104
Stratford-upon-Avon, 139
style
  epistolary, 106
  journals, 138–43, 182
  published, 107, 162–70, 180–2
  *see also* biography, journals, periodical essays, publication
suicide, 19, 22, 89, 146
Susette, Mlle, 54
Swift, Jonathan, 39, 89
  *Gulliver's Travels*, 26, 93–4, 144

*Tale of a Tub*, 93, 194n.19
Taylor, Jeremy
  *The Rule of Conscience*, 16, 151
Temple, Francis, 144
Temple, Rev. William Johnson, 9, 18–19, 27, 34, 40, 48–9, 56, 60, 68, 72, 75, 78, 105–6, 108, 109, 126, 142, 144, 181, 188
Thrale, Henry, 160
Thrale, Mrs, *see* Piozzi, Hester Lynch
Thurlow, Edward, 1st Baron Thurlow, 160
Tillinghast, A. J., 81, 114
time, 25, 89, 124, 126–8, 129, 132–3, 141, 142, 143, 148–9, 187, 192
  and identity, 99–100, 118–21
  and melancholy, 118, 120–1, 137–8
  *see also* imagination, journals, memory
Tinker, C. B., 199n.9
Toland, John, 173
Towers, Joseph
  *An Essay on . . . Dr. Samuel Johnson*, 170
Tunis, 77

Unwin, Rev. William, 103
Utrecht, 6, 19, 40, 42

Voltaire, François Marie Arouet de, 37, 42, 100, 102

Waingrow, Marshall, ix, 190
Walker, Ralph, 113
Walker, Rev. Robert, 29–30
Warburton, Dr William, Bishop of Gloucester, 173
Wauchope, (? John), 21
Webster, Capt. James, 21
*Westminster Confession of Faith*, 28
Wilkes, John, 92
Willis, Thomas, 14
Wimsatt, W. K., 151
Wolcot, John ('Peter Pindar')
  *Epistle to James Boswell*, 114, 166

Wordsworth, William, 183

Yeats, W. B., 95

Zimmerman, J. G.

*Solitude*, 24–5
Zuylen, Belle de ('Zélide'), 6, 40, 42, 106
Zuylen, Diederik Jacob van Tuyll van Serooskerken, Heer van (M. de), 106